Writing Mysteries

Writing Mysteries

Margaret Lucke

Self-Counsel Press
(a division of)
International Self-Counsel Press Ltd.
USA   Canada

Self-Counsel Press acknowledges the financial support of the Government of Canada through the Book Publishing Industry Development Program (BPIDP) for our publishing activities.

Printed in Canada.

First edition: May 1999

Canadian Cataloguing in Publication Data

Lucke, Margaret –
  Writing mysteries

   (Self-counsel writing series)
   ISBN 1-55180-205-8

   1. Detective and mystery stories — Authorship. I. Title II. Series.
PN3377.5.D4L82 1999   808.3'872   C99-910288-5

Material in From the Detective's Notebook 6 by Chelsea Quinn Yarbro is used by permission.

Material in From the Detective's Notebook 12 by Penny Warner is used by permission.

Material in From the Detective's Notebook 13 by Linda Mead is used by permission.

Material excerpted from *A Relative Stranger,* © Margaret Lucke, is used by permission.

Self-Counsel Press
(a division of)
International Self-Counsel Press Ltd.

1704 N. State Street
Bellingham, WA 98225
USA

1481 Charlotte Road
North Vancouver, BC V7J 1H1
Canada

In memory of my mother,

Valerie Bohnert Harris,

who introduced me to the pleasures

to be found between the covers

of a good mystery.

Contents

Part 2 Clues to Crafting a Compelling Mystery

From the Detective's Notebook

Samples

Introduction

Whodunit? And why do it? And the biggest question — how?

If you're thinking of writing a mystery novel, these questions probably loom large in your mind. This book will help you answer them. You probably already know a great deal about the subject, having absorbed a feel for the genre from the mysteries you've read. Most mystery writers begin as mystery readers. Being lovers of the form, they become inspired to create tales of their own.

I was introduced to the pleasures of mysteries early on. A bookish kid, I sought out escapades on the printed page in the company of Ginny Gordon and Nancy Drew. Soon I began raiding my mother's bookshelves, which were filled with enticing paperbacks by Agatha Christie, Erle Stanley Gardner, and Ellery Queen.

I wrote my first mystery at age 11 for my sixth grade's magazine. Entitled "Four Mysterious Twins," this tale is the one and only adventure of Nick Nixon, detective. Nick is hired by the richest woman in town to trace the origins of two sets of twins she plans to adopt. Even then I was familiar enough with the mystery genre to work into my story a number of private-eye clichés: the lone-wolf private eye, his devoted secretary, the opening scene in which a wealthy and beautiful client appears at the PI's office to beg for his help (because of my youth, I did neglect to put a bottle of booze in his desk drawer). I still had a lot to learn when it came to constructing a plausible plot, but I was clearly hooked.

For a long time after Nick Nixon solved his case and reunited the bevy of babies with their birth parents, I set mystery writing aside. I put my skills as a scribe to what I thought were more practical applications: technical editing, public relations, and marketing. But mysteries continued to work their allure on me. I read them in abundance and dreamed of someday writing a novel of my own. After a cross-country move, I joined the local chapter of Mystery Writers of America, hoping to find friends in my new hometown who shared my passion. And I did — wonderful people who gave me encouragement, both from their example (hey, mysteries are written by regular folks like me!) and their support. I have learned a great deal from my mystery-writing colleagues and offer them my heartfelt thanks.

Since then, my interest in mysteries has led me in many directions. I've traveled to New York, Seattle, Toronto, and various points in California to attend gatherings of mystery writers and fans. I've toured Hong Kong, Singapore, and Bangkok to research sites for a mystery-theme tour.

Most days, though, I journey no farther than my desk — and into my imagination. That is where I met Jess Randolph, artist and private investigator. She stars in my novel, *A Relative Stranger,* which was published by St. Martin's Press and nominated for an Anthony Award for the year's best first mystery novel. I've chronicled her further adventures in short stories that appeared in the Lethal Ladies anthologies published by Berkley Prime Crime and in solve-it-yourself mysteries for the Internet magazine *Salon.* I collaborated with another writer on a children's detective story and reading game called *Who Stole Travada?,* published by Adventure Press. I am now working on more novels and a screenplay. I also teach classes in mystery and fiction writing, which I delight in because I learn so much from other people who share my love of creating a well-told tale.

My first mystery to be published — or, a better word, produced — was The Silicon Valley Murders, a script for a mystery weekend. Forty would-be sleuths gathered at a hotel, where they witnessed an apparent murder, then spent the next two days chasing clues that would reveal who among them was the culprit. Instead of happening solely in my imagination, the story truly came alive. I sat in a fancy French restaurant and watched as the character I poisoned flopped face first into his chocolate mousse. I heard the gasps and shrieks of his flabbergasted companions. And I smiled enigmatically while everyone begged to know whodunit.

As my experience shows, the mystery genre embraces a number of formats and many kinds of pleasures. That's one reason it's so popular with readers and writers alike. Mysteries come packaged as short stories, movies, TV programs, radio dramas, computer games, mystery weekends, and party themes.

Yet when most of us think of a mystery, whether we plan to read one or write one, we think of a book. Therefore, in this book we'll be focusing on the skills, techniques, and information that will assist you in writing a novel. But you can apply the clues you'll find in these pages to any form of mystery entertainment.

Facts and figures about the mystery marketplace are hard to come by. In part this is because the publishing industry has no strict standards that define what a mystery is. One publishing house or collector of statistics might categorize all the possible subgenres as mystery while another reserves that term for traditional detective stories and lists figures for suspense novels or thrillers in a separate column. Also, as top-selling authors break out of genre boxes to find a wider audience, some gatherers of statistics may no longer count these authors' books as mysteries at all.

Still, it's possible to find clues to the genre's health and popularity. A look at fiction bestseller lists in *Publishers Weekly* (the North American publishing industry's news magazine) and major metropolitan newspapers finds that mysteries, broadly defined, habitually occupy one-quarter to one-third of the slots. More than 100 bookstores specializing in mysteries operate across the United States and Canada; most major cities have at least one. There are dozens of organizations for people interested in mysteries, ranging from associations of professional writers to small groups devoted to the life, lore, and literature of a single author. Half a dozen annual conferences draw mystery pros and fans by the hundreds. Hotels and cruise lines offer mystery-themed travel packages which give enthusiasts a chance to play tourist and detective at the same time. Fans who prefer to stay home with their computers can spend an entire night becoming cross-eyed and bleary-eyed trying to hit all the mystery-related Web sites on the Internet.

Trends and fashions in writing, as in any form of popular culture, are cyclical. When I joined Mystery Writers of America two decades ago, its members were moaning that the genre seemed dead. But by the mid-1980s, the genre was so vibrant that the years since have been hailed as the mystery's new Golden Age. Although there are now signs that some of the fervor may be cooling, mysteries have been a publishing mainstay for more than a century. Despite its periodic dips and rises, the category, on balance, tends to hold steady and strong.

A while back, a business trip took me to New York, so I seized the opportunity to play detective and try to crack The Case of the Mystery Market. Thirteen mystery editors at major publishing houses generously shared their perspectives for an article I wrote for the newsletter of the Northern California chapter of the Mystery Writers of America. I heard good news, not-so-good news, and lots of sound advice, which you'll find in the sections that follow.

The good news is that editors consider the mystery hale and hearty. The editors I spoke with were unanimous in their enthusiasm for the genre. They are bullish on mysteries for several reasons.

Over the past two decades, the mystery has been redefined — "reinvigorated," said one editor. Before, whether set on the mean streets or at Lord Pottingdale's country manor, the mystery was something of an intellectual parlor game, a puzzle that challenged readers to match wits with a clever detective. Now it is becoming a literature of character, ideas, and strong regional identities. It is the genre that best carries on a strong tradition of story-telling.

Part of the appeal, the editor continued, is "the sense of good and evil, the sense of rightness. Actions have consequences; you must take responsibility. The mystery is the modern-day forum for the morality play."

Another editor commented, "Mysteries have a lot of cultural insight that you don't find in other fiction — regional flavor, discussion of issues."

A third summed it up: "Nobody is doing better writing than mystery writers."

Attracted by the high quality of the writing, the mystery readership is growing, and it's a great audience. The editors I spoke with agreed that mystery readers as a group are loyal, discerning, and incredibly intelligent. And these readers love books, reading far more of them in the course of a year than the typical person.

The mystery remains an active and prosperous category for publishers. There has always been a solid, steady market for mysteries, and it seems to be growing. Readers are spending more dollars on them every year, and they can choose from an ever greater number of titles. One editor, who surmised that 800 books qualifying as mysteries had been published the previous year, also said that even his conservative number represented a 33 percent increase over the year before.

More books by mystery writers are landing on bestseller lists, especially hardcover bestseller lists, and this pleases editors greatly. It benefits not only the author in question but the genre as a whole, as readers who are drawn to the book by its high profile become mystery fans.

Even though the future for mysteries is basically bright, business upheavals in the publishing world are conspiring to make it more difficult for new authors, no matter what their field, to break in and stay in. The publishing and distribution of books is becoming concentrated in fewer and fewer hands as conglomerates and megachains increase their influence and power. While there are plenty of individual imprints (the publisher's name under which a book is published), more and more of them are coming to roost under the same corporate umbrella. Smaller and more specialized publishing houses are taking up some of the slack and offering new opportunities to writers, but they are finding it a challenge to distribute their books as the chain stores, with their centralized buying systems, push increasing numbers of independent bookstores out of the market.

Many publishers that remain are lavishing far more attention and dollars on acquiring potential blockbusters than on acquiring mysteries, which used to be publishing staples. And book prices are increasing, causing readers to be more selective in their purchases.

In some ways, new authors are victims of the mystery genre's success. Because mysteries are so appealing — to both readers and writers — more people are writing them. One editor speculated that there were three times more published mystery writers in the 1990s than in the 1980s. This speaks well for the opportunities the genre affords, but it means there's a lot of competition for an editor's interest.

Not only are editors receiving more submissions than they did a decade ago, but the overall quality of the manuscripts is higher. One editor commented, "It used to be that I could buy everything I thought was good. Now I have to turn down books I once would have bought. There's more to choose from. I've had to decline a lot of books from talented people."

Another editor agreed, saying, "You can't just be competent. You've got to be really good." And the implication was that there's no on-the-job training. You need to be good with your first book.

Writing and publishing are highly personal experiences, and the creative process works differently for every writer. You don't have the security of hard-and-fast rules. What you'll find in these pages are neither rules nor magic formulas, because there are none. Instead, this book shares my experiences of writing *A Relative Stranger* and other mystery works. It offers suggestions for discovering your own muse and developing a satisfying individual approach to writing mysteries.

The book is divided into three parts which correspond to the stages of a novel-in-progress. The first part, Clues to Getting Started, is intended to fire up your enthusiasm and help you make that important leap from thinking about writing to putting words on a page. The second part, Clues to Crafting a Compelling Mystery, will guide you through the wonderful voyage of discovery that leads to a completed, publishable manuscript. Finally, Clues to Selling Your Mystery, will help you present your manuscript to the marketplace and give it its best possible chance for success.

Throughout this book, I'll present various tools and techniques to help prospective mystery writers. Some will be in the form of From the Detective's Notebook features found throughout the book. To specifically help you capture, explore, and expand your ideas as you write, I've included short sections marked with an icon of a pencil.

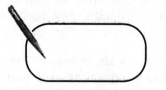

Want more information? At the end of the book, you'll find two appendixes, one on writing and publishing and one covering forensics, police procedure, and other matters directly related to crime and criminal justice.

The purpose of this book is to demystify the mystery-writing process and help budding mystery writers achieve their potential. So sharpen your pencil or turn on your computer, and let's begin.

"Whodunit?" When this question means, "Who wrote this mystery?," soon your answer could be, "I did."

PART 1
Clues to Getting Started

1
Unlocking the Mystery

"Mystery" is a tantalizing word. It suggests secrets and intrigue, an opportunity to peek behind closed doors, shine light into shadowy corners, and unlock truths about the human mind and heart.

In deciding to write a mystery, you are embarking on a great adventure. Between the moment the first idea for a story glimmers in your mind and the time you type "The End" on the final draft, ready to send it to a publisher, you will experience joy and fear, frustration and exhilaration, and a strong sense of magic. You will work hard, and you will have a great deal of fun.

The Pleasures of Mysteries

Why are mysteries so appealing? Each mystery fan, whether writer or reader, has an individual list of reasons, but most would include the following.

Good Storytelling

I believe that the mystery genre offers readers some of the best fiction writing being done today. That doesn't mean every mystery is brilliant literature, but, as a group, today's mysteries adhere to high standards of fictional art and craft. Unlike some of the more experimental types of fiction, mysteries have a plot and a purpose; a beginning, middle, and end. They resonate with story-telling traditions that have satisfied listeners and readers for thousands of years.

Order from Chaos

Mysteries comfort us with the illusion that there is order and logic in what is really a disorderly and confusing world. Real life is filled with unresolved problems, unexplained loose ends, capricious twists of fate, and wrongs that go unrighted. In a mystery, we have the satisfaction of learning the answers, discovering the truth, and seeing justice prevail.

Exploration of Diverse Subjects

Mysteries grab us because they deal with life-and-death matters — the kinds of fundamental issues we all wrestle with. But life and death are such vast subjects that the genre offers an unlimited canvas. In a mystery, you can create an intimate, personal story or one that is global in scope. You can examine the nature of people's relationships with themselves, with each other, and with society. You can probe the depths of goodness and evil. You can set a mystery against whatever background you choose and populate it with characters from any walk of life. The mystery is a framework that accommodates any theme or question you want to explore.

A Way to Taste Different Kinds of Lives

Who doesn't sometimes long for a life that's a little more exciting or colorful or adventurous than the one he or she actually leads? The heroes of mystery novels get to experience those lives. Moreover, by solving or preventing crimes and bringing the perpetrators to justice, they have an opportunity to make a real difference in the world.

You can assign your detective all the positive attributes you wish you had yourself and live vicariously through him or her. I once heard a panel of mystery authors respond to a question about how similar their protagonists were to the writers themselves. Each author conceded they had traits in common with their detectives except that the detectives were uniformly thinner and more courageous than their creators. Of course, you want your protagonist to come across as a real human being, so she should have fears and foibles as well.

> Mysteries have been likened to modern morality plays in that they force us to confront the consequences of criminal deeds and they reaffirm the notion that, in our society, justice is both necessary and desirable.

When you write a mystery, you can travel to new locales, fall in love with an ideal companion, and even take revenge — on paper, of course — on the girl who snubbed you in junior high or the boss who fired you without cause. You can take risks you never would in real life.

Superb Entertainment

Mysteries are first-class entertainment. Reading one provides a pleasurable escape while challenging our intellect, wit, and problem-solving skills. The best mysteries offer the added benefit of giving us insights into our world and the people who share it with us. Writing a mystery offers a great challenge to the writer. Instead of solving a puzzle, you construct one that will baffle your readers. You dream up characters and have the thrill of watching them come to life on the page. You learn new things about yourself and the world. And you have the great satisfaction of exercising your own creative powers.

What Is a Mystery?

So what exactly is a mystery? Once upon a time the mystery was considered a form of entertainment, not literature, and it was constrained by rules and conventions extending well beyond the rules of fair play that still apply. Revered mystery authors — Dorothy L. Sayers, Howard Haycraft, and S.S. Van Dine among them — cautioned aspiring authors to avoid cluttering their stories with distractions like romance, emotions, or psychologically complex characters. In an essay called "Detective Fiction: Origins and Developments," Sayers said, "The mystery-story is a pure analytical exercise . . . . it rarely touches the heights and depths of human passion." Another master of the genre, Raymond Chandler, in his "Casual Notes on Mystery Writing," asserted: "The mystery novel must have a sound story value apart from the mystery element." But he acknowledged in the next sentence that this notion was considered "revolutionary."

Nowadays, while the idea of the puzzle is still vital to mysteries, sound story value has become paramount. The genre has evolved far beyond the old formulas, both in the quality of the writing and in the kinds of stories that are told. No matter what your interests are or what issues concern you, you can find a mystery that addresses them — and if not, you can write one.

Why write a mystery? For the challenge of the puzzle. For the front-row seat it provides in the battle between good and evil. For the extra depth that intrigue adds to the story. For the insight it offers on human nature. For the solid entertainment that a mystery provides.

All novels and short stories have three basic elements in common: characters, plot, and setting. *Characters* are the fictitious people who carry out the action and whose lives are affected by what transpires. The characters create the story through their motivations, actions, and responses. *Plot* is the series of events that take place in the story. More than that, the plot is the way the author organizes and presents the events in order to achieve a dramatic impact. *Setting* is the context in which the story occurs. Setting goes beyond simply the location and time of the events to encompass the whole fictional world that the author creates and bids readers to enter.

These are the parts with which you create any story and all mysteries certainly contain these elements. However, to qualify as a mystery, a story must have suspense, a crime, a secret, a detective, and an orderly resolution.

Suspense

Suspense is a necessary ingredient in almost any story. In a mystery, though, the suspense is heightened and intensified to keep readers at the edge of their seats, unable to put the book down.

A Crime

A mystery is the story of a crime, its causes, and its effects. Most often the crime is a murder, though not always. Mysteries aimed at young readers usually do not involve death. Whatever the crime, though, it must be a wrongdoing of consequence, something that profoundly affects the lives of the people it touches — not only the victim, but others as well. With a spy thriller, the crime often has the potential to change the course of the world.

The mere fact that a story contains a crime does not make it a mystery. A story becomes a mystery when the attempt at a solution is placed front and center in the story rather than on the periphery or as a secondary issue.

A Secret

At the heart of almost any mystery there is a secret to be uncovered — often more than one. The process of discovering this secret drives the plot.

To me, this is one of the key traits that distinguishes mysteries from other types of fiction. Traditionally, the biggest secret concerns the circumstances of the crime, especially the identity of the perpetrator. The motive for the crime can also be a secret; the crime is committed in an attempt to prevent the secret from becoming known.

Usually, the secret is hidden from readers as well as from the characters, but not always. You can choose to tell the story from the viewpoint of the person who has something to hide.

A Detective

As we shall see, there are many types of mysteries besides traditional detective stories. But mystery readers expect to encounter at least one major character, usually the protagonist, who is actively trying to uncover the secret and solve the crime. This character performs the role of detective.

An Orderly Resolution

For a story to qualify as a mystery, it is essential that the crime is solved and order is restored. In writing a mystery, your task is to raise intriguing questions in readers' minds, keep them wondering about these questions, and then, at the end, provide satisfying answers.

Whodunit? is a key question in many mysteries, along with its cousins Howdunit? and Whydunit? But other questions can be equally critical. Often these questions involve an important issue that the detective or other main character is grappling with in his or her personal or professional life.

The Many Types of Mysteries

Watching my friends' toddlers explore the world, I'm always intrigued by how easily they master the concept of dog. Dogs come in a greater range of sizes, colors, and shapes than almost any other species of animal — compare a Great Dane with a Chihuahua, or an English sheepdog with a pit bull. At a glance, the different breeds resemble each other no more than cows look like horses. Yet, small children quickly learn to recognize dogs in all their wonderful variety.

There are almost as many breeds of mysteries as there are breeds of dogs. Definitions of the subgenres keep shifting over time, and the edges between them are blurry. Many mysteries straddle the lines, or jump back and forth, or incorporate elements from several types of mysteries. In a magazine article, author Lawrence Block offers his idea for two categories that would encompass the entire gamut: mysteries with cats, and mysteries without cats. (Dogs would work as well.) Block's system is probably as clear-cut and sensible as any. Either the story has a cat in it, or it does not. There would be no need to quibble about the fine points that distinguish different breeds or debate the issues raised by mixed-breed animals.

The division of the mystery genre into smaller slices is often more helpful to publishers' marketing departments, booksellers, and even readers than it is to writers. When you're selling or buying a book, it's convenient to be able to describe the story with a succinct word or two. But when you're writing one, such labels can be limiting. The best thing to do is write your story in the way you want to tell it and leave the labeling to others.

Still, it's worthwhile to be aware of the many kinds of stories that can be categorized as mysteries. The categories listed below are by no means definitive and are only a few among myriad possibilities. This list does, however, provide an overview of a versatile genre.

> Write your story in the way you want to tell it and leave the labeling to others.

Private Detective

The Private Eye Writers of America defines a private detective, according to the group's founder, Robert J. Randisi, as "anyone who investigates crime for pay but is not employed by the police, the FBI, or another government agency." The traditional private investigator (PI) certainly qualifies, but so might an insurance investigator, a journalist, a lawyer, or a corporate security officer, among others, if that person operates in the style of a PI. The big three writers who originally shaped this subgenre were Dashiell Hammett, Raymond Chandler, and Ross Macdonald.

Amateur Detective

In an amateur detective book, the detective is often referred to by the informal term "sleuth" and is someone who does not usually encounter crime in the course of a day's work. This type of detective usually takes on the task of solving the crime for compelling personal reasons, such as a threat to himself or herself or an injustice threatening someone the detective is close to. British writers Agatha Christie and Dorothy L. Sayers first brought this type of mystery to fame, so mystery fans often think of such mysteries as British-style, but many North American writers also write them exceedingly well.

Police Procedural

The police procedural mystery provides an inside look at police operations, showing how police officers go about cracking a difficult case and apprehending the perpetrator. Good examples of this type of mystery are Ed McBain's 87th-precinct novels and Collin Wilcox's series with Lieutenant Frank Hastings.

Other Procedurals

Police aren't the only professionals involved in bringing wrongdoers to justice; a mystery can focus on other aspects of the how-to of criminal investigation, such as forensic or legal procedures:

- The *forensic procedural* focuses on how criminalists (forensic scientists) and criminologists (sociologists and psychologists who study crime) collect, analyze, and use forensic evidence. Patricia Cornwell's mysteries are one example of a forensic procedural.

- The *legal procedural,* on the other hand, focuses on courtroom drama and the role of the prosecutor or the defense lawyer in the criminal justice system. An example of this type of mystery is Richard North Patterson's work. (Note: Books with lawyers as protagonists can be hard to categerize. Some are procedurals, some are thrillers; in others, the lawyer behaves more like a private detective.)

Suspense

While any mystery should be suspenseful, the suspense-story author works to create and sustain a particularly high level of tension. Often, the protagonist is trapped in bewildering, menacing, even life-threatening circumstances. Two subgenres of this type are the psychological suspense and the romantic suspense:

- Rather than focusing on the puzzle to be solved, the *psychological suspense* emphasizes the buildup of tension and the psychological effects of real or threatened crime on the people involved. An example of this subgenre is Marilyn Wallace's novels.

- A *romantic suspense* generally has a young female protagonist and a plot that is concerned as much with her developing relationship with a key male character as it is with the mystery. Mysteries of all types can include a romantic relationship; the difference is one of emphasis. Barbara Michaels' novels fall into the romantic suspense category.

Thriller

The fast-paced thriller emphasizes the excitement of the chase. It features plenty of action and very high levels of tension and suspense. Often, the plot is centered on political skullduggery or international intrigue, and it takes place in exotic settings around the globe. Classifications of thrillers include the following:

- The *espionage*, or spy, story was a staple of the Cold War, the decades in which the political and cultural enmity between the ideologically different Soviet Union and United States was the dominant force in international relations. Now that the symbolic Iron Curtain dividing these nations has fallen, authors need to come up with new villains and fresh sources of intrigue. Len Deighton and John le Carré are just two examples of espionage authors.

- The *technothriller* emphasizes the power of different electronic and computerized technologies, particularly in military applications. Both hero and villain use these technologies to conduct their battles against one another. Tom Clancy's books are considered technothrillers.

- In a *conspiracy thriller,* a megalomaniac with vast power, limitless resources, and hordes of loyal followers schemes to take over, control, or destroy a given country, region, or the entire world. Robert Ludlum's novels are good examples of this subgenre.

- Although the protagonist is usually a lawyer, the *legal thriller* is quite different from the procedural or courtroom drama. The legal thriller is really a chase or conspiracy novel in which a lawyer is the main character. John Grisham's novels can be categorized as legal thrillers.

- The *serial killer* subgenre describes a cat-and-mouse game between the detective hero and a diabolically clever serial killer. The works of Thomas Harris and John Sandford are examples.

Humorous Mystery

The humorous mystery takes a light-hearted approach to murder and other crimes. The best authors can make the book funny while not negating the seriousness of the crime. Lawrence Block's Burglar books are one example of humorous mystery.

Historical Mystery

Crime is hardly a modern phenomenon, and history offers plenty of material for suspense or detective stories. In the historical mystery, the circumstances of the period — its cultural, political, and social milieu — play a key part in determining the kind of crime or secret that is involved, the methods used to solve it, and the relationships of the characters. Anne Perry's Victorian-era novels are categorized as historical mystery.

Criminal Point of View

The criminal-point-of-view story provides a look at the planning, execution, or consequences of a crime from the criminal's perspective rather than from that of the detective or police officer. Donald Westlake's Dortmunder gang stories are written from this perspective.

Juvenile and Young Adult

Adults aren't the only fans of mysteries. Kids love them too. In fact, many adult mystery readers trace their love of the genre to sharing adventures with youthful sleuths like the Hardy boys and Nancy Drew. The juvenile mystery is written to appeal to readers aged 9 to 12. The young adult mystery is aimed at kids from 12 to 15 years old. Examples include works by Lois Duncan, Patricia Elmore, and Joan Lowery Nixon.

Mysteries: From Cozy to Hard-Boiled

Whenever you listen to mystery writers or fans discuss their favorite books, you're sure to hear the terms "cozy" and "hard-boiled." These terms don't refer to types of mysteries like the ones listed in the previous section; any of the above types of mysteries could be written in either a cozy or a hard-boiled style. The cozy and the hard-boiled mystery are the opposite ends of a continuum that runs from light to dark, from genteel to gritty.

Cozies are the direct descendants of the works of Sir Arthur Conan Doyle and Agatha Christie. Their tone is light and the solving of the puzzle is of prime importance. Violence is underplayed and often takes place offstage. The crimes involved are usually committed for highly personal reasons by people who otherwise might be pillars of the community. Many cozies feature amateur sleuths.

Hard-boiled mysteries bring violence to center stage. They are bloody and grim compared to cozies and more likely to be populated with characters who make a career of crime. The detective usually makes a career of crime too, as a cop or private eye. Hard-boiled mysteries move the murder from manor houses or village lanes to less elegant locations — dark streets and sleazy neighborhoods where a cozy's denizens would fear to tread.

Most mysteries are neither purely cozy nor relentlessly hard-boiled but fall somewhere between the two extremes. Jerry Kennealy, author of the Nick Polo private eye series, says his books are neither soft- or hard-boiled, but al dente.

In the past, cozies and hard-boiled mysteries shared one failing, in my opinion, which was a lack of emotional truth. In cozies, the characters often reacted to the murder either by exclaiming, "Oh boy, our very own mystery to solve," or by complaining peevishly about having to delay the croquet tournament for Scotland Yard's questioning. In fact, a murder in your own vicinity is an emotionally wrenching experience, even if you do not know the victim well. The lone-wolf detectives in

> Most mysteries are neither purely cozy nor relentlessly hard-boiled but fall somewhere between the two extremes.

From the Detective's Notebook 1
A Brief History of Mystery

1840s – 1910s: The Early Years

Edgar Allan Poe is given credit for being the first mystery writer. "The Murders in the Rue Morgue," published in 1841, introduced Auguste Dupin, who later appeared in two more of Poe's stories. The concept of the series character is one of Poe's many legacies, along with the amateur detective, the Watson-style narrator, and the locked-room puzzle.

Following Poe, a number of writers tried writing mysteries, notably Wilkie Collins, Anna Katharine Green, and even Charles Dickens with *Bleak House* and *The Mystery of Edwin Drood.* In 1887, came one of the genre's most important developments: the publication of Sir Arthur Conan Doyle's *A Study in Scarlet,* the first appearance of Sherlock Holmes. Further adventures of the redoubtable Holmes appeared over the next 40 years, and he became one of the most influential fictional characters of all time.

1920s – 1930s: The Golden Years, Chapter 1

By the 1920s, mysteries had gained a wide audience, and the genre flourished thanks to many innovative writers. In England, Agatha Christie and Dorothy L. Sayers established the cozy, the genteel drawing room puzzle that is solved by an amateur detective. While some Americans, like Rex Stout and Ellery Queen, followed the English example, others broke ground by taking murder "out of the drawing room and into the mean streets where it belongs," according to Raymond Chandler. Inspired by heroes of dime novel and pulp magazine stories, this era saw the creation of an American icon, the private eye.

1940s – 1970s: The Paperback Years

In the 1940s, paperbacks became available, making books inexpensive and easy to obtain, so the audience for mysteries grew. Cozies and private eye novels still had plenty of fans, and hard-boiled heroes like those created by

Mickey Spillane and Jim Thompson became popular. The Cold War gave rise to the espionage novel, with practitioners like Ian Fleming and John le Carré. Another favored category was the Gothic novel–romantic suspense of the kind that came from the pens of Mary Stewart and Phyllis A. Whitney.

By the end of the 1970s, general readers were turning to romance novels and science fiction for excitement. Publishers were buying fewer mystery manuscripts; fresh voices and new approaches were becoming rare. Some observers thought the mystery genre would fade away.

1980s – Now: The Golden Years, Chapter 2

Quashing the nay-sayers, mysteries not only have thrived, they're better than ever. An important factor in their revival was the rise of the female private eye, led by authors Marcia Muller, Sue Grafton, and Sara Paretsky. But the key is the variety and high quality of the books being published. Far more than just intellectual parlor games, today's best mysteries are keeping the traditions alive and drawing new readers with their solid characterization, strong evocations of diverse regions and cultures, and thoughtful explorations of social issues and interpersonal relationships.

hard-boiled mysteries, with their liquor bottle in the desk drawer and their disdain for personal relationships, took a different approach to ignoring emotions which seemed equally unrealistic. The best mystery writers today pay much more attention to how the crime affects the characters, portraying characters as real people with realistic emotional responses.

Some devotees of the cozy prefer to describe it by the term "malice domestic," a phrase borrowed from Shakespeare. This acknowledges that many such mysteries deal with personal issues and relationships within the home or other small-scale settings. But you can write a book that deals with larger societal or political issues, or send your characters trotting around the globe, and still have written in a cozy style. Conversely, you can write a novel of domestic violence that is as dark and grim as any hard-boiled tale.

The term "traditional mystery" has also been used for cozies, but that phrase could be applied just as accurately to hard-boiled mysteries, which also have a long and honored tradition that extends back for decades.

The abiding tradition in the mystery genre is the detective story, whether light or dark, nonviolent or bloody. The detective — private eye, cop, spy, or amateur sleuth — is challenged with a puzzle, and readers take up the challenge as well. In all its myriad forms, this tradition is alive and well. Even better, it has been expanded with greater attention to characterization, plot, setting, and literary style so that mysteries have become a richer experience for both readers and writers.

What Type of Mystery Should You Write?

With the abundance of options, what should you write? The answer is easy: whatever appeals to you most. It may be tempting to pattern your mystery after the type that is currently riding high on the mystery best-seller list, but editors caution against following trends. The books that are being published today reflect decisions made more than a year ago and choices made by the authors long before that. Trends and fads change quickly. By the time you identify a current trend and plan, write, and submit your book, there will be some new trend. That something new most likely will be a book that originated completely from the author's imagination as a fresh, original, and exciting new idea. Your motto should be: Don't follow fashion, follow your passion. Tell a story that you would like to read, one that speaks to your own mind and heart.

Don't follow fashion, follow your passion. Tell a story that you would like to read, one that speaks to your own mind and heart.

From the Detective's Notebook 2
Test Your Knowledge of Mysteries

Check all that apply:

1. A mystery novel is —

☐ Any fiction book that includes a murder

☐ A fiction book that combines elements of plot, character, and setting in a suspenseful way to tell the story of a crime, its causes, and its effects, and to bring that story to an orderly resolution

☐ A great book to curl up with on a stormy night in front of a blazing fireplace with a cup of tea (if it's a cozy) or a glass of whisky (if it's a hard-boiled private eye novel)

☐ One of the most popular forms of fiction, and a good way to break into the world of publishing

☐ A formulaic parlor game, the point of which is for readers to match wits with the clever detective

☐ The means by which you are going to becoming rich and famous

☐ All of the above

☐ None of the above

2. Plot is —

☐ The parcel of ground where the body has been buried

☐ The nefarious scheme by which the dastardly Nigel intends to bilk poor sweet Aunt Agatha out of her home, car, cats, and fortune

☐ The series of dramatic events that move your story toward its conclusion

☐ The skeleton of the mystery novel (as opposed to the skeleton in it)

☐ All of the above

☐ None of the above

From the Detective's Notebook 2 — Continued

3. Character is —

❏ The person in a mystery novel who looks, dresses, speaks, and behaves oddly, as in: "Watch out for Sadie, she's a real suspicious character"

❏ A letter, numeral, punctuation mark, or symbol on a page or computer screen

❏ The essential qualities of a person's personality, behavior patterns, and moral strength, as in: "It's hard to believe someone of such good character could be a murderer or a politician"

❏ Any person who makes an appearance in your mystery novel

❏ All of the above

❏ None of the above

4. Setting is —

❏ The locale in which your book takes place

❏ The china and silverware on the table where the victim is about to be fed a delicious meal laced with arsenic

❏ The framework of gold that holds the diamonds in the million-dollar necklace just stolen from Lady Armbruster

❏ Placing the murder weapon in the spot where it will most likely implicate someone who is innocent of the crime

❏ All of the above

❏ None of the above

5. Suspense is —

❏ The agony you go through while waiting to hear from the agent to whom you've sent your mystery novel

❏ The agony you go through while waiting to hear from the publisher to whom you've sent your mystery novel

❏ The agony you go through while waiting to receive the first copy of your published book, so you can finally see it between covers

❏ The quality in a story that keeps readers turning the pages, eager to find out what happens next

❏ All of the above

❏ None of the above

2
You Can Do It

You have a story to tell, a crime to solve, a mysterious fictional world you want to explore. A couple of characters are drifting around in your brain, tugging at your mental sleeve and demanding your attention. You're haunted by the image of a shuttered house, a dark alley, a lonely mountain cabin — a place where the air crackles with the energy of possible violence. Or some event — a news story, an occurrence in your neighborhood, an episode in your family history — has caught your imagination and won't let go. Perhaps, having enjoyed the pleasure of unraveling the puzzles posed by other writers, you're inspired to tackle a greater challenge: constructing a mystery of your own. Or maybe you heaved a poorly crafted book across the room and declared, "I can write a better novel than that."

Whatever your motive for writing a mystery, you're embarking on an exciting adventure. From where you stand now, completing a manuscript may seem like a faraway goal, shimmering way out at the horizon. Having it published may appear even more distant. But others have reached the goal, and you can too.

Making the Commitment

The first step to writing a mystery is simply to make a commitment to yourself that you will begin this project and carry it through. Well, perhaps "simply" is not quite the right word. Writing a mystery, especially a novel, takes time, energy, determination, and courage. It's a long-term investment, and you can't see when you start what the payoff will be. I can assure you that you will reap many rewards, even if your mystery isn't published. Still, you will encounter moments of distraction and discouragement, and the pledge you've made will give you an incentive to jump over those hurdles.

You might be able to toss off a short story in an afternoon, but more likely it will take days, even weeks. A novel can require a year or more. From the initial flash of an idea to a manuscript ready for submission, my first book, *A Relative Stranger,* took eight years to write. I worked in fits and starts, with months of dry spells between periods of production (not an approach I recommend). What kept me going was the determination to prove to myself, if to no one else, that I could actually write a novel.

Remember, a promise to yourself is no less binding than all the commitments you make to other people — your spouse, your kids, your boss, your coworkers, your friends. Make your commitment real, visible, and serious. State it out loud. Post it on your bulletin board or refrigerator. Draw up a contract and file it with your most important documents. Then get to work on your book.

Drawing on Your Resources

Who, me? you ask. Write a mystery? But I don't have any special background or qualifications to be a mystery writer.

Curiosity, imagination, and logic are the three mental qualities most important to writers who create mysteries.

Neither do most authors when they're first getting started. At one time, I made part of my living by producing résumés for job seekers. Although we often hear tales of people in high places who are caught lying about inflated credentials, I found the opposite problem to be far more common: people failing to recognize and take credit for genuine talents and accomplishments. It might help to take stock of the many assets and resources you need to bring to the task of writing a mystery.

Curiosity, Imagination, and Logic

Curiosity, imagination, and logic are the three mental qualities most important to writers who create mysteries.

Curiosity gives us the passion to understand more about ourselves, other people, and society at large. We want to make sense of the world we live in, to capture a glimpse of its hows and whys.

Imagination lets us apply the quality of make-believe to our search for understanding. It has been said that nonfiction is about facts but that fiction is about truth; imagination is what enables us to make the leap between the two. In this way, fiction writers are like detectives: we observe facts about the world or the people in it, then use our imaginations to analyze and interpret these facts so that we can discern and present the larger meaning.

A sense of logic is perhaps more important for mystery writers than for writers of other genres. By definition, a mystery involves analyzing information to solve a problem or puzzle. The sequence of events must be somehow physically possible, and logic is needed to devise a workable plot that leads to a sensible and fair solution.

Writing a mystery is a journey of discovery. The exploration draws you both inward, as you delve into your imagination and your subconscious mind, and outward, as you research all the details you need to give your story the ring of truth and organize them into a story. You'll learn a lot in the process — guaranteed.

Your Knowledge of Mysteries

Chances are, if you want to write a mystery, you're already a fan of the form. You've probably read and enjoyed dozens, perhaps hundreds, of mysteries, and this means you've absorbed a great deal of information about how one is written. You've developed a sense of the structure of a mystery, its rhythm and pace. You recognize which characters, plot elements, and devices have become standard or commonplace and which provide an innovative twist. You understand that readers expect the author to play fair when laying out the clues. All this knowledge may be unconscious, but it's there. The purpose of this book is to help you bring it to the forefront of your mind.

If you're not a mystery reader, now is the time to become one. Consider it the second step in your writing project, right after making the commitment. Range widely through the genre. If you think you want to write a cozy detective story with an amateur sleuth, read books of that type, but don't stop there. Sample some hard-boiled private eyes, taste some psychological suspense, savor a thriller or two. As you read, take notes. What did you like about the book, and why? What didn't you like, and why not? What would you have done differently if you were the author?

A helpful exercise is to choose two mysteries, one you think was especially well written and one you didn't care for, and analyze them both. How did the author bring the characters to life? Make the setting vivid? Create suspense? Plant the clues? Divert suspicion from the killer? At what point did you begin to suspect who the killer was and what gave you the clue?

Reading with care and attention is one of the best ways to learn how to write. It's like baking a cake — much easier to do if you know how a cake looks and tastes, if you know the difference between angel food and devil's food. The idea is not to imitate other writers or be derivative in any way. You want to do what they do but do it differently, honoring the conventions of the genre with your own fresh, original story and style.

Your Personal Knowledge

You may think you lead a dull, ordinary life. But, in fact, you are an expert in some field that would make an excellent background for a mystery. You are already familiar with places where mysteries can happen. You have experienced or observed relationships that have taught you something about the workings of the human mind and heart.

Look for the possibilities in your own line of work, hobbies, and daily activities. Almost any form of human endeavor has the potential to make a good background for a mystery, and if you find a subject intriguing, many readers will too.

Try this as a confidence booster: Make a list of the topics about which you have a reasonable base of knowledge. You'll probably be surprised at how many there are. Consider, for example: What did you study at university? What have you learned on the job (any job, not just your chosen profession but even the burger-flipping or gas-pumping you did in high school)? What leisure-time interests or activities do you pursue? Where have you traveled? In what way are you involved in your community? What groups do you belong to? What topics do you read about avidly? On what subjects do people ask your advice? What do you do in the course of a typical day?

Here's a quick list I came up with for myself, drawing on my non-mystery-writing life: acting, architecture, art history, banking, baseball, bookkeeping, camping, chocolate, cooking, cross-country travel, driving in heavy traffic, friendship, gardening, genealogy, graphic design, the health-care industry, historic preservation, interior design, investing, literature, marketing, marriage, movies, nonprofit organizations, painting, photography, printing, psychology, public speaking, small-business management, swimming, tea, theater production, and urban planning.

Don't forget to list your research skills. If you know how to use a library, surf the Internet, or make telephone calls, you can fill in any gaps in the information you need to write your story.

Your Family, Friends, and Acquaintances

If you don't have the knowledge you need for your mystery, tap into the skills and interests of your friends and acquaintances. Mystery author Linda Grant, describing one way she looks for ideas for her mysteries, says that when she meets people at a party or gathering, she asks, "In your profession, why might someone want to kill someone else, and how would they go about doing it?" At first they think the question odd, but once Grant explains that she's a mystery writer, they get into the game. And almost everyone can provide examples of motives, means, and opportunities for murder that are specific to their field.

Your Love of Language

Language is the writer's means of expression, just as paint is the artist's. Most writers love words — their sound and rhythm, their literal and implied meanings. We use words like brushstrokes to express not only the content of our ideas but their color, shape, and texture, their interplay of light and shadow.

People who want to write generally have solid verbal skills; if they didn't, writing wouldn't appeal to them as a means of self-expression. When I teach classes for beginning writers, I find that most students, even those who have never penned one word of fiction before, have a powerful command of the language. Those whose skills are rusty improve with practice and a bit of gentle instruction.

It helps to have an appreciation for grammar and the structure of language — the way that words are put together to create meaning. This doesn't mean, however, that you must be able to accurately define a subordinate clause. You have probably honed a sharp instinct for the fine points through your love of reading well-written books. Take heart from an experiment I participated in way back in the ninth grade. The school district wanted to test a pilot program developed to increase language skills. Two English classes, matched in ability, were selected to participate in a test of the program. For 20 minutes each day, kids in one class did specially created grammar drills. The other class (the one I was in) received no formal grammar instruction; instead, we read lots of stories and essays and turned in weekly writing assignments. In September and then the following June, both classes took standardized tests that measured our grammar skills. You can guess the result: to the dismay of school officials, the grammar drilling made no discernible improvement in the first class's test results, while we readers and writers improved by leaps and bounds.

Making Time to Write

The alarm rings, yanking you away from your dream. Eyes still shut, you stumble to the shower and fumble through your morning routine. You wrangle the kids out of bed and off to school, toting homework and lunchboxes. Pouring coffee down your throat, you dash out the door to battle through snarled traffic to work. All day long you have projects to start, telephone calls to answer, memos to write, meetings to attend, customers to satisfy, projects to finish, papers to push, and never a moment to catch your breath. After work, you pick up the dry cleaning, stop at the grocery, round up the kids, inch home through worse traffic, throw dinner on the table, check homework, study for your night-school class, field telephone calls about your community group's fundraiser, collapse in front of the TV for a few minutes, and fall into bed.

Does this sound like a typical day in your life? If you're like most of us, you have plenty of ways to spend your time besides writing a mystery. You have a family, a job, volunteer activities, and a social life. You may have classes to attend, exams to study for, and papers to write. Your hobbies and interests clamber for attention. How can you cram one more thing into your packed schedule? When are you going to find time to write?

You don't find time. You make time.

It's easy to regard writing as a guilty pleasure, an indulgence, a treat that steals time from more pressing obligations. As soon as your schedule clears, as soon as you have the luxury of unfilled blocks of time with no competing demands, then you'll get started.

If you think this way, your book will never get written, because there will always be something else to do, some other priority that tugs on your sleeve and insists it's more urgent. Something I've noticed is that frequently people who profess the desire to write are in fact busily arranging their lives to ensure that they have excuses (not enough time, too many other obligations) to avoid writing. I fell into this trap for a long time myself, and I mention it to urge you to avoid it.

Even when your intention is strong and sincere, sitting down to write a novel can stir up a lot of fear. Why? Because it puts you to the test in so many ways. Can you actually write a whole book? Will it be any good? Will your family or friends feel slighted or angry when you lavish attention on your mystery instead of on them? Will your novel expose dark aspects of your psyche that you'd rather keep hidden?

It is much easier to not run the risk and to avoid the whole issue, consoling ourselves with thoughts of the books we could have written, if only we'd had the time. That's why making a commitment to yourself is essential. You don't want to let yourself down by reneging on your promise. And as writing becomes a habit and you begin to make steady progress, you'll find that the joy and excitement you experience will overcome the fear.

Following are four things you need to do to make time to write.

> As writing becomes a habit and you begin to make steady progress, you'll find that the joy and excitement you experience will overcome the fear of writing.

Schedule a Regular Writing Time

British mystery writer Michael Gilbert penned 23 novels while on the train riding back and forth to work. Janet Dawson, author of the Jeri Howard series, wrote half a dozen mysteries at dawn, rising early every morning to write for two hours before leaving home for her regular job. My friend Bette takes her laptop computer to the office and sits in her car every lunchtime, eating yogurt and writing her novel.

Most successful mystery authors start out this way, squeezing in their writing around the pressures of earning a living and raising a family. Eventually some reach a cherished goal — giving up their day job and writing mysteries full time. Others continue for years to juggle writing with other demands. You can do the same thing. Somewhere there is a chunk of time you can carve from your busy schedule and devote to your mystery. Turn off the TV. Order in pizza instead of cooking elaborate meals. Catnap in the early evening and take advantage of late-night hours when the house is quiet.

Beginning writers are often advised to write every day. That's excellent counsel, but frankly it's not always practical. So I'll be easier on you and tell you to write at least once a week. You won't finish your book as quickly, but a weekly writing session still allows you to maintain momentum and make steady, measurable progress.

Every week, identify one block of time for writing, mark it on your calendar, and consider it sacrosanct. This is your appointment with yourself to write. Put a "Do not disturb" sign on your door or the back of your chair and let voicemail take your calls.

If you can, make your writing date at least two hours long. An hour, even 45 minutes, is better than no time at all. But two hours will let your characters really stretch their muscles and push the story forward. You'll have time to chase an idea and see where it leads. You'll be surprised at how quickly the time passes.

Determine Your Prime Writing Time

I admire writers like Janet Dawson and others I've known who can work well at sunrise. I'm so muddle-headed in the early morning that if I fall out of bed, I have a hard time finding the floor. No matter what time I get up, my brain refuses to awaken until 10 a.m. Before then, it's useless for me to try to string words into coherent sentences. On the other hand, I've been known to get on a roll about midnight and keep up a good pace until 2 or 3 a.m. But my prime times for working — the hours when my wits and energy are at their peak — tend to be in the late morning and in the early evening.

Everyone's body clock and mental rhythm are different. Experiment by scheduling your writing session at different hours; this will help you figure out when you tend to be at your sharpest and most productive. Your own prime time could be in the morning, at noon, or at night (and when it turns out to be may surprise you). Once you determine your prime time, reserve it whenever you can; your book deserves and demands that you work on it when you're at your best.

If your prime time happens to be booked solid, that's no excuse to skip out on a writing schedule. Writing at less-than-perfect moments may not be ideal, but it's much better than not writing at all.

Learn to Say No

To complete any project as substantial as writing a mystery novel, you must make it a priority. And that means saying no to demands that don't serve an equally important personal goal. Let someone else chair the committee or host the holiday dinner or captain the softball team. It's amazing how difficult it can be to say a short, simple word like "no." So practice now, reciting this sentence out loud until it comes easily: "No. I need to spend that time working on my mystery."

Set Mini-Goals

Your goal is to write a whole book. The very thought of it strikes you as a huge, almost overwhelming endeavor — an enormous investment of time and energy. The sheer size and scope of the enterprise can intimidate you into not even getting started.

As with any large project, the way to handle it is to break it down into small, manageable chunks or mini-goals that are easy to focus on and achieve. A mini-goal might be to complete a scene or a chapter, or to write a particular number of pages or words, or to spend two hours on planning, or to find a particular piece of information you need.

Attaining mini-goals helps you measure and acknowledge your progress. Take them one at a time, and when you've stacked up enough of them, the book will be finished.

Facing the Blank Page

Few things are more terrifying than a blank page or a blank computer screen. It sits there in front of you, empty, pristine, taunting, daring you to sully it with your inadequate words. You're up to the challenge. Go ahead. Pick up your pen, or poise your fingers on the keyboard, and begin.

One warm-up technique many writers use is to retype the last couple of pages they wrote during their previous session; by the time they reach the point where they broke off, they're ready to just keep rolling. I've heard of writers who stop writing halfway through a sentence when they quit work for the day, just so they'll be in midstream when they start again the next morning.

If you're just getting started and have no midstream to jump into, start writing whatever pops into your head. If you're distracted by negative thoughts or counterproductive concerns (I'm not a good writer, I should prepare for the meeting tomorrow, did I ever answer Uncle Fred's letter?), write them down; that will help clear them out of the way.

Gradually, something worthwhile will evolve out of what initially seems like incoherent rambling. Here's how I started one scene in the book I'm currently writing. My detective, Jess Randolph, arrives at another character's office:

> *All right so what's happening here, what's going on in this scene? Darned if I know. Caroline Webster's office. I can't think of anything to say. Jess, jess, jess, jess, what are you doing there? Okay. Caroline Webster high-powered executive big fancy office what does it look like? I don't think these two are going to like each other. What to say? I haven't got a clue. Okay, here comes Webster stiff and starchy frowning lips pursed busy annoyed at the interruption tapping a pencil on her big rosewood desk. The eraser tip, wouldn't want to scratch it. The desk was vast; I could imagine a dinner party of twelve seated around it . . .*

The beauty of working with a word processor is that once I'm into a scene, I can zap all the extraneous verbiage. Here's how the opening of the scene reads in the final manuscript:

> *Caroline Webster, executive vice president of Moritz Investment Associates, tapped out a rhythm on her desktop with her pencil as I spoke. The eraser tip, I noticed — she wouldn't want to gouge the highly polished rosewood surface. The desk was vast; I could imagine a dinner party of twelve seated around it, eating foie gras and truffles from gold-rimmed porcelain.*

Even if you're not ready to work on an actual scene — for instance, if you're still in the planning stages — such an approach give you a jumpstart. Or, try this exercise: Get a kitchen timer, one that chimes quietly and turns itself off, so that it's not too jarring. Set it for five minutes, then start to write whatever comes to mind. Don't lift your pen from the page or your fingers from the keyboard. Write quickly, and don't backtrack to change a word, correct a spelling, or add a punctuation mark. Quality is not the point here; the purpose is to get the ideas flowing, to shift your brain into writing mode.

Suppose the timer is ticking but your mind is as blank as your page. Pull a work of fiction from your bookshelf, open it to a random page, and copy the first sentence you see. When you reach the end of the sentence, flip the book shut and keep writing. This tactic works best if you haven't yet read the book; that way you can't be influenced by the sentence's contextual meaning.

Or, you can try one of the idea starters below. Set the timer, copy one of the sentences in the list below, and don't pause when you reach the ellipsis:

- "Don't open the door!" yelled Chris. Too late. Lee had already twisted the knob. The door creaked open and . . .

- Pinewood Lane was more like a deer track than a road. Rain-heavy boughs hung overhead. In the flashlight's beam, Alex saw . . .

- Face to face with Dale at last, Terry had never been so angry. Here was the person who . . .

When five minutes is up, you may have a head start on a brand-new story. Or a fresh thought about one you're already working on. Ideas generate words, but words also lead to ideas. When you put words on the page, even if at first they seem silly, trite, inaccurate, or off the mark, you are making good progress.

The Joy of Writing

Hard work. Frustration. Fear. If that's what writing a mystery is all about, why bother?

You make the effort because those drawbacks pale in comparison to the benefits. You feel great satisfaction when you successfully conclude a major project like writing a book — and possibly publishing it, although your achievement is real whether it's published or not.

Equally as important are the ample pleasures you encounter along the way. There's a saying that the journey is as important as the destination, and that's certainly true of writing a mystery. The rewards are many: the exhilarating high you experience when a writing session goes well, the pleasure of keeping company with people who exist only in

Warning: Mystery writing can be addictive. Once you try it, you'll keep coming back for more.

your imagination but seem as real as your family and friends, the insights that bubble up to surprise you, the bits of wisdom you didn't even know you knew. You get to dig into research, becoming knowledgeable in fascinating subjects like forensics, psychology, and criminal law. You have the opportunity to join the mystery community, where you can take classes, attend conferences, discover bookstores devoted to your favorite genre, and come to count like-minded writers as friends.

An exciting fictional world awaits in your imagination, ready for you to explore. If you want a challenge, a sense of joy, or a thrill of accomplishment, it's hard to beat writing a mystery.

3
Developing Your Story

A friend of mine who teaches business communication tells her students to break writing projects into three phases: prewriting, writing, and revising. She maintains that prewriting — carefully planning all aspects of the document — is as important as the actual writing, and she advises writers to take time to define audience and goals, gather supporting data, and organize material in a way that guides readers to the main points. This way the memo or report is much more likely to achieve the desired results. All this is true of fiction writing too. Once you're fired up with enthusiasm and ideas, you may be tempted to plunge in and begin flinging words onto the page. Better to channel your energy into planning; the time and effort will pay off.

Writing a mystery is like taking a journey to a place you've never visited. This is especially true of your first novel, though every book will take you into unexplored lands. The journey will go more smoothly if you're prepared. You want to figure out your itinerary, map your route, and decide what essential gear to tuck into your duffel bag. Of course, once you start writing, the story will take unexpected twists, turns, and detours, and you may well arrive at a destination far different from the one you originally intended. But if you plan ahead, you'll endure fewer false starts and wrong turns.

Planning usually comes before writing, but it is also an ongoing task even after the serious writing has begun. Don't check it off your to-do list once you've made a few notes and feel ready to write the first draft. Creating a book is an interactive mix of planning and writing. You move back and forth, planning, writing, then planning some more, based on the new things you discover along the way.

Finding Ideas

Where do you get your ideas? Readers and aspiring writers are fascinated by this question. As your writing experience grows, you discover that ideas are everywhere. The trick is to snag them as they fly by and then to find the time to write about them all.

The Birth of a Mystery

One of my own answers to the question of where to find ideas is, "At the corner of Franklin and Jackson Streets in San Francisco." I was once crossing the street on my way to a bus stop when a brief scene played out in my head:

> *A woman is awakened late at night by a telephone call. The caller identifies himself as her father — he was not her step-father, as she first assumes, but her real father. She hangs up on him, but he calls back and begs to see her. Giving him an angry retort, she slams down the telephone again. The third time the telephone rings, she pulls her pillow over her ears and lies quaking in the dark, refusing to answer.*

When I got off the bus and reached my destination, I wrote down the scene. I could picture the woman amidst her jumble of blankets, hear the tone of her voice and that of her father's. I knew her dog was in the room with her. I had a sense that she'd had little or no previous contact with this man. And that's all I had.

I was faced with a challenge: to figure out who these people were, why the woman's father was breaking a 30-year silence to call her in the middle the night. Why did she react so strongly? What led to his call, and what would it lead to? In other words, what was the story?

This impression of a telephone call, almost word for word as I wrote it down after my bus ride, became the opening scene of my novel, *A Relative Stranger.*

Story Triggers

When an idea — a scene, an image, a snatch of conversation — pops into your head, it's a gift from your subconscious mind and you should pay close attention. But you needn't wait for an idea to hit you spontaneously. The world abounds with story triggers that can fire your imagination. What you need to do is train yourself to recognize them.

Story triggers can present themselves in a variety of guises; they may appear in the form of a person, a premise, a place, or a passion.

A person

A character wanders into your mind; you encounter or read about someone who intrigues you; an acquaintance provides a model for a detective or perhaps for a villain.

Sometimes, your own relationship with another person can trigger an idea. More than one mystery has been inspired by the angry thought, "I would really like to get even with him." Writing a mystery lets you carry out that impulse safely, on paper, with no actual harm done to anyone concerned.

A premise

You run across a situation or incident that seems fraught with dramatic possibilities. The source could be an event in your own life, a news story, or simply a flash of inspiration. An early story of mine was sparked when my grandfather, a judge, told me about a time when he gave a ride to a hitchhiker, only to discover hours later that the man was a convict escaping from prison.

Neither my grandfather nor the convict appear in my story; all I used was the premise: a driver picks up a hitchhiker who turns out to be a fleeing convict. If your story is born of an actual occurrence, reduce it to bare bones before you turn it into fiction. Encapsulate the idea in a single sentence, then let your imagination fly. Come up with fresh details and new characters. You're writing fiction, so what really happened, and to whom, is not relevant. Trying to stick to the facts will only hinder your creative process.

A story trigger for a mystery could center on the murder itself. For example, you might be intrigued when you read about an unusual poison, or you could try to devise how to commit the perfect, undetectable crime. Then ask yourself, who would use this method, and why? Most often, though, an author doesn't work out exactly what the crime will be until further along in the planning process.

A place

As you're walking down a city street, hiking in a rocky canyon or dense forest, or taking tea in the library of a Victorian mansion, a thought occurs to you: "Hey, this place would make a great setting for a mystery." For example, in the early 1990s, a number of poker palaces opened in the San Francisco Bay area. Local officials were eager for the tax revenues these cards-only casinos would generate. Where they saw the solution to a budget crunch, I saw a mystery waiting to happen. The fictitious Royal Court Casino was both the setting and the starting point for my story "House of Cards."

Mysteries can turn up in exotic locations. Sue Henry, in *Murder on the Iditarod Trail*, used the setting and background of a famous Alaskan dog-sled race. Aaron Elkins has traveled the world with his sleuth, forensic anthropologist Gideon Oliver, who has solved cases from Egypt to Tahiti to Mexico's Yucatan Peninsula. (Sometimes you can guess where a writer spent a recent vacation by the setting of his or her latest book.)

A passion

Look for story triggers in your own emotions and the things you feel strongly about. What is the most thrilling thing you've ever done? What frightens you the most? What makes your blood boil? What cause do you fight for? The answer to each of these questions is a potential story trigger. What's more, it will be a story you're likely to get excited about writing because you feel strongly about the subject.

Here's an example of a story trigger of mine and what I did with it. One day in San Francisco's Chinatown, I encountered a four-foot-high wooden statue of Buddha on the sidewalk outside a shop. Next to the statue was posted a sign reading, "Rub my head for wisdom or my belly for luck." I noticed the belly was much shinier than the head, indicating it had been rubbed more often. This intrigued me: What is it about human nature that makes people desire luck more than wisdom? I scribbled a note to myself, thinking I might use the statue sometime to add a little local color to a story.

> Look for story triggers in your own emotions and the things you feel strongly about. You're likely to get excited about writing when you feel strongly about the subject.

Several months later, the statue came back into mind, but not as an image of local color. The wooden Buddha and its sign became the main motif of a short story, providing both the setting (Chinatown) and the theme (wisdom versus luck). Playing around with the idea of luck led me to think about gambling and from there the story situation evolved: a man starts gambling for fun and gets in over his head. The resulting tale, "Dreaming of Dragons," appears in the anthology *Lethal Ladies II*.

What turns a random thought or observation into a story trigger is curiosity. Whenever you wish you knew more about something or want to explore further, that's the sign of a potential story. Ask yourself, Who? What? When? Where? Why? How? For example, when you read a newspaper article and find yourself thinking, "What would make someone behave like that?" you have a story trigger. When you see a stranger across a crowded room and wonder, "What is he doing here?" that's another. If something intrigues you, ask yourself a question about it and imagine what the answer might be. That's how a story begins.

Capturing Ideas

Finding an idea is only half the battle; the challenge is keeping it. In both of the examples I gave from my own experience, note the key words: I wrote it down.

This is important advice. If you don't write down your idea, you're likely to suffer from what I call the Brilliant Idea Syndrome. This annoying affliction struck me recently: On a Wednesday afternoon, driving along University Avenue in San Francisco, with a Beatles' oldie playing on the radio and a silver Toyota in front of me, an idea for a story pops into my head. It's a Brilliant Idea, so wonderful and powerful that there's no way I'll possibly forget it.

On Thursday, I can recall that I had a Brilliant Idea. I can recollect everything about the moment it struck — University Avenue, the music, the silver car. But I cannot remember my Brilliant Idea.

Don't rely on your memory to store ideas for you. Memory can be capricious and fickle; it can forget your best thoughts as casually as it presents them to you. The only way you can be certain of keeping your ideas is to make sure you write them down.

> Whenever you wish you knew more about something or want to explore further, that's the sign of a potential story. Ask yourself, Who? What? When? Where? Why? How?

Turning Ideas into a Story

Okay, you have an idea and you've written it down. How do you take that vague notion in your head and turn it into a 75,000-word book? Or even a 5,000-word short story? Simple: Find more ideas to add to it.

Nonwriters sometimes have the misconception that once an idea has flashed into their mind, the rest of the story is there too. All they need to do is grasp it and write it down; the story will unfold from the idea in an inevitable progression.

Nothing could be further from the truth. A story is a product of a multitude of ideas; the initial idea or story trigger is an essential one, but it is only the first of many. You add a second idea, then a third, then another, until gradually the story begins to take shape.

The key to this process is asking that magical question: What if? Once this question has been asked, answers come bubbling forth that will help you figure out what your story is.

Take, for instance, my opening scene for *A Relative Stranger*. My vision on the way to the bus stop introduced two people about whom I knew almost nothing. I also had a situation — the unwelcome middle-of-the-night telephone call. What was going on here? Why would a man suddenly, at half past one in the morning, call a daughter he had not been in touch with since she was a toddler? It would have to be a more than a whim.

I began by asking myself these questions:

☞ What if he was in trouble, and serious trouble at that? He must think for some reason that his daughter could help him.

☞ What if he realizes that the police are about to arrest him for a murder — one he insists he didn't commit?

☞ What if his daughter is a private detective, someone with the investigative skills to help him establish his innocence?

☞ What if he is in an unfamiliar city and has no one else to turn to for help?

And so the mystery that became *A Relative Stranger* began to reveal itself — the story of the daughter, Jess Randolph, and how she is affected when the father who walked out on her when she was a small child suddenly reappears in her life as a murder suspect.

Sample 1 uses a different story trigger to show the possibilities of What if? questions in greater detail.

Not every What if? question yields a valid answer. Like jigsaw puzzle pieces, some you try won't match the knobs and notches on the pieces you've already put in place. Keep trying; you'll find the ones that fit.

The Starting Points: Characters, Conflict, and Crime

A story is an account of what happens when a character confronts a conflict. A mystery is created when the conflict results in one or more of the characters committing a crime.

The first pieces you need to begin to put together your story are some characters, a conflict, and a crime. The first two are essential ingredients in any story. Indeed, you could define a story as an account of what happens when a character confronts a conflict. A mystery is created when the conflict results in one or more of the characters committing a crime — often a murder. When these three elements come together, you have the basic situation from which to develop the plot of your mystery.

Very likely, your story trigger or your initial idea for the story will give you a nudge toward either the characters, the conflict, or the crime, and your story will develop from there. Your next task is to come up with ideas about the other two ingredients. As you pose your What if? questions, consider the potential answers in each of the areas listed on the following pages.

Sample 1
What If? Story Development

Story trigger: A letter in an advice column from an employee concerned about a coworker. It's a social office, but the man in question refuses all invitations to join the others in after-work activities, claiming he has other plans. He does not talk about his outside interests and while he claims to have girlfriend, no one has seen her. Office mates have concluded he's lying and really has no social life.

What if . . .

The concerned colleague is a woman named Donna who has decided she is in love with the reticent coworker, Paul?

Donna pursues Paul, writing him letters, inviting him to lunch, and otherwise giving him persistent attention.

What if . . . (Story 1)

Donna is married to an abusive man named Larry who is prone to jealous rages?

Her crush becomes obvious to coworkers, and one of them takes it upon himself to tell Larry what is going on.

Larry arrives at the workplace with a gun. He shoots several people, killing at least one of them.

Who is killed? Donna, Paul, someone else?

What happens next?

OR

What if . . . (Story 2)

Donna is unmarried but has set her mind on marrying Paul?

Donna begins secretly following Paul after work, trying to get a glimpse of the purported girlfriend.

What if . . .

The company that Paul and Donna work for is an importer and retailer of fine jewelry? Paul is a new employee who sought the job to learn the firm's systems and its points of vulnerability in order to set up a heist.

Tailing Paul one night, Donna follows him to a meeting of major-league jewel thieves.

Sample 1 — Continued

What if . . .

Donna is discovered by the thieves? After a struggle she gets away, but fears they will come after her to kill her.

    Afraid to go home or to work, she must find shelter elsewhere.

    What happens next?

OR

What if . . .

Having followed Paul to an out-of-the-way location, Donna watches as he meets a woman there? They are obviously lovers.

    Donna recognizes the woman from news photos as the wife of a prominent politician who is running for reelection.

    Donna and Paul are employed by a news organization, or by a political-consultant firm working for the politician's opponent?

    What happens next?

OR

What if . . . (Story 3)

The first person to arrive at work on Monday morning, Donna discovers the body of a murdered coworker in the lobby?

    The police cannot find enough conclusive evidence to arrest anyone for the crime.

    The suspicion of all their coworkers falls on Paul, in part because he has insisted on making himself an outsider.

    Donna agrees to help Paul as he tries to find out what really happened and prove his innocence.

    Who was killed? What is assumed to be the motive? What happens next?

Note: An endless number of stories can evolve from a single story trigger. The What if? questions shown here gets three of them rolling; they are far from complete. All three derive from a single scenario: casting Donna and Paul as two principal characters and assuming that Donna is in love with Paul.

Characters

Without characters, there is no story. Characters are the life blood of any story. No matter how intriguing a situation you come up with, until some characters begin to walk around and experience it, the story won't come alive.

The important triumvirate of characters in a mystery — the ones who play the greatest part in determining what the story is — consists of the detective, the villain, and the victim. The detective is usually the protagonist: the central figure of the story and the person who ultimately will solve the crime. The villain is the perpetrator of the crime whom the sleuth is seeking to unmask and bring to justice. He or she is the antagonist, the principal opposing force pitted against the detective. The victim is the person who is killed or otherwise suffers a wrong at the hands of the villain. The victim's sad fate incites the story's main action. His or her actions, relationships, and circumstances are given careful scrutiny throughout the book in the hunt for the villain.

Many mystery writers add a fourth character to this list: someone whose life is turned upside down by what happens, perhaps a member of the victim's family or a person who is wrongfully accused. I think of this character as the secondary protagonist. Other characters will come along to play major or minor roles, but these three or four characters are the ones to concentrate on as you start planning your story.

Conflict

Conflict is the blood that flows through the story and gives it energy. It sets up the basis for the interactions of your characters by giving them problems to resolve or difficulties to overcome.

Mystery writers are fortunate in that right from the start, they know the nature of the two fundamental conflicts that define their story, even if they're still hazy on the details. The first conflict is the one that has caused one person (the villain) to commit a grievous offense against another (the victim). This conflict is the wellspring of the hidden story. The other conflict is the basis of the surface story: the battle that ensues as the detective endeavors to identify the killer and the killer attempts to get away with the crime. The victim's death is the pivot point that connects the two. The hidden story and the surface story are discussed later in this chapter.

These are far from the only conflicts in a mystery, however. Mysteries are rife with clashes and discords, large and small. Few characters are spared. Of particular concern are the problems that beset your protagonist, whose struggles to surmount them form the spine of your plot.

What kinds of conflicts can you put your major characters up against? Here are the principal sources; tap into them for What if? ideas.

Other characters

When one person bears enough ill will toward another to contemplate murder, certainly that qualifies as a major conflict. The villain, feeling in some way threatened or impeded by the soon-to-be victim, resorts to violence, believing somehow that this will resolve or eliminate the problem.

For the detective, the problem posed by the killer is the major issue of the book, but not the only one. Conflict can arise in any relationship, even the most loving or altruistic one, and including other interpersonal difficulties can enrich and enliven the story. Other characters who might present your detective with obstacles could include:

- Friends or family members who, for whatever motives, discourage or distract the detective from pursuing the investigtion wholeheartedly

- Persons the detective should be able to trust, but whose actions raise suspicion about their loyalty or their possible involvement in the crime

- Associates of the killer or victim who, though innocent of the crime, have their own personal reasons for impeding the investigation

- Police officers or other persons who are conducting their own investigation and see the detective as a competitor or an interference

Societal attitudes, expectations, and trends

We live in an imperfect world. Until we achieve a better one, societal conditions will hand mystery writers plenty of material: controversial issues, prejudice and intolerance, cruel or unfair treatment of individuals and groups, unequal opportunities, clashes over lifestyles and values.

Including conflicts like these can establish the place and time of your story and add to the richness and verisimilitude of the characters. But remember, such conflicts are abstract. If one figures in your story, pull it from the background to the foreground, and humanize it by assigning particular characters to represent the opposing sides.

Forces of nature

Fire, flood, storm, drought, harsh terrain. While these impersonal forces of weather, climate, and geography don't commit crimes, they can certainly impose hardships and place people in danger. You can use them to provide dramatic complications for your detective and other characters. The suspense novel *Snowbound,* by Bill Pronzini, is an example of a story incorporating this type of conflict. A blizzard and avalanche imperil the residents of a mountain village by cutting off access to the outside world, leaving the residents trapped in the company of vicious killers.

Internal struggles

As a character in Walt Kelly's comic strip Pogo used to say, "We has met the enemy, and it is us." Many people find that their most serious and persistent conflicts, the ones most difficult to overcome, are those that spring from within. Through the course of the story, your detective's own flaws and weaknesses may get him or her into trouble — a hot temper, a tendency to leap before looking, loyalty to someone undeserving of it.

Another source of internal conflict is the moral or ethical dilemmas engendered by the situation. For instance, what if someone you love has committed a serious crime: To what length should you go to protect that person? Or what if your efforts to save one person's life will place a different person in grave danger: How do you choose between them?

Internal obstacles provide a deep well of material for a mystery writer. They make your characters more complex and lifelike, and they invest your story with layers of interest that are hard to achieve with external conflict alone.

Crime

In a mystery, the story's main conflict or conflicts result in crime, usually a murder. Although other crimes may also occur during the story, the focal point of the story is the murder and the protagonist's efforts to solve it.

You can approach the What if? questions about the crime from several angles. Start with a character (under what circumstances might this person become mixed up in a murder case, and what role would she play?) or a situation (under what circumstances would someone be so desperate that he would kill another person?). Or, you could play around with the traditional tests used as standards against which to measure the proof of a culprit's guilt:

- *Motive.* Who would want to murder Lord Chesterfield, and why?

- *Means.* How would the villain go about killing Lord Chesterfield without getting caught? Mystery writers enjoy the challenge of devising a perfect crime — of finding exotic and undetectable poisons which can be slipped into the victim's drink or suggesting unusual and unexpected murder weapons.

- *Opportunity.* Under what circumstances could the villain get close enough to Lord Chesterfield to accomplish the dastardly deed, and what sort of alibi might the villain contrive?

Which Comes First: Characters or Plot?

Mysteries have a reputation for being driven by their plots rather than by their characters. That may have been true once; it is far less so now. Many mysteries, upholding tradition, still rely primarily on the plot for their impact. Over the past couple of decades, however, characterization has gained in importance and become steadily stronger.

In a plot-driven mystery, the emphasis is on the puzzle, à la Agatha Christie; on action for its own sake; or on the author's manipulation of an elaborate house-of-cards arrangement of people, places, and incidents. The author predetermines the sequence of events, then selects the characters on the basis of how well equipped they are to do carry out the plan.

In a character-driven mystery, the puzzle is present, of course, but the characters are of most importance. The focus is on the psychology, emotions, and motivations of the protagonist and the people around him or her. These factors determine what the mystery is and how it will be solved. Marcia Muller, Sara Paretsky, and James Lee Burke are a few of the mystery writers who take this approach.

Both plot-driven and character-driven stories can be rewarding — to both readers and the writer — when skillfully written. If poorly written, each has its pitfalls. A plot-driven story can seem forced and hollow, with characters merely stereotypes or pawns. A character-driven story can meander with no apparent plot, point, or purpose. The best mysteries derive their energy from their characters *and* their plot, combining and balancing both. The characters dictate the plot by performing actions, making choices, and responding to situations in ways that are true to their natures. The plot in turn sets up situations that require the characters to take new actions, to make new choices and have different responses, and in the process, to change and grow.

If your initial idea for a story involves a character, ask yourself this: Given this character's background, personality, and motives, what sort of conflicts or crimes could this person find himself or herself mixed up in? Once involved, how would this person behave in those circumstances? Or, to turn it around, for an idea associated with some aspect of plot, ask: What kind of person would naturally act in the way the plot calls for? What background, personality, and motives would such a person need to have?

The Surface Story and the Hidden Story

To help you get your book in focus, keep in mind that a mystery is actually two stories in one. I refer to these as the surface story and the hidden story.

The Surface Story

In a mystery, the surface story is the narrative you write, the one your readers will read. It describes the investigation: the process by which your detective uncovers the truth about the crime that has been committed or the secret that has been concealed. Instead of focusing directly on the crime, the way a news report would, the surface story angles in on the crime's consequences. It examines the crime's impact on the lives of the people involved, including the detective.

The Hidden Story

The hidden story lies submerged beneath the surface story. It concerns the underlying secret your main character is trying to discover. This effort to find the truth is what defines your protagonist as a detective, no matter what his or her profession might be. The hidden story describes the circumstances surrounding the crime to be solved. It answers these questions:

- Who did what to whom?

- When, where, and how did the crime occur?

- Why was the crime committed?

The hidden story can have its own characters, plot, and setting. If you chose to, you could write a narrative that depicts the facts of the crime and its causes in a straightforward way. But when you choose to present them in a mystery, you want to bury these details and then reveal them slowly, letting your reader accompany your detective in a process of discovery.

Weaving the Surface and Hidden Stories Together

The surface story and the hidden story walk hand in hand — one in light and one in shadow. Readers experience the surface story in full as it unfolds, but for most of the book, they see the hidden story only in fragments, hints, and half-glimpsed movements. Yet the pursuit of the hidden story drives the action of the surface narrative throughout. The detective's purpose is to discover all the details of the hidden story. Once that has been accomplished, the surface story draws quickly to an end.

In some mysteries, the two are sequential, with the hidden story representing the past, and the surface story, the present. When this is the case, the crime (usually a murder) occurs before the curtain rises on the surface story, or early in the first act. The surface story is then a process of investigation which pieces together the details of the past event — the hidden story.

In other mysteries, the two stories play out side by side in the present time, mutually influencing each other: The surface story opens with an event that leads to one character, whose identity is unknown, committing a crime; an investigation into the crime begins; the detective's hunt causes the villain to do something more; the villain's response forces the detective to change course. In this way, the two stories interweave throughout the book.

Like many mystery authors, I like to know the rudiments of the hidden story before I begin writing. This provides me and my protagonist with a valuable sense of direction. It's much easier to keep the book on track if I know what destination I'm trying to reach.

One of my first steps is a game of What if? to sketch out some preliminary thoughts on the hidden story, starting with the basic questions: who, what, when, where, how, and why? I then write a brief description of the circumstances surrounding the crime — brief because I don't yet know many of the details. As the novel develops, I revisit the hidden story several times, filling in the blanks. When new suspects show up on the story's doorstep, I add a paragraph or two about them: What is their relationship to the villain or victim? What do they want to accomplish? What secrets of their own are they trying to hide?

The hidden story gives me insight into the surface story. It suggests possible scenes and settings, characters and clues. I gain ideas about how the detective gets involved, what information the detective must have to solve the crime, and how he or she might discover those key facts. The surface story, in turn, influences the hidden story. As the surface story develops, I learn things about the characters and the situation, and this new knowledge adds to and sometimes changes my understanding of the hidden story.

The hidden story

A good way to get your story rolling is to begin at the end and sketch out the hidden story first. Think about the questions: Who did what to whom? When, where, and how did the crime occur? Why was it committed? You don't need to write the hidden story in detail; a paragraph or a page may be enough. As your story develops and you know your characters better, you'll fill in the particulars. When you write the surface story, you won't reveal these details until close to the finish and probably not all at once. But working out basics of the hidden story ahead of time will give you a valuable sense of direction. You'll know what your detective needs to uncover, so you can guide his or her actions more effectively.

To Outline or Not to Outline?

Some writers swear by outlines. Some writers swear at them.

At a mystery writers' conference I attended, an author described the extensive outlines he creates for each book he writes. Running as long as 200 pages, the outline contains voluminous notes on the plot, descriptions of characters and settings, and lines of dialogue. The author knows every detail of the story before he starts writing.

The sense of being completely in charge, of knowing for sure exactly what you're doing (as this author does), might give you confidence to write. However, there are pitfalls. The story can lose its freshness for you long before you finish writing it. Moreover, you can lose out on exciting possibilities of discovery along the way, and miss the surprising events that unfold while you are writing which add new dimensions to the mystery.

A second writer at the same conference commented that he never outlines a story in advance but plunges right in. His theory is that if he can't guess what's going to happen next, neither will readers. Certainly this approach guarantees that the story will retain its freshness and its ability to surprise everyone.

The danger to this approach is realizing, 100 pages into the manuscript, that you've written yourself smack into a dead end. That means plodding back to figure out where you went wrong. You may discover you need to toss out the last 80 pages and start over.

What Is an Outline?

The term "outline" means different things to different writers. It's simply a convenient shorthand designation for the personal planning system, whether it's sketchy and slapdash or intricate and thorough, that an author has devised to help with the process of figuring out the story and keeping track of the details.

What "outline" rarely means to a fiction writer is the rigid format you were taught in school. While you're writing your novel, you can forget what your eighth grade teacher told you about Roman numerals and capital letters, or major points and subsidiary ideas. That method has its uses for other kinds of writing, but it's not well suited to the process of creating a mystery.

Planning systems are highly individualistic, and you must ultimately come up with your own. Possible components include:

- *Characters:* detailed biographies, charts listing physical descriptions and personality traits, interviews in which you ask questions and let the character "answer"

- *Plot:* lists of scenes, brief scene summaries, a synopsis of the action

- *Setting:* descriptive notes on the physical layouts of places and their sights, sounds, and smells; floor plans and maps

- *Clues:* lists or charts indicating what clues and items of infomation the detective and readers must have to solve the mystery, and the points in the story at which they will appear

- *Time line:* charts that track the order of events; lists showing where various characters were at crucial times

The Three-Stage Outline

My own approach is using what I call the three-stage outline, a model I developed while writing *A Relative Stranger.* Even after I had worked out a rough idea of the hidden story, I wasn't comfortable leaping right into the first draft, so I began to plot the novel in some detail, using the notebook system I describe below. But by the time I'd figured out the first third of the story, I'd grown impatient to begin writing. In outline form, the story seemed static and pale. I was eager to see the characters in action, to see my vision take shape on the page. I put aside my outline and wrote several chapters.

Soon, though, I reached uncharted territory. Writing grew difficult, and I found I couldn't move forward because I didn't know what the next sequence of events was going to be. So I went back and outlined another chunk — the middle third of the book as it turned out. Satisfied that I'd reestablished my sense of direction, I wrote those middle chapters. Finally, I stopped writing again, plotted the ending, and then completed the first draft.

This back-and-forth process, alternating stages of planning with stages of writing, worked well for me, and I've used it for my fiction writing ever since. It gives me control of the story while keeping it fresh, vital, and open to change. It lets me take advantage of serendipity — those fortuitous notions and ideas that would never occur to me while outlining. For example, early in *A Relative Stranger*, Jess Randolph enters the murder victim's apartment. Because she is an artist, her eye is drawn to a painting on the wall. When I wrote the scene, I hung the painting on the wall simply to decorate the set; it was a prop to give readers a tidbit of insight into both Jess and the victim. Imagine my surprise when, several chapters later, I found having that painting stolen worked well as a key twist of the plot. The placement of the painting was just a minor detail in my mind during the planning stage. Had I outlined the whole book straight through, I would not have known it was there, and I would have lost a valuable opportunity.

What form does my outline physically take? When I begin planning a novel, I set up a looseleaf notebook. It includes my first sketchy telling of the hidden story, lists of possible scenes in various sequences, and initial thoughts about characters. I add random ideas, doodles, and inspirations as they occur to me (writing a mystery is not always an orderly process).

As the story sorts itself out, I add to the notebook a separate page for each scene. At the top of the page, I write a summary of the scene, indicating where it takes place and describing what I expect is going to happen. These descriptions run anywhere from two or three lines to half a page; the rest of the page is left blank. In the course of writing the book, I fill up the empty space with notes to myself about changes to make and points to include later, when I write the second draft. That way, I can capture the ideas without interrupting the momentum that is carrying the story forward.

Having the scenes on individual pages has several advantages. Besides giving me plenty of room for further thoughts, it means I can re-arrange scenes, toss them out, and add new ones with ease. It's a flexible system that accommodates both linear and nonlinear thinking processes and brings a little order to the chaos of creation.

Sample 2 shows a page from my notebook for *A Relative Stranger*. As it turned out, the scene as first outlined bears only a marginal relationship to the one that appears in the book. Remember, your outline is not a set of rules and regulations. It's more like a guidebook or a map, and it's of your own devising. You can deviate from it, alter it, or ignore it whenever you please.

No matter how carefully you plan, if you are like most writers, much of your creativity will occur while you are writing. Once your characters are moving around in the story and living the lives you've created for them, they will surprise you with what they think and do. They will become real to you. You'll make other happy discoveries along the way and experience moments of genuine exhilaration when a crucial piece of the story falls into place. It's these rewards that will sustain you through the rough spots and keep you returning to your desk or computer until you can say, "Hey, I wrote a mystery."

Sample 2
A Page from the Planning Notebook

The first three paragraphs describe the scene as I originally envisioned it. The lines in italics represent the pencil scribbles I added to the outline page based on developments in later chapters and feedback I received from friends who read the work in progress.

Jess attends Deborah's funeral with Allen and meets Deborah's family: Brad, the father, who is Allen's business partner; Isabel, the mother; and Bradford, the college-freshman brother.

The funeral is something of a circus. Nick Gardino, the homicide detective assigned to the case, is at the funeral, observing. He and Jess talk; she explains her interest by saying Deborah's parents are friends of relatives she has in New York. During the conversation, Nick mentions that Deborah was found dead wearing flat shoes.

Brad gets into an argument with a newspaper reporter, during which he mentions he will be staying for a while in Deborah's flat. *(This gets printed in newspaper — gives credence to idea of return-of-necklace scheme.)*

J. sees both Brockway and Sanmarco at funeral.

Sees Ibanez at funeral talking to Brockway?

Nick gets pestered by press.

Lois Whittlesey, society grande dames are there.

Some kind of negative encounter between Brad and George.

"Brad, this is all your fault."

Allen mentions hat.

D. was murdered somewhere else, body dumped under freeway — reference to homeless character? Purse with missing keys.

From the Detective's Notebook 3
Novel or Short Story?

I've been using the terms "book" and "novel" in my discussion of writing mysteries, but what I've been discussing applies as much to writing short stories as it does to writing a novel-length story. How do you decide which to write?

A short story usually entails a smaller time commitment than a novel, but a writer should bring just as much care, attention, and skill to the task of writing one. A short story requires a tight focus and control. It must be told with great economy and precision of words. You have a limited scope to work in: a small cast of characters, just a handful of scenes, a single plot.

A novel gives you room to stretch. You can develop your characters slowly and more fully, bring in interesting background information, and tell a complex story with multiple plots and story lines. Though not necessarily harder to write than a short story, a novel will certainly take longer, and you'll need to keep track of many more characters and details.

If you're just starting out as a mystery writer, composing a short story or two (or more) can be a useful warm-up exercise, giving you practice working with story triggers and ideas, limbering up the muscles of your imagination, and honing your writing skills before you tackle a novel. A short story can also be a good testing ground for a new character, a place where you can become acquainted and observe that character in action before giving him or her the job of protagonist for a book-length project.

The marketplace shouldn't determine your choice. Decades ago, writers benefited from a thriving pulp-magazine scene that published short stories in abundance: detective stories, adventure yarns, science fiction, and westerns. The pulp magazines, which got their name from the cheap pulp paper they were printed on, usually had a dozen or more tales printed in each issue. They filled a demand for entertainment that is now served in large part by TV, and, lamentably, nearly all of them have died off. The number of publications where short mystery fiction finds a home has shrunk considerably, so these days a short story is not necessarily easier to sell than a novel.

The deciding factor in whether to write a short story or novel should be the tale itself. Some ideas require a big arena in which to play. Crammed into a short story, they can't develop their full potential. Such a story feels rushed, forced, or incomplete, and its readers end up perplexed and dissatisfied. If your story involves many characters, complicated circumstances, or intricate subplots, a novel is the better bet.

Other ideas work best on a small scale. If the essential conflict that the story deals with can be resolved in 5,000 words, there's no point in dragging it out to 80,000 words.

From the Detective's Notebook 3 — Continued

Or, perhaps your story idea is inherently implausible. Readers of a short story are more willing to suspend their disbelief for the brief amount of time that it takes to read a short story. The same implausible notion might well lose its believability over the course of a novel. In my short story "Identity Crisis," a woman discovers that everyone she knows thinks she is dead. Her obituary has appeared in the paper, her bank account has been closed, and her driver's license canceled. Worse, her identification has been stolen, so she can no longer prove who she is. This dilemma would have been difficult to make believable for the length of a novel. In a short story, however, I found that I could make her plight seem poignant and real.

How Long Is a Short Story? A Novel?

While there are no hard-and-fast definitions, these are commonly accepted categories and their approximate word counts:

- *Short story:* fewer than 7,500 words. Many publishers of short fiction prefer fewer.

- *Novelette:* 7,500 to 20,000 words. Novelettes are rarely encountered in the mystery genre. They are more common in other genres, such as fantasy and science fiction.

- *Novella:* 20,000 to 50,000 words. These, too, are rarely encountered in the mystery genre.

- *Novel:* More than 50,000 words. A typical detective story runs between 70,000 and 85,000 words. Thrillers tend to run longer. Juvenile and young adult mysteries, on the other hand, are generally shorter, in the neighborhood of 40,000 words.

PART 2
Clues to Crafting
a Compelling Mystery

4
Choosing Your
Cast of Characters

Whose story is it? Yours, of course, but in a very real sense, the book belongs to your characters. It's their lives that are changed by the events in your story and their choices and actions that determine the course of the mystery and its outcome. The cast of characters in a mystery includes the big three — the detective, the victim, and the villain — along with a full supporting cast. This chapter provides an overview of the roles each typically plays.

The Detective

Sherlock Holmes. Jane Marple. Lord Peter Wimsey. Philip Marlowe. Nero Wolfe. Lew Archer. Travis McGee. Sharon McCone. Kinsey Millhone. George Smiley.

When we look back on our favorite mysteries, it's usually the detectives we recall first. Fictional detectives are some of the most memorable characters in all of fiction.

Whether a private investigator, a police detective, a forensic specialist, or an amateur sleuth, it's customary for some sort of detective to be given the starring role in a mystery. When I refer to "your detective," I mean the protagonist or main character, the answer to the question, "Whose story is this?" This is the character whose actions the story will focus on, the one your readers will identify with and root for, the one for whom they will bite their nails when danger threatens.

More than one character in your book may actively investigate the crime. Rarely does an amateur sleuth, for example, hunt down a killer that no one else is seeking; most likely the police are also on the job too, working either in concert with the amateur, at cross-purposes, or some combination of both. But regardless of how many others are trying to solve the crime, your detective is the character who will ultimately learn the truth and bring the villain to justice.

What Makes a Good Detective?

Mystery novel detectives have several characteristics in common: they are typically intelligent, curious, resolute, and tenacious. To some extent, they understand human nature. The story usually reveals them to be courageous, resourceful, and strong, though they don't always believe that of themselves at the outset.

Beyond that, anything goes. Fictional detectives come from every conceivable cultural background. Some are highly moral and responsible members of society, others are criminals at heart or in fact. They can be male or female, of any age, race, religion, or sexual orientation. They can be dreamers or schemers, optimists or pessimists, straight arrows or free spirits. In short, there are no rules, no models your detective must conform to, no patterns he or she must fit. You may fashion this character out of whatever cloth you choose, but what you are seeking is a character who fits three criteria:

- Someone who can serve the purposes of the story you want to tell (or can provide you with an interesting tale of his or her own)

- Someone who is real and believable to you, and whom you can make real and believable to readers

- Someone you find intriguing and likable. After all, during the long journey of writing your book, you'll be spending a lot of time with your main character. The trip will be much more pleasant if you find him or her an enjoyable traveling companion.

Professional or Amateur?

Will you create a professional or an amateur detective? If a professional, will your detective be in the public service like a police detective, or in private practice like a private investigator? This is one of your earliest decisions, because your detective's professional status or lack of it will affect many aspects of the story: your detective's reasons for taking on the investigation, the methods used to conduct it, and his or her relationships with other characters.

The public-sector professional

Police officers; FBI agents; investigators for the coroner, district attorney, or Crown; postal inspectors; CIA operatives — what they all have in common is that they are employees of a public agency with a peace-keeping or law-enforcement mission. Professionals like these are a natural choice for the protagonist of a mystery novel: Who has a greater right or reason to investigate a murder? Moreover, as professionals, they are well trained for the task and have a network of experts to aid in the investigation. Their techniques for solving the crime can make for fascinating reading.

If you're considering a police officer or a similar professional for your principal character, there are a couple of points to keep in mind. Police officers must conduct their investigations according to well-defined laws, regulations, and standards. They do so for sound reasons: First, to protect the rights of the individuals they deal with, including persons accused (perhaps falsely) of a crime. Second, to avoid missteps that could jeopardize the investigation or the prosecutor's ability to obtain a conviction.

This is admirable behavior in real life but sometimes awkward in fiction. When your detective is committed to obeying the rules to ensure the case will stand up in court, his or her actions are constrained to some degree. These limitations might help your story by giving you some interesting complications to work with. Or, they might be hindrances, interfering with action that's necessary to your plot. For example, what will your detective do when she cannot obtain the search warrant she needs to collect evidence essential her case? How far will he go to entrap a suspect when he is certain the suspect is guilty but doesn't have proof?

The other consideration is your own level of expertise and knowledge of professional operations. Making your main character a public-sector professional requires you to have or acquire a reasonable understanding of police procedure or the operations of whatever agency employs your protagonist. Don't think that you can get away with faking it; mystery readers are a bright and knowledgeable bunch and will catch your mistakes. If you have a professional background in this area, you're a step ahead. If not, thorough research will be very important to you as you develop your story line and characters. Chapter 10 will help you get started with your research.

The private-sector professional

Private investigators (also informally known as private eyes), lawyers, journalists, and insurance company investigators are all considered private-sector professionals. (There are others as well.) As with police officers, the common element with private-sector professionals is that someone is paying these individuals a salary or fee to investigate and solve the crime.

Choosing a private investigator (PI) as your main character gives you some advantages. Serving the interests of a client or employer gives the investigator a reason to become involved in unpleasant or dangerous situations that other people would shy away from. Like a police officer, a PI has investigative expertise plus a network of helpful contacts. A police officer can back up his or her actions with the weight of official authority, an advantage the PI doesn't enjoy. The trade-offs for the PI — in fiction at least — are independence and the freedom to take action that might land a police officer in hot water fast.

Real PIs operate according to laws, professional standards, and proven investigative techniques, and the author who writes about one should learn what these are. Because the rules governing PIs are less stringent than those that bind the police, a mystery writer who is just beginning to acquire in-depth background knowledge might wish to consider using a PI as the protagonist.

In real life, PIs rarely get involved in murders. In some jurisdictions, private investigators are not permitted to investigate homicide cases that are active police matters. The concern is that the PI could, either deliberately or inadvertently, influence witnesses or contaminate evidence, thus damaging the prospects of building a sound legal case against the perpetrator that will stand up in court. Directly engaging in a murder case could put the detective's investigating license at risk.

That means you may need to contrive another reason for your PI to become involved in the murder case. You might create an investigation that initially does not involve a murder or is related to a murder only tangentially. The PI's intention might be to find a lost child, for example, or to recover missing heirlooms, or to uncover a fraud.

The amateur detective

An amateur detective gives you perhaps the greatest flexibility in your story. An amateur is not bound by rules of evidence or the need to build a solid legal case the way a professional detective is, nor by the need to protect her license or livelihood, as a PI would be. An amateur is limited only by what's legal and what's not — and perhaps even that won't restrict his or her activities if your story provides your detective with sufficient justification to break the law.

On the other hand, the amateur sleuth typically has much less expertise and experience in investigating crime than a professional and few outside resources to draw on for help with the task. This might pose a challenge for your detective, but it can be an advantage for a writer who is just learning about crime-solving techniques and practices — you and your sleuth can learn together.

If you are an expert in a field, or a particular subject intrigues you, that's a good choice for your sleuth's profession or background. The professions followed by amateur sleuths range from A to Z: from advertising executive, bookstore owner, and cab driver, all the way to zoologist.

Matching the Detective to the Case

All fictional stories, reduced to their most basic element, follow a classic pattern: they tell of the protagonist's struggle to overcome a conflict and achieve a goal. The details about the goal, the conflict, and the struggle generally constitute the plot. Will the protagonist succeed or fail? How will the outcome be determined? The desire to find out these answers is what keeps readers glued to a book.

As the character who will be your detective starts to take form in your mind, think about why his or her story, and not someone else's, is the tale you want to tell. The detective in a mystery, especially a police officer or a private investigator, is rarely the character affected most directly and profoundly by the crime. To justify taking the role of protagonist and being the focus of the story's attention, your detective needs a compelling and persuasive goal. Ask yourself, what does the detective hope to achieve by becoming involved in this investigation? Yes, the detective wants to solve the mystery, to unmask the villain. But why? What does he or she have at stake personally?

Curiosity, or a vague desire to see justice served, or even the challenge of outwitting an evil-doer are rarely sufficient reasons to become mixed up in a crime, especially a homicide case. No ordinary person would get involved on a whim. To take on the arduous and possibly dangerous task of investigating a crime, your detective needs a compelling personal reason.

This is especially true for an amateur sleuth. But even if your detective is a professional, the crime you're writing about should somehow mean more to your detective than just an assignment, and it should demand more from him or her than the usual detached professional interest. Of all the cases in which your detective has been involved, why choose this one to write about? What makes solving it so important? What gives it a personal twist, making it deserving of readers' attention? Something about the case should touch your detective in a profound and personal way.

Here are some possible reasons for a detective's involvement in a murder case:

> The detective or someone close to him or her has been wrongfully arrested or accused of the murder.

> The detective's life or someone else's life is threatened unless the detective becomes involved.

> The detective seeks to assuage the guilt he or she feels for having done something that may have inadvertently placed the victim in harm's way.

> The detective feels a strong sense of obligation to the victim or to a person who asks for help.

> The detective's professional competence has been called into question or livelihood is threatened.

> The detective needs to prove himself or herself in some way to someone significant, or to release himself or herself from that person's power.

> The crime you're writing about should mean more to your detective than just an assignment.

The case has created a personal crisis that must be resolved before the detective can move forward with his or her life.

The case has raised important issues from the detective's past that need to be settled.

A Detective Is Born: A Case History

When I began writing *A Relative Stranger*, I knew only three things about Jess Randolph, the young woman who would be the protagonist:

she has been awakened at 1:30 a.m. by an unwelcome telephone call from a man claiming to be her father,

she has a dog, and

she will solve a murder.

Playing the What if? game, I decided that the man, Allen Fraser, telephones Jess because he is in trouble. The daughter of his business partner has been found murdered. As the last person known to have seen the victim alive, Fraser is suspected of being her killer.

But Fraser has not seen or spoken to Jess since she was a small child. What reason would he have to think she would, or could, help him? Because she is a professional investigator. That way, she has the skills to assist him. Not only that, if she chooses, she can keep their relationship strictly businesslike.

Making her a police officer wouldn't work, though. As the suspect in a murder case, Allen has to avoid contact with the police. I concluded that Jess would be a private investigator. This appealed to me; writing about a PI seemed less daunting than writing about a police officer.

However, this decision told me little about Jess. Determining the detective's professional status — police officer, PI, amateur sleuth — is only a tiny part of creating a fully realized character. I wanted Jess to have a complex life, with interests and obligations and connections to characters beyond the boundaries of any one case. After all, in the real world, people are multidimensional, and I find fictional worlds most satisfying when their inhabitants are multidimensional too. I wanted a protagonist who had come to investigative work by a route other than the typical ones: ex-cop, ex-security officer, ex-lawyer. The idea of involving Jess in the arts came naturally because that's where many of my own interests lie.

I first thought that I would make Jess a musician — a cellist in a chamber ensemble. I barely know an arpeggio from an accordion, but I was eager to learn. I reasoned that writing a novel about a musician would be a great excuse for indulging in extensive research about the music world. Fortunately, I hadn't gone far with this idea when a writer friend convinced me that placing my main character in a field I already know and understand would make my life much simpler.

Then I wondered about making Jess an amateur actress or a player in a local theater group. Having worked in college and community theater, I could draw on my own background. I've acted, directed, painted sets, stitched costumes, made props, and hauled things around backstage. The problem with the theater is that the demanding and rigid schedules would require too much of my protagonist's time. If she wasn't at rehearsals and performances when expected, she would let herself and other people down. I figured my detective's schedule needed more flexibility than a theater career could offer.

Finally, I thought about making Jess a painter. I come from a family of artists, which gave me insight into Jess's world. My grandfather was a commercial artist in New York, and, as a child, I was fascinated by his studio — the pungent smell of turpentine, the canvases stacked six deep along the walls, the half-formed images on his easel.

In terms of my detective, painting is something she could do on her own time, so it wouldn't interfere with her schedule. Further, painting requires passion and dedication, and it hones the skills of observation and attention to detail that can benefit a detective. Having made the decision that Jess would be a struggling young painter, she came alive for me.

It was Jess's mother, a struggling single parent, who encouraged her interest in art. On graduating from art school, Jess realized she couldn't rely on painting to pay the rent, so to support her art, she took a part-time receptionist job with a small (three people, one dog) investigative firm.

Jess's role in the firm grew until she decided to get her PI license. At the beginning of my story, Jess has two careers which she loves. They mesh well: "I like it when a painting is finished," she says, "just as I like it when an investigation is done. In each situation, some truth has been discovered, some sort of order achieved. To me, that's the heart of both art and detection: finding some bit of underlying logic that helps to explain what this crazy world is all about."

Jess's life is going well until her father's telephone call turns it upside down, placing difficult demands on her mind and heart, calling into question many things she had accepted as true about herself and her family. Her goal is to deal with the issues raised by her father's long absence and abrupt reappearance. She becomes involved in the murder investigation as a means to that end.

I gave Jess my sister's red hair and moved her into an apartment with a sunporch to use as a studio. It's located in San Francisco's Haight-Ashbury district, a neighborhood where I once lived. Although the novel is by no means autobiographical, my own tastes and experiences suffuse hers. When I sent my sister a copy of the completed manuscript, I assured her that Jess wasn't me. After reading the book, she wrote me a letter pointing out all the various ways my heroine and I are similar, from our love of art to our shared taste in clothing to our preference for tea over coffee. Yes, to a degree, Jess is an alter ego, but that's true of each of my characters; like most fiction writers, I find that all my characters, even the villains, reflect aspects of myself. But that does not diminish the fact that Jess stands apart from me as a separate and unique character, with a heart and mind of her own.

The Victim

The victim is arguably one of the most important characters in a mystery — even if he or she never appears alive within its pages. After all, if weren't for this character's death, there would be no story. If readers are to understand and care about what happened (or happens) to the victim, that character must be as vividly drawn as any of the other characters in the book. Even in serial-killer stories, where the victims are more significant as numbers in a series of deaths rather than as individuals, the author often depicts at least one of the victims in some detail, giving readers a glimpse of the victim's family and daily life so they can develop the essential empathy.

The victim I created in *A Relative Stranger* is Deborah Collington, a young woman with an appetite for glamour and scandal. On the Saturday night before the novel opens, she attends the Beaux Arts Ball, a high-society fundraising event for the benefit of local arts organizations. She is seen leaving in the company of a man who is a stranger to everyone present. This man turns out to be the detective's father. Her body is found in an alley in a seedy part of town on Sunday morning; she has been strangled and the valuable diamond-and-emerald necklace she had been wearing is missing.

Although Deborah's death has already occurred when the novel begins, I tried to make her a vital presence in the story. Jess comes to know her through newspaper stories, as well as anecdotes from Deborah's ex-husband, fiancé, and other associates, but these secondhand sources alone could seem a bit dry. I wanted Jess, and readers, to have a strong visual impression of Deborah alive, not dead, so that whenever her name came up they would see her clearly and feel a sense of the loss caused by her death. So, in an early scene, I had Jess come upon a candid photo of Deborah at a party on a yacht:

> *Her backlit head nearly filled the frame. It was thrown back and slightly to one side; she appeared to be laughing. The long blond hair, wind-tossed, glinting in the sun, surrounded her face like a wild fiery halo, while her eyes seemed to project a light of their own from within. How could anyone who looked so alive, so loving of life, ever be dead?*

Some writers prefer to not make their victims too likable. That way, they figure, readers will object less when they die. With Deborah, I tried to create neither a saint nor a sinner but a real woman who has flaws (as we all do), which lead her into trouble.

This doesn't mean that murder victims in mysteries must be knowingly flirting with danger or that they have traits that make victimhood inevitable. Your victim can be any type of person you choose. (Mystery readers in a general, however, have an aversion to violence toward animals and children.) The only commonality mystery victims share is that they run afoul of a criminal. The conflict that leads to the crime — usually murder — is sometimes overt; the passions or purposes of the two individuals clash in a fateful way. But sometimes it is one-sided, for instance, when the killer sees the victim as an impediment to something he or she desires: I could use the money now; why not bump off Uncle Walter and speed the inheritance along? or, If I kill this guy, he can't testify against me in court and I'll get off scot-free.

The Villain

Every story needs an antagonist: the opposing force the protagonist must face and overcome to bring a resolution to the story. In a mystery, the villain is the character who has committed the crime, usually a murder. You must make your antagonist a worthy opponent, someone whose strength, resources, and power are equal to or greater than your detective's. You want to cast a villain who will inspire the detective's best effort.

Mysteries are sometimes regarded as stories of good versus evil: detective versus villain. To some extent, this generalization is valid, but rarely are the villains purely evil and nothing more. You want the villain in your story to be a complex and realistic human being, just like your other characters are, with at least a few positive qualities to temper the negative ones. The psychology of the villain is often one of the fascinating aspects of a mystery: What kind of person believes that killing someone will solve a problem? This belief may be the main quality that mystery villains have in common. As with victims, villains come in an infinite variety.

Motive: The Urge to Kill

Criminal investigations focus on individuals with the motive, means, and opportunity to commit a crime. Means and opportunity are matters for the plot, but motive is an essential part of your characterization of the villain. To achieve a credible villain, you must convince readers that someone who has this character's personality, temperament, and background, and who finds himself or herself in the situation you describe, would choose to commit a crime or kill another person. Casual violence occurs far too often in our society and is devastating to its victims, but it has little place in a mystery novel. A fictional killer must have good reasons, at least in his or her own mind, to resort to murder. Most mysteries feature villains who do not commit murder lightly. There must be good reasons, often involving strong emotions — such as rage, revenge, greed, betrayal, self-defense — for even the toughest character to commit murder.

> Motive is an essential part of your characterization of the villain.

Be cautious about blaming your killer's vicious acts on the fact that he or she is crazy. "Not guilty by reason of insanity" receives a lot of publicity as a defense strategy but, in fact, it's used rarely. The vast majority of murderers are not mentally ill individuals. If you select mental illness as a reason for someone committing murder, take care to depict the character's condition in a medically accurate way. Likewise, if you set up an insanity defense, make sure it's believable. Otherwise, it can look as if you, the writer, chose the easy way out.

Playing Fair with the Villain

One of the mystery genre's rules of fair play is that the villain be introduced to readers early in the story. It's considered cheating to wait until page 356 of a 360-page novel to introduce the villain from out of the blue. The villain should take an active role, though not necessarily a predominant one. He or she should certainly have more to do than stand around waiting to be accused.

Just in Case: The Backup Villain

A veteran mystery writer once gave me a valuable piece of advice: When you're planning your book, choose a backup villain. Have someone in mind who can step into this pivotal role in case your first choice doesn't pan out. That way you won't be stymied if, halfway into the story, you discover that things haven't gone as you intended. Perhaps the plot has veered in an unexpected direction, or your villain becomes so obvious that your detective would have to be a fool not to have the solution to the crime by the middle of the book.

Besides giving you a handy fallback position, designating an understudy for the villain's role enriches your story. You must set up this character as a viable alternative villain who also has the motive, means, and opportunity to commit the crime, just in case you need him or her to take over the lead. In this way, you create a suspect capable of legitimately fooling your detective and readers, and leading them off the trail of the real villain.

Moreover, determining the backup villain can give you insights into your story. I quickly realized that my standby villain had even better reasons to kill Deborah Collington than the character I had originally chosen as the perpetrator. Not only that, those motives fit better with the story's evolving theme. I quickly promoted the backup villain to first place and relegated the original villain to the status of a suspect.

The Supporting Cast

You could create a successful and intriguing mystery short story with no more characters than a detective, a victim, and a villain. But in most short mysteries, and certainly in any that are novel length, these three can't sustain the whole story alone. They are aided and abetted by an assortment of sidekicks, scoundrels, and suspicious characters.

Secondary Protagonist

Suppose you were to remove the detective from your mystery and then ask the question, "Whose story is this?" Your answer designates the secondary protagonist. Not every mystery has one. Whether or not yours will depends on your plot and your approach to storytelling. But frequently, it makes sense to have a major character who is nearly equal to the detective in terms of eliciting readers' interest and concern. The secondary protagonist is someone whose life has been torn asunder by the crime — perhaps a close family member of the victim or an innocent person in danger of being jailed for the crime.

Whether or not this is the character who originally involved the detective in the case, the detective usually comes to see himself or herself as the secondary protagonist's ally and advocate. Often, although not always, readers are drawn to this character just as the detective is. Sympathy and reader identification don't exempt the secondary protagonist from suspicion, however; the secondary protagonist can certainly be a suspect, and in some cases might even prove to be the villain.

The Usual (and Unusual) Suspects

If the villain stands alone as the sole character who could have committed the crime there is no mystery. Your cast must include other characters who also may have had the means, motive, and opportunity to do the deed. This category can include just about anybody connected with the victim — family members, business associates, current and former lovers, rivals from any area of the victim's life.

In my observation, writers fall into two camps when it comes to handling suspects. I've come to think of them as the closed-circle and open-circle approaches. Although mysteries written from either kind of approach present readers with a puzzle, the way that it is presented in each is quite different.

The closed circle

In some mysteries, particularly traditional detective stories, the list of suspects is restricted: a closed circle of possibilities. Half a dozen or so individuals are quickly identified as being the suspects, and both the detective and readers concentrate their energies on narrowing the list from six or seven to one.

In its purest form, this approach involves physically isolating the characters, for instance, by gathering them all in a remote country house during a violent storm. That way no one from the outside world has access to the victim and the villain clearly must be a member of the assembled group. Agatha Christie's *Ten Little Indians* is one of a number of classic examples; Lawrence Block recently paid homage to this tradition in *The Burglar in the Library.*

There are other ways to formally define a list of suspects. For example, when someone bumps off wealthy Uncle Walter, suspicion will naturally fall on the nieces and nephews mentioned in his will. Often, authors use the closed-circle approach informally; although the suspects do not fall neatly into a category, the writer makes it clear that the pool of possible villains is limited to certain characters.

The open circle

Writers who take the open-circle approach leave the roster of suspects wide open. While the villain will turn out to be someone who plays a role in the story, the list of suspects is not quickly or easily narrowed down. The possibility exists — in the minds of the characters if not of the readers — that the villain could be someone else, someone unknown to them, someone beyond the apparent boundaries of the story. After all, characters don't realize they are only participating in a story and not in the real world. This type of mystery leaves open the possibility that the killing resulted from some hidden facet of the victim's life, that it may have been a random street crime, a robbery gone wrong.

When writers take this approach, the characters wear their suspect label more discreetly; their other functions in the story demand more of their attention. In fact, in the investigator's eyes, some of them might not be considered suspects at all. The story focuses less intently on the mechanics of the detective's sorting through the clues, working out the crime's logistics, and speculating on the various candidates' likelihood of guilt.

I chose this approach for *A Relative Stranger* because I thought this particular story would be well served by the open circle's flexibility and lack of restrictions. While I wanted to create a valid mystery puzzle, whodunit? was only one of the questions the book explores. The other, at least equal in weight, was whether and how Jess would come to terms with her father, and I didn't want the puzzle to obscure it. I also felt this approach would help me make the plot more convincing. In real life, the circumstances in which Deborah's murder occurs wouldn't suggest that there was a closed circle of possible perpetrators.

This leads to another way of comparing the two kinds of stories: the closed-circle stories bring the puzzle front and center, while open-circle stories let it reside in the background.

> ### Photo file
>
> Looking for inspiration for characters? Scan magazines, catalogues, and other sources for photographs of interesting faces that suggest mystery characters to you. Photographs that include some background context work best. Clip them out and file them. When you need a character, check this photograph file. It's amazing how staring at a photograph of someone's face can set your imagination humming.

Witnesses, Police Officers, and Others

A homicide investigation is a major-league enterprise, one that involves the coordinated efforts of many people — police officers, coroners, crime lab personnel, prosecutors, defense attorneys, witnesses — the list goes on. So you have a rich array of characters from which to choose. Some may play major roles in your story; others may never appear.

What if your detective's hunt for the villain is independent of any official investigation? Even so, all these individuals are hard at work, and to be realistic, you should at least let readers hear the hum of their activity in the background. Your characters might converse about what the police and others are or are not accomplishing, they could observe news accounts, or they might mention being brought in to police headquarters for questioning; in other words, let them demonstrate in some way that they, and you, are aware of the official activities.

If your protagonist doesn't work for the police department, he or she will most likely cross paths at some point with the police or other officials, and their separate investigations will impinge on each other. How they work with or against each other — whether they cooperate, compete, or collide — can provide excellent complications for your plot. For example, my detective Jess endeavors, against her better judgment, to hide information about her father from the police inspector in charge of the investigation of Deborah Collington's murder. In doing so, she jeopardizes her productive working relationship with the police and risks losing her private investigator's license. But cooperating with the police would be seen as a betrayal of her father and ruin her chance to resolve troubling issues from her past.

Sidekicks and Supporters

As mysteries have developed more and more into novels of character, the context of the detective's life has been accorded greater importance and emphasis than in the past. When Ross Macdonald, one of the creators of the private-eye prototype, wrote his Lew Archer novels, he told us nothing about Archer's personal life. Archer fought in World War II, he was divorced; over the course of many novels, that's just about all readers learned about the man. He had few known friends or continuing associations. Today's mysteries recognize that even lone wolves have histories, hopes, homes, and present and past relationships.

Think about the people who play important parts in your detective's life: significant others, family members, friends, coworkers, neighbors — an assortment of potential allies and enemies. These relationships add color and texture to your detective's life. You can draw on them to enrich the character, to provide subplots, and to give your detective resources for the investigation. An example of this last point (one that is no longer terribly original): Many amateur sleuths become romantically involved with a police officer, a situation that gives them access to details about the crime and the official investigation they might otherwise be denied.

Whose Point of View?

Once you have a sense of who the main players in your story are, you have another important decision to make: Who will be your point-of-view character? In other words, who will tell the story? Whose eyes will your readers look through? Whose thoughts and feelings will readers know?

The point-of-view (or viewpoint) character defines the vantage point from which readers observe and understand the events. There is always more than one side to every story, and, in your mystery, the viewpoint character's side of the story is the one that readers will see and hear.

Working with students in writing classes, I've realized that many new writers find dealing with point of view to be a particular challenge, yet it's a skill worth developing. When you handle point of view properly,

Decide on a point of view. Who will tell the story? Whose eyes will your readers look through? Whose thoughts and feelings will readers know?

From the Detective's Notebook 4
"Elementary, My Dear Watson"

One type of sidekick, unique to mysteries, merits particular mention. This is the Watson, named after Dr. John Watson, the friend and admirer of Sherlock Holmes who chronicled the master detective's adventures.

The use of this device predates Sir Arthur Conan Doyle, going back to the nameless "I" who recounted Edgar Allan Poe's Auguste Dupin stories. Other more recent examples abound. Writer Rex Stout recruited Archie Goodwin to play the Watson to detective Nero Wolfe. In Lucille Kallen's mystery series, reporter Maggie Rome served as the Watson to newspaper editor C.B. Greenfield.

While the detective is the star, the Watson character narrates the tale and serves as the detective's chief deputy. The Watson character is generally saddled with the bulk of the legwork, gathering clues and interviewing witnesses, while the detective remains behind in comfortable seclusion. The Watson character presents the same information to both the detective and readers and challenges both to come up with the correct solution.

Using a Watson character enables you to achieve intimacy yet distance. Just like the Watson character, readers are close to the heart of the investigation, yet none are privy to the workings of the detective's mind as he or she ponders the clues and comes to brilliant conclusions. Writing from the detective's point of view, you can run up against the dilemma of how to sidestep parts of his or her thinking process. You don't want to reveal too much, too soon, but neither do you want to annoy readers or make them feel cheated. With a Watson character, you can avoid this problem.

readers readily identify with the characters and are pulled into the story world quickly and completely.

You have several choices when it comes to point of view, each with its benefits, drawbacks, and special applications.

First-Person Point of View

When you write a mystery using first-person point of view, you appoint one of the characters to tell the story for you. The narrator, the person telling the story, is both the "eye" and the "I" of the story. Readers walk in the character's footsteps, listen to that character's thoughts, watch from that character's perspective as events unfold, and share not only his or her experiences but his or her understanding of them. Here's an example:

> *Parking was tight as always around Union Street. Finally on a side street, I got lucky. A Volkswagen Beetle pulled out of a space between two driveways and I pulled in, centering my Toyota carefully so that it didn't block either driveway by more than a few inches. I muttered a brief prayer to the parking god that neither resident would get irked and have the car towed. Getting out, I surprised myself by slamming the door shut. I patted the fender in apology and tried to shove the last of my anger way into the deepest, coolest recesses of my mind.*

The first-person narrative has a long and honorable tradition in mysteries, particularly in detective novels. Writers use it because it is such a strong and involving way to tell a story. Readers' experience is direct and immediate, and a high level of intimacy with the character is easy to achieve. Readers partake in everything the narrator observes, does, thinks, feels, and knows.

Moreover, readers *should* partake in just about everything. Implicit in a first-person viewpoint is the notion that the narrator is not concealing important information from readers, even if he or she is hiding it from the other characters in the story. If readers discover that the narrator has been keeping secrets, they feel cheated. A famous example is Agatha Christie's novel *The Murder of Roger Ackroyd*, in which the narrator waits until the end of the story to reveal an important fact about the killer that he clearly knew from the beginning. The book generated tremendous controversy among mystery fans when it was first published in 1926, and you can still incite a lively debate today about whether or not Christie played fair in the book.

The drawback to writing in the first person is that the narrator is the only source of readers' information. If the narrator doesn't notice the lingering smell of a suspect's pipe tobacco in the murder victim's kitchen, readers will never be aware of it. Your narrator can't be two places at once, so if he or she is at home in bed at 3 a.m. Thursday, readers are too; they can't watch at that same hour as a band of thieves breaks into a jewelry store but will have to wait to learn about it later when the narrator does. There is no "meanwhile, back at the ranch" with first-person viewpoint. Nor can the narrator read the minds of other characters; this means readers can't know the actual thoughts and feelings of any other character, only what the narrator surmises them to be.

The narrator in a mystery written in first-person is usually the detective, but not always. If there's a Watson character, one of the sidekick's functions often is to narrate the tale.

Whichever character you choose as the narrator, you must know that character and his or her voice extremely well — and remember, that character is not you. The narrator doesn't use language quite the way you do but expresses himself or herself in an individual way. The details the narrator points out about people and places are different from the ones you'd notice and mention. For instance, Jess, being a painter, comments on colors and shapes, and the quality of light and shadow. The first thing she observes on walking into a room is the art, or the lack of it, on the walls, and from that she draws conclusions about the room's occupant. I, on the other hand, am more inclined to notice the style of the architecture and furnishings and the type of books on the shelves, although Jess has helped me pay attention to artworks with a more appreciative eye.

It's tempting to let your own voice slide into the narration, but you must maintain your narrator's autonomy. In a first-person narrative, every detail, even every word, should be consistent with the narrator's unique personality, perspective, background, and style.

Third-Person Point of View

When you write using the third-person point of view, you reserve the role of narrator for yourself, the writer. There is no "I" character; every player, even the detective, is a "he" or "she," as in the opening of my short story "The Hitchhiker":

> The kid stood just past the Clearfield exit, long-haired, bearded, thumb thrust out. A cardboard sign taped to his ragged knapsack read: NEW YORK CITY. Blinded by the rising sun, Carol didn't see him at first. Then, spotting him, she thought, Why not? This trip was an adventure, after all: the first time she'd traveled without Stephen since their marriage, nineteen years ago.

In a third-person narrative, the protagonist's thoughts are filtered through the author's voice. This sets the character and readers a greater distance apart than does a first-person narrative. While this is a limitation, you, as the writer, gain something in exchange: greater flexibility and a much larger theater of operation. You can let readers listen in on the thoughts of more than one character, or show them what is happening at two different places at the same time. You can set two lines of action going simultaneously and let readers have the fun of watching them both.

Third-person point of view is not one approach but several; it's a category that offers choices. Although there is any number of subtle variations, there are three principal ones.

Restricted-third-person point of view

Although it uses the pronouns "he" or "she" to refer to the viewpoint character, rather than "I" or "we," the restricted-third-person point of view resembles the first-person point of view in the way it closely focuses on a single character. In a restricted-third-person narrative, readers hear one character's thoughts and follow that character's actions, and no one else's.

So why choose restricted third person rather than first person? One reason is that it lets you more easily conceal information about the viewpoint character without making readers feel cheated. This can be especially effective in short stories, which don't give readers time to attain the close allegiance to the character that develops over the course of a novel. "The Hitchhiker" is told from Carol's point of view. It begins with the passage quoted above and builds quickly, in 1,700 words, to a surprising revelation about her — a surprise readers might not accept if the story had been longer or been written in the first person. With the story so short, I could restrict it to a brief time span and limit Carol's actions; in a longer tale, her behavior would have given her secret away. Similarly, if I'd let her tell her own story, I would not have been able to edit her thoughts to the extent that I did. Readers would rightfully expect her to tell them what was on her mind.

A second reason for using restricted third person could be that you would like to combine some of the intimacy of first-person point of view with a dispassionate distance. You can shift the point of view just slightly so that readers are not looking quite through the character's eyes, but rather, over his or her shoulder. You can grant readers a little insight into what the character sees, thinks, and does that the character himself or herself may be lacking.

For example, in my short story "Dorothy Ann, I Love You," the viewpoint character is a middle-aged woman who is receiving mysterious telephone calls at home:

The next morning at break time she told Bertie about the calls while they pushed their trays down the line of pastries and doughnuts in the company lunchroom. Bertie was her best friend. They'd taken their break together every day for nearly twenty years.

"Probably crank calls," said Bertie as she unloaded coffee and juice and two apricot Danishes onto a table.

Dorothy Ann sat down in front of her own cup of coffee and a cinnamon twist. "I guess," she said. "But I thought crank calls were, you know . . . dirty. I thought they said things to you about, well, you know . . ."

"And this guy didn't?"

Dorothy Ann shook her head.

"You can be glad of that, anyway." Bertie shoveled three scoops of sugar into her coffee and stirred.

Dorothy Ann considered. What would she have done if the caller had whispered obscenities into her ear? Screamed? Slammed down the telephone? Whispered back?

By using the restricted third person for this story, I can show readers aspects of Dorothy Ann's character — timidity, discomfort about sex, loneliness — that she might not be aware of and certainly could not articulate herself. Readers realize, long before Dorothy Ann does herself, that her friendship with Bertie, despite its longevity, is based on habit and a mutual fondness for sugar rather than real affection. When Dorothy Ann needs real help and Bertie doesn't come through, she is surprised, but readers are not.

This doesn't mean that the restricted third person always puts readers two steps ahead of the characters. Most often it doesn't. But using this viewpoint gives you extra control over readers' responses and understanding.

Multiple points of view

To broaden readers' perspective, and your own perspective as a writer, you might try revealing your story through the eyes of more than one viewpoint character. Using multiple viewpoints, you can uncover your story in the following ways:

- ☞ Run parallel tracks through your book, one following the detective's hunt, another focusing on the villain's misdeeds and attempts to elude capture.

- ☞ Show the activities of several characters whose separate efforts contribute to the investigation.

- ☞ Depict the crime or the events leading up to it from the victim's point of view.

Suspense novels and thrillers frequently employ multiple viewpoints. This approach is less common in detective novels, but there is no reason not to use multiple viewpoints if this style suits your story. Here are some tips for handling multiple viewpoints well:

- ☞ Choose your viewpoint characters carefully, and limit their number. Pick those who have a unique and important perspective to contribute.

- ☞ Be economical about how much you reveal about the different characters. Readers don't need to know what each and every character thinks.

- ☞ Assign each character certain chapters or scenes. When you write a scene, decide to which character it logically most belongs, and keep within that character's viewpoint from start to finish. When you want to switch to someone else's point of view, do it at the beginning of a new scene. That way, readers will move readily from one character's head to another's, because the transition comes during a natural break.

- ☞ Present each character's point of view using the restricted third person. This allows you to achieve a first-person style of intimacy and immediacy for several characters.

Occasionally in a multiple-viewpoint book, the author writes one character's sections in first person instead of third, as Rosellen Brown did to great effect in *Before and After*. This novel describes the turmoil wrought upon the lives of three members of a family when the girlfriend of the teenage son is murdered and the young man, assumed by the whole town to be guilty, runs away. The viewpoint characters are the teenage boy's father, mother, and younger sister. The father's sections are written in the first person, the mother's and sister's in the third. Brown sets a good example for other writers by limiting herself to a single first-person character. If you have more than one, it's a challenge to make each character sound distinctive and individual. You and your readers are likely to find it difficult to keep the various "I"s straight.

Omniscient-third-person point of view

Omniscient means "all-knowing." Rather than present the story from the vantage point of one or more characters, the writer presents it from his or her own perspective. The writer, of course, knows the entire story and the thoughts, feelings, and observations of every character and can present as much or as little of this information as he or she pleases.

While the omniscient viewpoint looks easy to write, I think it's perhaps one of the most difficult viewpoints to handle effectively. For one thing, it's hard to control. When you give readers access to every character's head, the danger is that you'll bounce readers from one character's thoughts to the next without establishing a clear point of view at all, as you can see in the following example:

> Jay Faulkner scurried up to Chief Reinhard, who was standing near the first-base line. "Hey, Chief, what's new on the Alistair Guthrie murder?" he asked, pulling out a spiral-bound notebook and pen.
>
> Reinhard frowned. Jeez, I hate reporters, he thought. "No comment, Faulkner. This isn't the time or the place. We're here to watch these kids play ball."
>
> Faulkner was disappointed. When he'd realized that both their sons played on the Blackwood School softball team, he figured that might give him an in with the taciturn chief of police. No such luck. With a sigh, he shoved his notebook back in his pocket. Then he spotted Reinhard's wife sitting alone in the stands. Maybe the chief was more forthcoming at home over the dinner table.
>
> Watching Faulkner approach, Marilyn Reinhard fluffed her hair and unbuttoned the top of her blouse. What an opportunity. She'd been looking for a way to get back at her husband ever since she found out about his last "little fling." Well, I'll fling him, she thought. "Hello, Jay," she purred as he sat down. "Looking for a story? Well, I think I've got a scoop for you."

Michael Reinhard looked around for his parents as he stepped up to bat. His father stood near first base, fists clenched and red-faced, just daring him to strike out. His mother was in the bleachers, talking to some strange man. They were right in the spot where his favorite teacher, Mr. Guthrie, always used to sit. A wave of sadness swept over Michael. Why did someone go and murder the only person in the world who understood him?

In this passage, we're pulled to and fro from Faulkner's head to Chief Reinhard's to Marilyn's to Michael's. Before we can settle into any one point of view, we're plopped into the next one. This can be disorienting, and it deprives us of the chance to build a strong bond with any of the characters. The omniscient viewpoint creates a greater distance between readers and the story than does either first person or restricted third. The author is not a participant in the story but describes the action from the outside looking in. Readers, regarding the story from the author's vantage point, are outsiders too. Sample 3 presents another omniscient viewpoint scene and shows how it might be reframed in the first-person and restricted-third-person points of view.

The omniscient viewpoint works best when the author's perspective is not simply all-knowing but flavored with a strong, distinctive attitude that guides readers' response. The crime novels of Carl Hiaasen, for example, with their overlay of humor and social satire, offer readers a far larger and much funnier understanding of the events that transpire than any of the individual characters could possibly achieve.

Changing point of view

If you're having trouble developing a character, a scene, or the story as a whole, try writing from a different character's perspective. This exercise can bring new insights that help even if you decide to return to the original point of view. Or, switch from first-person to third-person point of view, or vice versa. In one critique group I belong to, two colleagues were struggling to make their protagonists, written using the third-person point of view, come alive. In both cases, the novel improved when the author switched to first person and allowed the main character to tell the story in his or her own voice. This isn't to say that first person is preferable — only that experimenting with point of view might get you over a hurdle or two.

Sample 3
Points of View

First-Person Point of View (Joanna's Point of View)

Naturally, when I arrived at the Tuesday night meeting of the Blackwood School Carnival Planning Committee, Alistair Guthrie's murder was topic number one.

"I can't believe Guthrie's actually dead," Emily whimpered. "It must have been terrible for you, Joanna, walking into his classroom and discovering the body like that."

Such a little fussbudget. If she'd been the one to find Guthrie's body, she would have fainted on the spot. Of course, I hardly did better myself. I shuddered, remembering the horrid sight and, worse, the smell of all that blood.

"I handled it okay." It was a lie, and I knew it.

"Who do you think killed him?" Nora asked. Before I could warn her, she dipped a celery stick into the cheese dip Alexis had brought. I'd already tasted it — way too salty. You'd think by age forty a woman would learn to cook.

Alexis said, "The murderer was probably his wife."

The shock I felt was mirrored on Emily's and Nora's faces. Alexis smirked with satisfaction.

I caught myself fiddling nervously with the ends of my scarf. "What are you talking about? Guthrie wasn't married." Then I remembered his cryptic remarks after the faculty meeting, and wondered.

**Restricted-Third-Person Point of View
(Alexis's Point of View)**

Alexis was delighted to find that Alistair Guthrie's murder was topic number one at the Tuesday night meeting of the Blackwood School Carnival Planning Committee.

"I can't believe Guthrie's actually dead," Emily said. "It must have been terrible for you, Joanna, walking into his classroom and discovering the body like that."

If it had been me, Alexis mused, how would I have handled it? She tried to imagine it, the sight and smell of all that blood. That mouse Emily probably would have fainted on the spot.

Joanna shuddered. "I handled it okay," she said. It was a lie, and Alexis knew it.

"Who do you think killed him?" Nora asked. She dipped a celery stick into the cheese dip Alexis had brought, then made a face as she tasted it.

Sample 3 — Continued

Alexis frowned. Damn, what had she done wrong this time? She'd followed the recipe to the letter. No matter how hard she tried, she'd never impress these women with her domestic skills.

Tonight, though, she had something better to impress them with. She leaned back into the soft sofa cushion and said, "The murderer was probably his wife."

What fun to see the shock on the other women's faces. Joanna was fiddling with the ends of her scarf. She must be nervous. Good.

"What are you talking about?" Joanna asked. "Guthrie wasn't married."

Omniscient-Third-Person Point of View

Naturally, Alistair Guthrie's murder was topic number one at the Tuesday night meeting of the Blackwood School Carnival Planning Committee.

"I can't believe Guthrie's actually dead," Emily said. "It must have been terrible for you, Joanna, walking into his classroom and discovering the body like that." If it had been her, Emily thought, she'd have fainted on the spot.

Joanna shuddered, remembering the horrid sight and, worse, the smell of all that blood. "I handled it okay," she said. It was a lie, and she knew it.

"Who do you think killed him?" Nora asked. She dipped a celery stick into the cheese dip Alexis had brought. Way too salty. You'd think by age forty a woman would have learned to cook.

"Probably his wife," Alexis said, and she smirked with satisfaction at the sight of shock on the other women's faces.

Joanna fiddled nervously with the ends of her scarf. "What are you talking about? Guthrie wasn't married." Then she thought about his cryptic remarks after the faculty meeting, and wondered.

5
Creating Characters
Readers Will Care About

One of the best compliments readers can pay a fiction writer is to say that the characters in a story really come alive. Your characters don't exist, of course; they are constructs of your imagination. But you want readers to believe in them as if they were real. Cardboard cutouts won't do. Neither will stereotypes, nor collages pasted together from randomly selected personality traits and quirks. You want to make your characters as complex and individual as real human beings are.

When you succeed, a strong and vital bond is established between readers and characters; readers identify with the characters and care about them. However you go about luring readers into the world of your mystery, it is your readers' interest, empathy, and concern for the characters that will keep them turning the pages until the end of the story. If your character is truly successful, you may be able to start a series of books based on that character. At the end of this chapter, From the Detective's Notebook 5 discusses some of the issues involved with working with series characters.

The Secret to Creating Great Characters

Characters begin as shadows. Their wispy forms drift into your imagination. As your story takes shape, they grow more distinct and solid. In a good mystery — or any good fiction — the characters begin to live and breathe on the page.

The secret to creating great characters, characters readers will believe in and care about, is intimacy. It's a twofold process: First, you must know your characters intimately. Then, you must share that intimacy with your readers.

When you know your characters intimately, you present them on the page with confidence so that their personalities, emotions, and actions come across as true. The plot unfolds smoothly and credibly. Readers become willing to accept even plot elements that might be inherently implausible, because they are happening to what seems to be real people.

The secret to creating great characters is intimacy.

You must also have intimate knowledge of your characters to make them leap off the page. Achieving an intimate knowledge of your characters requires that you understand them in four critical ways. While this is especially important in the case of your detective, you should ask yourself these questions about each one of your characters:

- Who is this person?

- How does this person feel about himself or herself, about his or her life to date and present situation?

- What led this person into the story?

- How will this person behave, and why?

The next four sections in this chapter discuss these clues in detail.

Once you know your characters well, sharing your understanding of them with readers is vitally important. Especially with your detective, there should be no holds barred; the best mysteries work because a truly intimate relationship is created between the main character and readers. Even if your detective is shy, reserved, secretive, or deceptive in the story, or keeps other characters at a distance, he or she needs to be upfront and outgoing with readers. No secrets allowed. This is how the identification between readers and the detective is achieved.

Who Is this Person?

The first clue to developing a character concerns the basics that define a person. Ten keys will help you unlock the mystery of each of your characters in this regard.

Physical attributes

Physical attributes include the obvious: sex, height, weight, body type, color of skin, hair and eye color, identifying marks. But these attributes also go beyond appearance. Another consideration is the state of the character's health: robust or frail, infirmities or physical challenges. In addition, there is the manner in which the character presents himself or herself: habitual mode of dress, position on the sloppy-to-neat scale, gesturing and body language.

Personality and temperament

Shy or bold? Generous or selfish? Fretful or a devil-may-care attitude? Confident or insecure? Cool-headed or hot-tempered? Bold or timid or indecisive? This key covers all the aspects of a character's personality: mental and emotional qualities, disposition, way of responding to the world.

Pay particular attention to the traits that you would consider to be strengths and weaknesses, especially for your detective. Weaknesses will contribute to your detective getting into trouble; strengths are resources your detective can use to get himself or herself, and others, out of trouble.

Consider, too, the contradictions that are built into a character's nature: the man who is kind to his family but cruel to his associates at work; the high school football star who prefers classical music to rock but is afraid to admit this to his friends; the conservative, timid young woman who cuts loose with reckless abandon behind the wheel of her sports car; the cool, collected lawyer who is prone to sudden, unpredictable bursts of anger. Ambiguities like these are often the quirks that make characters interesting, sympathetic, and believable. It is especially important to give a few incongruities to your detective and villain. Readers find it equally hard to relate to flawless heroes and totally evil villains. A mix of positive and negative qualities will make stronger, and more memorable, characters.

> Characters' contradictions and ambiguities often make them interesting, sympathetic, and believable.

Background

A person is the product of the cultural, societal, and economic conditions from which he or she springs. Family, ethnic background, childhood, neighborhood, education — all these circumstances mark a person with an indelible stamp.

You don't need to interrupt the telling of your story to provide readers with a character's background. Much of it you can make obvious by the way you depict that character's behavior, style of speech, attitudes, and present circumstances. Where details about a character are needed, divulge them to readers in the natural course of events: through dialogue, documents (such as a news article or police file the detective reads), or one character's observation of another.

Relationships

Whether the character is a social butterfly or a lone wolf, there are other characters who, now or in the past, have been important in his or her life. To understand their influence on the character, consider not only who these other characters are but also how the relationships were conducted. How someone behaves when interacting with others can be tremendously revealing of other aspects of that person's nature: emotions, prejudices, moral or ethical position, self-confidence or lack thereof, to name a few. Charting the nature and progress of his or her various relationships is one good way to track how a character changes or grows during the story.

Profession

A person often defines himself or herself, and is defined by others, by his or her role in society. When meeting a new acquaintance, the first thing we often ask is, "What do you do?" This key is your character's answer to this question.

A number of characters in your novel may be in professions related to crime or criminal justice, while others are not. The detective could fall into either camp. Amateur sleuths may not think of themselves as detectives at all; they are simply taking necessary steps to solve a problem.

A character's profession does not refer to his or her role in the story but to the principal way in which that character earns a living or spends the working hours.

Talents, hobbies, and passions

Adjuncts to "What do you do?" are other equally important questions: "What are you good at?" "How do you most enjoy spending your time?"

"What really turns you on?" How a person earns a living is often secondary, at least in that person's mind, to other pursuits that he or she finds more engaging and more expressive of the "real me."

The things that excite a character lend color and verve to the character, whether it's a fondness for playing cool jazz, sipping a perfectly brewed cup of tea, snorting cocaine, growing exotic roses, saving redwood forests, or setting up a successful swindle.

Environment

The kinds of places where a character chooses to live and work are very revealing. Even more so is the sort of environment your character creates, especially at home, with freedom to choose the furnishings and adornments.

Another aspect of this key is the kinds of places where the character feels most comfortable. The cocktail lounge of a swank hotel attracts a different clientele than a back-alley gin mill. Someone who is most content in a rustic mountain camp will differ in many respects from someone who relishes the bustle of a big-city neighborhood.

Beliefs, attitudes, and opinions

The eighth key to developing a character is the lens through which a character looks at the world. It also describes how a character understands what he or she sees. It covers religious and political views, prejudices or biases, and assumptions about what is or ought to be true. The nature and strength of your character's beliefs will determine what he or she is willing to fight for, and how hard.

Preferences, habits, and routines

A character's life, like our own, is a quilt pieced together from the minutiae of daily existence. The small day-in-day-out choices your character makes are telling. Is he or she a night owl or an early bird? A beer guzzler, a whisky sipper, or a teetotaler? Does your character listen to Rachmaninoff or the Rolling Stones? Choose red shirts or blue ones? Gobble coffee and toast for breakfast or linger over bacon and eggs? Drive a Mercedes or commute by bus? Details like these reveal a lot about the character's economic circumstances, self-image, and personal taste.

Ambitions, dreams, and fears

Ambitions, dreams, and fears are important aspects of character because they are strong incentives to action: they give a character both a sense of direction and a push to get there. Ambitions and dreams impel your character forward. Fear, on the other hand, may shove him or her backward. When a character starts to move, on whatever course it may be, that's when stories begin to take shape.

Play private detective

Who is this person? Here is one way to discover the answer: pretend you're a PI conducting surveillance on the character for three days — a typical workday, a typical day off, and the character's ideal day. Make note of the details: what the character wears, eats, his or her mode of transportation, how the character spends free time, the people he or she associates with. Eavesdrop on conversations. At the end of the three days, write your report. By then, you'll know the character quite well.

How Does this Person Feel?

Whatever a character's circumstances, relationships, and beliefs might be, they are only the first step in defining that character as a realistic person. What lifts these facts and figures from being lifeless notations in a biography is the character's feelings about himself or herself, his or her life to date and current situation. For each of the ten character keys, one question is pivotal to your understanding of a character and the way you depict him or her in the story: How does your character feel about that particular area of his or her life?

To expand on this idea, consider:

- Does the character like or dislike his or her physical self, job or profession, home, other characters in his or her life?

- Is the character pleased or displeased with the choices he or she has made in life up to the point where the story begins?

- Is the character proud of his or her background or trying to deny or escape it?

- Does the character feel like an insider or outsider in his or her current milieu?

- Does the character feel appreciated and appropriately rewarded for his or her efforts in the various arenas of life, or does the character feel undervalued, belittled, or taken for granted?

- Is the character basically content with life, or does he or she feel bored, restless, or burned out?

- What are the character's chief regrets? Greatest longings? About what past events does he or she still harbor anger?

- Two particularly telling questions: How would the character change his or her life if possible? How much power does the character feel he or she has to make those changes?

What Led this Person into the Story?

Shakespeare remarked, "What's past is prologue." This means that present events are rooted in earlier ones; what happened yesterday was the opening act for what will take place today.

Your characters haven't been standing in the wings waiting for you to raise the curtain. They have been out in the world living full lives right up to the moment your mystery begins. The term "back story" is used to refer to all the circumstances that have brought the characters together and set them in the right place, at the right time, for the story to occur. Every character has a back story; a personal chain of events has resulted in that character becoming involved in the situation in some large or small way.

> Every character has a back story; a personal chain of events has resulted in that character becoming involved in the situation.

Every fictional tale, whether a mystery or not, has a back story. The back story is not the same as the hidden story (which is described in chapter 3), though they may overlap. How much of the back story should you weave into your book? For your detective and other major characters, quite a lot; knowing the key elements will help readers understand and identify with them. For minor characters, too many details may just clutter up the pages. But, as the writer, your awareness of all your characters' personal stories is essential — it will help you depict their behaviors in a way that will seem natural and true.

How Will this Person Behave, and Why?

Your characters drive the action and events of the story forward through their actions, behaviors, and responses. To develop the plot plausibly and carry it through to its logical conclusion, you need to understand not only what each of your characters would do under the circumstances but — very important — why each would do it. In other words, you need to understand their motivation.

When the reasons for your characters' actions are clear to you, you'll be able to portray more lifelike characters, and your plot will be more believable. When mystery fans hear the word "motive," right away the villain comes to mind: Why did the villain commit this terrible crime? The villain's motives are vitally important, for they form the rationale for the hidden story. However, you need to understand the motives not just of the villain but of each character.

You can gain clues to characters' motives from who they are, how they feel, and what events led them into the story. There are four more factors that contribute to the reasons why people, and fictional characters, act the way they do: their goals, their problems, their patterns of behavior, and their emotions.

Goals

In chapter 4, I discussed the detective's goal. The detective is not alone in having one. Each character has goals he or she wishes to attain or a problem that needs to be solved. What is the character trying to accomplish during the course of the story? What does he or she hope to gain, or stand to lose, as a result of being involved in these events? A character's actions are governed by what that character believes will best further his or her own self-interest.

Consider the villain, for instance. The villain would not commit the crime if he or she did not feel there was an advantage to gain: If the victim dies, the killer would be able to:

(a) inherit the fortune,

(b) take over the company,

(c) have custody of the child,

(d) keep a dark secret hidden,

(e) feel avenged for some insult or wrongdoing the victim committed, or

(f) _____ (fill in your own villain's motive).

Once the murder is accomplished, the villain takes on a new goal: to hide his or her guilt and elude arrest and imprisonment.

Or, consider the various witnesses and suspects. When questioned by the detective, each will react differently, according to that character's goal. If a character is concerned about seeing justice served, or wants to repay a favor, or hopes to exonerate himself or herself, that character may be cooperative and truthful. But if a character desires to protect someone he or she thinks might be guilty, or is concealing a personal secret, or simply wants to avoid getting tangled up in a hassle, that character may lie, or balk at answering, or behave rudely.

Problems

Fictional characters tend to be beset by problems. This is a good thing. If they all were living happy, carefree lives, we would have precious little to write about.

The behavior of your characters is strongly influenced by the nature of their problems: what caused them, how serious they are, how long they've endured, and who else might be affected.

Problems are different from goals, because a goal implies an intent to take action. A character may be more anxious to hide, deny, or avoid problems than solve them. Moreover, characters establish their goals voluntarily, while problems are thrust on them. Even self-inflicted problems are rarely situations characters would consciously choose.

Although the difficulties faced in your characters' present lives count for a lot, the adage "Once burned, twice shy" also applies. Few people get very far in life without at least one shattered dream, broken heart, or deep disillusionment. Unresolved issues from the past may still stymie or haunt your characters. The lessons, some of them bitter, that the characters have learned from problems of the past will affect their actions and attitudes.

Patterns of behavior

Like real people, fictional characters are creatures of habit in both large and small ways, whether it's drinking their ritual glass of orange juice in the morning or choosing an unsuitable romantic partner time and time again. Their training and upbringing, expectations and personal tastes, strengths and weaknesses, and psychological makeup all contribute to establishing what is, for them, normal and consistent behavior. And most characters will consider themselves normal, no matter how bizarre or frightening their habits or behavior may seem to outsiders.

Emotions

No matter how often we tell ourselves that what we do is based on logic, sound reasoning, and good sense, often our most powerful actions come out of our emotions. When our heads tell us one thing, and our hearts whisper the opposite, frequently it's our hearts we believe and obey.

Fictional characters operate this way too. The things they do that give them the greatest joy, cause the deepest regret, and land them in the most trouble are rooted in love, loyalty, greed, anger, hatred, jealousy, humiliation, and especially fear. These emotions are a great boon to the mystery writer. Your characters' emotions are the source of high drama and excellent story material.

Your Characters' Motivational Problems

One reason some stories fall apart is because a character, or several of them, doesn't act believably. The author fails to convince us that a character like this would behave in this manner under these circumstances.

This happens for two main reasons: the character is either acting out of character or behaving like a dolt.

Out-of-Character Behavior

Behaving "out of character" means the character does something that is neither logical nor sensible for that particular individual. Of course, what constitutes logic and sense varies from person to person and depends on each character's physical and psychological capabilities, emotional makeup, and background. Even when a character has a solid reason to do something, you will have a hard time making readers believe that character's behavior if it is out of keeping with what we know of him or her.

For example, suppose your character is a woman (we'll call her Virginia) who has led a sheltered middle-class life. Safe under her family's wing, she is shy, unassertive, and embarrassed if the spotlight of attention focuses on her. She believes that the way to get along in life is to play by the rules, to do what is expected of her. One day, Virginia is brutally assaulted by a stranger. She discovers the assailant's identity and, outraged, she mounts a vigilante campaign to terrorize and shame him in a very public way.

Certainly Virginia's fierce anger is understandable, but her response to the assault is completely at odds with her nature. We simply don't believe she would react this way. To make this scenario work, you need to lay the groundwork for Virginia's abrupt transformation from mouse to lion. For example, you can show us an incident before the assault where she surprises another character, and herself, by showing unexpected spunk or a white-hot flash of anger. That way, we will understand that, however timid Virginia may seem, she has a hidden wildness that could emerge with the right provocation.

Readers quickly develop a sense of how a character would behave in a given situation. When a character's actions are totally at odds with what readers expect, readers can lose trust in the author and in the story. Such a loss of trust could lead to readers setting down the book, never to pick it up again.

Characters who behave in strange and suspicious ways are an integral part of a mystery: their puzzling actions move the story forward and contribute to the suspense. But this is different from having them act out of character. Their behavior must be perfectly logical; it strikes readers, and other characters, as dubious or peculiar only because they don't yet know the rationale behind it. The reasons for the aberrant behavior are part of the hidden story. Once the hidden story is revealed, what seemed strange will be understandable.

Stupid Behavior

Stupid characters are rarely interesting or engaging. And while it's true that some people act without considering the consequences, don't let your detective be one of those that does; it's a quick way to lose readers' sympathy.

Your detective returns home to discover that the window has been broken, the light left burning has been extinguished, and strange noises are emanating from within. Any reasonable person would head for a brightly lit place from which to call the police. If the detective goes inside, even with a gun, readers will question his or her good sense.

Another example: Following the break-in, your detective receives a telephone call from a murder suspect who wants to meet to talk. In spite of having good reason to believe this person is the killer, your detective agrees to meet the suspect in a private, out-of-the-way location. Worse, your detective goes alone, without a colleague for backup or letting anyone know what's up. Readers' stupidity alarm, already buzzing after the first incident, begins to clang loudly.

Everyone takes calculated chances from time to time, and a dire situation might well push someone to riskier behavior than he or she would usually undertake. But your detective must have a compelling and convincing reason.

Avoiding Pitfalls

Often problems in characterization arise from an incompatibility between the characters and the plot. The plot demands that event A take place: the detective must enter the violated home or must be trapped by the killer in a remote place without hope of rescue, in order for the rest of the events in the story to proceed as the author has planned. Yet event A requires the character to behave in a way that is contrary to that character's nature, inclination, or good sense. If you force the character to behave as you wish, the result will be a scene — perhaps a whole book — that seems stiff, contrived, or unbelievable. When up against such a dilemma, you have three alternatives:

- *Rethink the character.* You might be able to change certain aspects of the character so that he or she can fulfill the assigned role more plausibly. Revisit the ten character keys of the first clue: What qualities must a person have to carry out this part of the action believably? Can those attributes logically be incorporated into this character? If they can, that's great. But you'll have work ahead, revising the story to ensure that the character is presented consistently throughout.

- *Recruit a different character.* Perhaps the character you first had in mind is not the right one for the role. Another character already in your story might be a better choice to carry out a particular action. Or you may need to invent a new character, one who would naturally act in the way the plot calls for. The original character might remain in a different role, or you could decide that he or she doesn't belong in the story at all.

🔫 *Change the plot.* If the character balks at doing what you want, consider changing the plot to be in keeping with the person's nature and motivation. Ask this: What would the character do in this situation if the choice were his or hers alone, unencumbered by any knowledge of what's supposed to happen next? The answer might lead your story in a direction even better than the one you had planned.

Getting Acquainted

You've assembled some traits and troubles, some patterns and quirks, some feelings and goals. How do you make the alchemy happen, the magic that transforms these bits and pieces into a plausible character, akin to a living, breathing human being?

For some writers, characters don't begin to come alive until they see the characters in action on the page, walking around, stretching their muscles, saying what they have to say. This is true for me. In the planning stages, I simply jot down a few brief notes about the main characters, just enough to give me a feeling for the story situation. Later, I may go back and flesh out these scribblings, especially for characters who are involved in the hidden story or who are suspects and whose own secrets affect the plot.

When I was planning *A Relative Stranger,* I wrote a detailed biography of only one character, a private investigator named David Patrick O'Meara, a partner in Parks and O'Meara, the investigative firm that employed my detective, Jess Randolph. Other than Jess, O'Meara was the character I knew best in the planning phase. I could see the man clearly: six foot three, lean and lanky, reddish hair shagging over his ears, tortoise-shell glasses that he'd pop on when he wanted to impress one of the firm's corporate clients by appearing erudite. I knew his history: He came from a Texas family that had made a minor fortune in oil before turning to law and politics. The family sent this scion to law school at Stanford University, expecting him to return to Austin and take his place in the family's budding political dynasty. But he deeply disappointed them by dropping out of school and staying in California to found a private investigative firm with his friend and partner Tyler Parks.

When O'Meara strolled on stage in chapter 1, I thought I knew him well. But after he said a few lines, he disappeared. He dropped out of the story as decisively as he had dropped out of Stanford. All that remained of him was the partnership's name on the plaque by the office door: Parks and O'Meara.

When I wrote the second draft, I came up with a new character called O'Meara to account for the firm's name. The only resemblance of this O'Meara to his predecessor is the reddish hair; in his new incarnation, O'Meara is an Irish setter. While transforming a character from a law school dropout with Texas roots into a dog may seem extreme, O'Meara is happier this way, and he fits better into the story.

Other writers, though, find it helpful to get well acquainted with their prospective characters before starting to write, using techniques like the ones described in this and other chapters. Because they have become intimately acquainted with the characters in advance, they have greater confidence that the story will progress smoothly, without hitting snags or potholes. You'll have to experiment to find out what sort of magic wand to wave or incantation to chant in order to bring characters alive for you.

First-person biography

If you'd like to try getting to know a character by developing his or her biography, why not let the character do the work for you? Write the bio using first-person point of view (i.e., from the character's point of view), and do it stream-of-consciousness fashion. In other words, just start writing and let the character spill out whatever he or she has to say. Don't stop to fiddle with style, spelling, or punctuation, and don't worry about arranging the events you describe in chronological order. What's important is the character's perspective on his or her own story. This exercise can yield great insights and is worthwhile even if you're writing your story from a third-person point of view.

Listening to Your Characters

Your characters are your best friends in the writing process. They know what the story is; trust them to tell it. Your mystery won't work if you force them to dance to your tune. Listen to them and get out of their way.

Beginning writers sometimes ask if characters can develop minds of their own and take over your book. The answer is yes, and that's exactly what you want them to do. *A Relative Stranger* would never have been finished if the characters hadn't persisted in tiptoeing into my mind at night as I drifted asleep and whispering bits of information to me about the story: "Oh, by the way, did we mention what happened on the boat?"

Characters you thought would play prominent roles might turn to dust, as the original O'Meara did. Or you could have an experience like I'm having with the manuscript I'm currently writing, another novel featuring Jess Randolph. As I was writing chapter 5, a freelance reporter unexpectedly sauntered into the scene. From the way he and Jess interacted, it was clear that they'd encountered each other earlier. I realized they had met in chapter 2, although I hadn't known it when I wrote chapter 2. In fact, when I outlined the first third of the book, this fellow didn't exist. Yet, to my amazement, once he appeared, he brazenly muscled his way into scene after scene. Finally, I realized he was an important character, but I was more than halfway through writing the book before I discovered his purpose in the story.

What most interferes with an author's ability to trust his or her characters is fear. On this score I offer two pieces of advice: don't be afraid *of* your characters and don't be afraid *for* them.

Don't Be Afraid *of* Your Characters

A wise person once said, "Writing is easy; just sit at the typewriter and open a vein."

Writing is tantamount to laying your soul down on the page. It can make you feel exposed and vulnerable, to yourself as well as to your readers. There's no telling what might get dredged up when you probe your unconscious in search of a story. Therefore, it's tempting to hold back. After all, if you create a truly intimate relationship between your detective and your readers, what's to stop your detective from revealing all your secrets? But holding back will ruin the story. The bond between readers and the protagonist is very different from the relationship readers have with the author. If you do the job right, readers will be so absorbed in the story and the characters that they'll scarcely be aware of you, the author, at all.

The most valuable advice I received when writing my first novel came from a college professor of humanities who was also the author of

> Sometimes, characters can develop minds of their own and take over your book.

> Writing takes courage. Let go and give your characters free rein.

several popular novels. "The problem with this book," he said, "is that the characters are tiptoeing around, trying not to disturb each other. They're much too genteel and polite. They apologize for the slightest ruffling of feathers. When I read a novel, I want the characters to let emotions out. I want to know how they feel. I want to see them fight and yell and laugh and weep."

On consideration, I concluded he was right. As I rewrote the novel, I let the characters scream and throw tantrums and run around like mad creatures. I was sure I was overwriting terribly, perpetrating the worst sort of purple prose. Yet, when I read it, I realized that although the book was better this round, the emotions in it were still quite restrained. So I rewrote some scenes yet again.

Writing takes courage. You need to let go and give your characters free rein. They will make capable collaborators if you trust them to tell the story.

Don't Be Afraid *for* Your Characters

It's been said that an author's job is to get the characters into trouble, and then get them into worse trouble. That is how plots are made.

This can be hard to do, especially in the case of your detective. Chances are that you like this character or you wouldn't have chosen him or her to be the focal point of your mystery. As you write the book, you'll come to regard your detective as a friend. Kind, gentle soul that you are, your instinct is to protect your friend and yourself from sorrow and suffering. You flinch from deliberately hurting anyone.

Tough. Do it anyway. If you soften your blows, you undermine the story's conflict. Tension sags, issues go unresolved, and readers close the book dissatisfied. For the story to succeed, you must let your detective and the other characters confront the challenges that beset them, no matter how difficult or painful. Trust your characters. They know the story, and they are willing to determine their own fates.

From the Detective's Notebook 5
Writing about Series Characters

Sam Spade, Dashiell Hammett's archetypal private eye, appeared in only a single book, *The Maltese Falcon*. But just about every other notable fictional detective stars in a mystery series.

Mystery publishers, writers, and fans all like series. For publishers, a series is a good way to build an audience; with each new volume, the author gains a greater following, enlarging the cadre of fans who will buy the books. For readers, savoring a new book featuring a favorite detective is like a satisfying visit with an old friend.

For a writer, a series offers several opportunities:

- You can explore the dimensions and themes of a character's life beyond the confines of a single story.

- You have an established framework within which to develop future mystery plots.

- By developing a following of readers of your series, you increase your chances of attracting long-term interest from publishers and fans.

How the Series Detective Has Changed

Mystery series written today differ from older ones in one important respect. Up until the last two or three decades, series detectives tended to remain static from one book to the next. Each volume was completely independent of the others, and the detective and his or her circumstances changed very little over time.

That has changed. It's still true that each plot of each volume in a mystery series must be self-contained. Readers should be able to pick up any book in the series, whether it's the first or the tenth, and fully comprehend the story and the characters on their own merits, without feeling as if they've missed some essential bit of information.

But just as real people change as they move through life, the contemporary detective evolves from book to book. The circumstances of life alter. Your detective learns things from the challenges he or she has faced, from successes and disappointments. Perspectives change. Relationships with other people begin, end, shift gears, or move into new stages. While your detective wraps up the mystery by the end of each book, some personal issues may be left unresolved, providing a common thread that runs through several volumes. The individual books in a series are independent works, yet at the same time, they are episodes in the ongoing chronicle of the detective's life.

From the Detective's Notebook 5 — Continued

When You're Considering a Series

If you think the story you're writing has series potential, keep the following pointers in mind:

🔫 *Choose your detective wisely.* If you plan to write a series, you need a detective who will sustain readers' interest and your own through several books; a strong, intelligent, complex, and likable character. Not only that, it needs to be a character who can come up with plausible reasons for continuing to stumble over corpses. This is less a problem with professional sleuths, more so with amateurs. Unless they are employed as full-time crime fighters, most people do not become tangled up in the investigation of a single homicide, let alone murder in multiples.

Often in the first novel of a series, the amateur detective is touched personally by the crime and is highly motivated to solve it. As the series continues, the author becomes hard pressed to come up with believable ways to involve the sleuth. Mystery writers refer to this as the Jessica Fletcher Syndrome, after the lead character in the TV program *Murder, She Wrote*. Everywhere Jessica Fletcher goes, a murder is sure to follow. You'd think her friends would catch on after a while and quit issuing her invitations.

I'm not suggesting you avoid making your detective an amateur; many successful series have been built around nonprofessional sleuths. But considering at the outset of your first book how your detective might become involved in future cases can help you establish your detective more solidly from the beginning.

🔫 *Find a way to keep tabs on your characters.* Here is a true story: A friend was rereading an early volume in her writer husband's long-running mystery series. Two characters I'll call Jones and Smith appear in each book in the series. "I didn't know Jones was the godfather of Smith's kids," my friend commented. "Smith doesn't have kids," her husband replied. My friend: "In this book he did."

It can be difficult enough to remember from page 12 to page 254 what you wrote about a character. Hanging onto details from book one to book five can be even trickier. Losing track of the children may seem extreme, but even larger discrepancies than that have occurred in some mysteries. And while you may not catch them, your readers will. It's not uncommon for an author to meet a fan at a book signing or conference who knows the details of the detective even better than the author does.

If you think certain characters may pop up again in subsequent books, keep whatever notes you developed on them in a file or notebook. When your detective is locking horns with the same police captain once again, you won't have to scour your first manuscript to locate that paragraph where you so eloquently described him.

From the Detective's Notebook 5 — Continued

☞ *Finish the first book, first.* If while you're writing, story triggers and ideas occur to you that would suit future books in a series, that's great. Jot them down and file them away until you need them. Then get back to your top-priority task: writing book number one. If a publisher is intrigued by a series concept, you might be offered a contract that includes more than one book. But the publisher will make such a decision only with a first book in hand that is well written and filled with fascinating, believable characters.

6
Constructing a Convincing Plot

The plot is the structure of the mystery, the bones on which you hang the rest of the story. Like the skeleton inside your body, the plot gives shape and substance to all the story's disparate parts, enabling them to function together as a living entity, whole and complete.

Sometimes fiction, especially a short story, can succeed brilliantly without a plot. The author has found some other way to make the story elements coherent and cohesive, for instance, by uniting a series of images with a common theme or a shared mood, or by developing an extended portrait of a character by focusing on his or her emotional life. While these approaches can be very insightful, a traditional plot is the best way to support a mystery's demands for character development, suspense, and entertainment.

So, how do you come up with a plot? This question probably ranks second on the mystery-writing frequently asked questions list, after "Where do you get your ideas?" The answer: One step at a time. A writer approaches the plot in much the same way readers do, by asking, "What happens next?" Slowly, event by event, clue by clue, the plot takes shape.

The Purpose of a Plot

The good thing about bodies is that they come preassembled. Coming up with a plot for a mystery is like being handed a box of bones and being told to join them into a working skeleton.

The work you did in chapter 3 gave you the starting pieces: characters, conflict, and crime. To these you have fitted some What if? questions that have helped you see more of the story. But you're still a long way from having a complete mystery novel. Some puzzle pieces are scattered; others are missing, and you'll have to fashion them. To decide which bones will fit and which should be discarded, it helps to understand how a plot organizes them into a comprehensive whole.

To Depict a Series of Dramatic Events

Plot is often defined as a series of dramatic events moving forward in time. Let's examine that definition more closely.

A plot is a chronological progression of events (the *time* element), but it is more than that. The events constitute a series: a sequence of related occurrences with a defined beginning, middle, and end. Something happens to initiate the sequence; something else happens to bring it to a close. The intervening events are connected by some common element.

The starting and ending points of a person's life are birth and death. What relates the events in between is that they all involve the same person. A war between two countries begins with the first act of aggression and ends with a treaty of peace; the middle consists of battles and diplomatic negotiations. The thread that runs through it is the desire of both combatants to prevail.

Mystery writers are lucky in that our favored genre lends itself naturally to this pattern: a crime is committed, an investigation ensues, and the crime is solved. In many mystery novels, the structure is just about that simple, with the events of the surface story presented in straightforward chronological order.

Other mysteries, though, demand a more complicated, less linear, presentation. A good working definition of plot might be "a dramatic arrangement of related events."

The key word here is *dramatic,* often defined as full of action, highly emotional, having conflict, vivid, exciting. The events of a mystery are like those in real life, but heightened and intensified. Whatever is boring or irrelevant should be left on the cutting-room floor. The rest should be arranged and presented in the way that best allows you to serve the requirements of the story: to elucidate your characters, explore your story's theme, establish the right mood, build suspense, and elicit the desired emotional response from your readers.

To Raise Questions and then Answer Them

Early in any story, and in a mystery in particular, the author quickens readers' interest by posing questions. The unfolding of the plot is the process of discovering the answers. By the end of the story, all the questions should be resolved; this is what yields the sense of closure essential to a satisfying mystery-reading experience.

In a mystery, three sets of questions drive the plot. The author chooses the characters and events according to their ability to raise, discuss, or answer these questions.

Questions about the hidden story

Whodunit? This question is so fundamental to a mystery's purpose that the word has been adopted into popular parlance as a synonym for a detective story. Its cousins are Howdunit? and Whydunit? — questions about the villain's means and motives. Together they form the heart of the hidden story. By the end of the novel, all the pertinent details of the hidden story should be fully revealed to readers.

Questions about your characters' goals

What keeps readers turning the pages is the desire to know if the detective will succeed; not whether the detective will solve the mystery — readers assume this will happen — but whether he or she will accomplish the larger goal that pulled him or her into the investigation. If your mystery has a secondary protagonist, readers will be concerned about the outcome of that character's goal as well.

The detective's struggles to achieve the goal are the essence of the surface story. The answers to the following questions are like the picture on the cover of the jigsaw puzzle box: a glimpse of what your story will look like once it's fully assembled. You can use them as guidelines for matching and fitting the pieces.

(a) *What is the detective's principal goal or desire?* As I've discussed in previous chapters, solving the mystery is a means to a larger end for your detective. Besides unmasking the villain, what does your detective hope to achieve by participating in the investigation?

(b) *Why is the goal important to her?* A person's stated goal is only half the picture. Equally important is why that goal matters. Here's a simple example many of us can relate to: Three people have a common objective of losing ten pounds. Although these three people desire the same result, they each want it for different reasons. One is looking for health benefits, the second hopes to feel more attractive, the third is trying to appease a nagging friend.

You can often find an important clue to a character by finding the goal behind his or her goal. Frequently, the real issue is buried deep in the character's subconscious; often, it is hidden from the character as much as it is from other people. The expressed goal may seem logical and rational, but often it's rooted deep in the character's emotions, in some fear, loss, betrayal, or unmet need.

(c) *What will be the consequences of success or failure?* Either outcome will make a difference, positive or negative, in the detective's life and perhaps in the lives of others. What does the detective have at stake? What does the detective expect will happen if he or she does or does not achieve the goal?

(d) *What is the detective willing to risk to achieve the goal?* Any effort to gain something entails the risk of losing something else. When the risk exceeds the payoff, the character will cut his or her losses and move on. The purpose of the plot is to keep raising the bar as the stakes get higher, the character has more to gain and more to lose, and the story's tension increases.

(e) *Who or what gets in the way?* The bones of the plot are the challenges and obstacles that the detective encounters while striving to achieve the goal. Conflict occurs when other characters' goals and personal agendas clash with those of the detective's, but the detective's own desires, fears, and failings may well be a source of problems too.

> ### "Why do you want this?"
>
> To discover the goal behind a character's goal, use the stream-of-consciousness technique to ask that character. Write the direct question to your character at the top of the page: "[Character's name], why do you want to achieve/attain/acquire thus-and-such?" Then, writing with the first-person point of view, let the character tell you.
>
> Ask again: "Why do you want [whatever was named in the previous answer]?" In this way, you can work down through the layers of motivation.

The primary question

In addition to your questions about the crime and the characters, there is a larger question that needs to be answered. It addresses your own motivation as a writer: What is the central issue of the story, the one you are writing this mystery to explore? You don't need to know the answer before you begin. Discovering it is one of the rewards and joys of writing. It may take you more than one draft to fully grasp what this key question is.

When I began writing *A Relative Stranger,* I focused on the elements of the mystery: what the hidden story was, and how my protagonist, Jess, would uncover it. But as the work progressed, I found that the issue of Jess's relationship with her father intrigued me much more than the questions surrounding Deborah Collington's death. The primary question became, "What impact will the sudden reemergence of her father have on Jess's life and her understanding of herself, and how will she come to terms with her relationship with this man and the issues it raises for·her?"

The primary question provides a touchstone as you make decisions about the plot. Does this character, this scene, this event contribute to the answer or detract from it? If it contributes, it belongs in the story. If it doesn't, boot it out.

The Structure of a Mystery's Plot

Most mysteries are constructed along the traditional lines of a well-told tale. This does not mean you must resort to a formula, any more than an architect has a formula in designing a building. All buildings have certain elements in common: a floor, roof, walls, windows, and doors. These components are assembled in a similar sensible arrangement — the floor on the bottom, the roof on top, the walls in between — that makes the building functional and keeps it from falling down. Yet infinite variations in size, style, and purpose are possible. You can construct a palace, a garden shed, or a highrise office tower.

The same is true of mysteries. Their structural elements comprise six basic categories of events and circumstances universal to stories with plots. To construct the story, the author arranges these parts so they fall into a logical and dramatic sequence, from beginning to middle to end. Within this basic framework, countless stories can be told.

The six constituent parts of a mystery's structure are the inciting incident, the involving incident, the development and complications, the plot points or turning points, the climax, and the denouement or resolution. Let's consider each one in detail.

The Inciting Incident

The inciting incident is the event that ignites the action, that sets up the main conflict the story will deal with. Often this event is a murder. If not, it starts the chain of events that leads up to a murder.

In *A Relative Stranger,* the inciting incident is Deborah Collington's murder. She is killed offstage, two days before the events in the book begin. The crime doesn't occur in the narrative; readers can't picture what happened until the perpetrator describes it, seven pages before the book ends. But everything that takes place in the novel occurs as a result of this murder.

Many mystery writers insist that a murder should occur as early in the book as possible, preferably in the first few pages. Others prefer to push it to a somewhat later point so they can show readers the circumstances that led up to it. If you decide to delay the murder, be sure to make some sort of conflict or problem evident in the first chapter. That way, you will establish the tension you need to propel the story forward.

The Involving Incident

The involving incident is the event that pulls your detective into the conflict. If your detective witnesses the crime or is present at the event that sets the story rolling, the inciting and involving incidents can be the same. Often, though, they are not. A classic (and by now somewhat clichéd) way to involve a private detective is to have a client show up at his or her office to ask the detective to take on the case.

Because Jess's father fears being suspected of a murder he insists he did not commit, he contacts her after years of silence to ask for her help. This call to Jess is the event that involves her in the case. If he had not telephoned her in the middle of the night, Jess would have been no more concerned about Deborah Collington's fate than about any other event that made headlines in the morning paper.

Development and Complications

Development of the plot and complications along the way make up the bulk of the story, as the detective endeavors to solve the crime and achieve his or her larger goal. At the same time, the criminal is trying to thwart the detective, as well as other investigators, to avoid discovery and elude capture.

The detective's path to a resolution cannot be smooth. Your job is to make his or her life difficult. You set up barriers, place roadblocks in the path, dump your detective into messes, create problems that must be solved before he or she can move on. You can also engage your detective's weaknesses so that he or she compounds the troubles.

As the story progresses, these complications should become increasingly dire and harder to overcome. You keep raising the stakes, increasing the tension, and building the suspense. You want to challenge your detective's ingenuity and make him or her draw on all personal strengths and resources while solving the mystery.

Plot Points (Turning Points)

Plot points are major complications that have some special significance to the story. A plot point might:

- Call into question key information that the detective or other characters have understood or assumed to be true

- Mark a turning point in the fortunes of the detective or another major character

☛ Raise the stakes significantly, putting substantial additional pressure on the detective to succeed

The plot point is also called a turning point. Because it occurs, the story's line of action veers in a new direction. As a result, the detective must rethink what has gone before and adjust the course. Here are some examples of plot points:

☛ A second murder occurs and damaging evidence is discovered.

☛ A major character, whom readers have assumed to be innocent, is arrested.

☛ A character disappears under suspicious circumstances.

But don't limit yourself to these examples; the possibilities are boundless.

The Climax

The climax of the story is the moment of greatest drama, the high point toward which all the tension and suspense have been building. The opposing forces of the story — good and evil, protagonist and antagonist, detective and villain — face each other at last to resolve the conflict and determine which will prevail. In the climax, the main points of the hidden story are revealed, and the detective's success or failure is determined once and for all.

The climax is sometimes referred to as the confrontation. This synonym embodies something important about the climax: it must be a face-to-face encounter. It's no fair having the detective write someone a note explaining who the killer is and then fly off to the Bahamas, out of harm's way, before the envelope can be opened.

The Resolution (Denouement)

Once the climax is over, the tension drops sharply, and it's time to wrap up the story. In a brief chapter, or a short scene in a short story, tie up any loose ends, answer any dangling questions, and drop the curtain.

In detective stories in the past, it would sometimes take pages after the villain was revealed for the sleuth to expound on his or her deductive reasoning process and the significance of each clue. Not any more.

The preference is to push the climax to the last possible moment and provide just enough of a resolution to give readers a sense of closure.

Putting It Together: The Plot's Chain of Events

Between your story trigger and What if? questions, it's fairly easy to come up with the inciting and involving incidents. If you've figured out the hidden story, you may have a good idea of how the confrontation should play out. But what about the events in between — all the complications and turning points? How do you decide what happens, and then what happens next?

Ask the characters. After all, it's their story. The plot grows out of their actions and interactions. When something happens, each character responds to it in an individual way, depending on his or her personality, temperament, previous experiences, and personal agenda. One character might respond conservatively and cautiously to the situation while another might rush into it headlong.

Whatever the character does, his or her action has consequences; something else happens as a result. This might or might not be the result the character was hoping to achieve. But the consequences set up a new situation, and that requires the character to do something more in response.

> A plot is a chain of events linked together by actions and consequences.

So, at its simplest, a plot is a chain of events linked together by actions and consequences, or causes and effects. Because event 1 occurred, event 2 happens as a result. Because event 2 occurred, event 3 happens as a result. And so on. Here's an example:

(a) Because he has been accused of killing his wife, Jack Lambert needs to hide from the police.

(b) Because he needs to hide from the police, Jack returns to the childhood home he fled years ago and asks his mother to take him in.

(c) Because Jack is her only child and she is lonely, Matilda Lambert lets him stay, despite her misgivings about breaking the law by harboring a fugitive.

(d) Because Matilda has misgivings, she goes to the office of her church to seek her minister's advice.

(e) Because Matilda speaks to the minister in the thin-walled office, she is overheard by Dolores Wilcox, the busybody church secretary.

(f) Because telling other people's secrets makes Dolores feel important, she tells her sister Marie, a reporter for the town's newspaper, that a murderer is staying at the Lambert home.

(g) Because Marie smells a hot story, she decides to visit the Lambert home.

(h) Because Marie goes to the Lambert home . . .

What happens next? That depends on whom Marie encounters when she arrives at Matilda's and how that person responds to finding her on the doorstep.

Note that at any point, this story could have evolved differently. Jack Lambert could have chosen to hide elsewhere. His mother could have refused to take him in. Once she gave him shelter, she could have kept quiet about his presence. Instead of telling her sister, Dolores could have shared her juicy secret with the police, or her boyfriend, or the women in her bowling league.

Try the What if? exercise to determine various chains of events — the various answers that could be given to the question, "What happens next?" Then test the possibilities you come up against the factors listed below:

☞ Based on your intimate knowledge of the characters, does this sequence of events accurately reflect what the characters involved would do under these circumstances?

☞ Do these events arise logically out of what has occurred?

☞ Is this course of action consistent with the hidden story? Will it either move the detective closer to discovering the hidden story or place a significant obstacle in his or her path?

☞ Will this sequence of events keep the story on track toward a climax and a resolution?

☞ Do these events move the story forward in the direction set by the questions that drive the plot? Do they contribute to establishing, explaining, or answering one or more of those questions?

When your plot ideas yield yes answers, you'll know you are on the right track.

The Three-Act Structure

When I was writing *A Relative Stranger*, I struggled with the idea of how to put all the plot elements together in a way that would sustain interest. Finally, the puzzle pieces began to fall into place when I read about the screenplay paradigm — the way that movie scripts are structured. I had a model to follow that allowed me to anticipate the events to come, build in moments of high drama that would keep my readers guessing, and bring the story to a satisfying close.

Although it is not always apparent when you're watching the movie, a screenplay is structured in three acts, each with specific story objectives to accomplish. Hollywood designates the acts as the setup, the development, and the resolution. But it is easier to think of them simply as the beginning, the middle, and the end.

A clue from Hollywood

The three-act structure corresponds neatly with the three-stage outlining process I described in chapter 3. I've also devised a related tool to help me play around with the events of the plot: the three-act chart shown in Sample 4 at the end of this section. The chart helps me keep the big picture in view as I test, discard, arrange, and rearrange various events that I might include in my mystery. Does this incident belong at the beginning, in the middle, or at the end? What sequence will best serve the dramatic purposes of each act? Is any crucial event missing? Using the chart, I can come up with an order of events that feels satisfying and right.

As with all my planning tools, I return to the chart from time to time as I progress with the writing, revising it to reflect new developments in the story. I draw it on a large sheet of paper, making entries in pencil or on sticky notes so I can move them around easily from act 1 to act 2 to act 3. I know a writer who employs a similar technique but prefers a larger surface on which to spread out his ideas; he uses colored markers on a whiteboard mounted on the wall.

You need not make any formal designation of the three acts in your book, no more than a movie drops a curtain to show when one act closes and the next begins. Indeed, you don't need to follow a structure at all; the structure of novels has fewer rules than screenplays, which are expected to follow a form almost as rigid as a sonnet in poetry.

But for a mystery, thinking in terms of three acts is a helpful way to get over plot hurdles. If you'd like to have fun while learning about story structure, watch some mystery movies after you read the sections below and try to identify the points at which the three acts begin and end.

The Beginning: Hooking Readers

Like a fisher with a rod and reel, your objective at the beginning of the book is to snag readers and lure them into the world of your story. Readers are busy people, with many competing demands on their time and an abundance of entertainment options. You need to convince them that, of all their alternatives, your mystery is worth their attention. A strong beginning to your story is essential, and that takes more just an intriguing opening scene.

Your objective at the beginning of the book is to snag readers and lure them into the world of your story.

Hollywood calls act 1 the setup, and its purpose is to establish the basic elements of the story in a way that engages viewers' interest and curiosity. In a movie, the setup is the first 20 to 30 minutes, about one-quarter of the total running time. By the end of act 1, most viewers will have already decided whether or not they like the movie.

Act 1 of your mystery serves a similar purpose. You have a lot to accomplish in the beginning section:

(a) *Hook readers' interest.* Once readers have picked up the book, you have only a paragraph or two, a page at the most, to convince them to continue reading. The easiest way to do this is to jump right into the middle of the action. This doesn't mean you must write about gunfire or explosions on the first page, but your characters should be busy and in motion, acting, speaking, and doing things. Drop your readers right into the scene and let them spy on what's happening. Describe the action clearly, but save the elaborate explanations of who the characters are and what they're doing for a later moment, after readers are hooked.

(b) *Introduce the characters.* Bring all the important characters on stage, including the villain. Perhaps you have a character who will play a significant role, but who, for sound plot reasons, should not come on board until later in the story. In that case, make readers aware that this character exists, perhaps by having other characters talk about him or her. In the fairy tale "Cinderella," Prince Charming does not appear until Cinderella, transformed from tattered waif to beautiful princess, appears at the palace ball. But he is a strong presence in the story from the opening scene, when Cinderella's stepsisters receive the invitation to the ball and start to dream about captivating him.

(c) *Establish the story's milieu.* Let readers know where the mystery takes place. By "milieu," I mean more than the setting; I mean the kind of story world you are presenting. This includes its locale, its key background elements (for instance, your story might be set within the environment of a particular profession), and its atmosphere — light or dark, comic or tragic.

(d) *Present the inciting and involving incidents.* The inciting incident should happen quickly, perhaps even before the story begins. If it occurs offstage, be sure to have a character explain to readers what starts the story rolling. Show the involving incident early on as well. If you wait until chapter 7 to bring the detective on scene, readers will have already identified with another character; once that's happened, it's hard to persuade readers to switch their allegiance to someone new.

(e) *Define the problem.* Tell readers what your detective is up against, and why. By the end of act 1, you want to have posed the story's primary question and the important questions surrounding the hidden story and the detective's goal.

(f) *Commit a crime.* If the inciting incident or the involving incident do not involve a crime, be sure to kill a character or perpetrate another life-or-death act before proceeding too far. Give the detective a mystery to solve; after all, that's one of the main purposes of the book. Crank up the suspense and tension right away.

(g) *Propel readers into act 2.* Conclude act 1 with a significant plot point or turning point, a new problem for your detective to solve. This increases the suspense and creates the forward momentum to push both the characters and readers into the next part of the story.

The Middle: Keeping Readers Turning the Page

In screenwriting terms, act 2 is the development. It is usually twice as long as acts 1 and 3, and it takes up the middle half of the movie.

Some writers prefer to call this section the "muddle." It can be the most difficult to write. Many aspects of an investigation, even a homicide investigation, are, frankly, a bit dull, with endless rounds of asking questions and sifting through objects and information in the hope that something will provide a clue. Unless you have a clear sense of where your story is headed, the middle can easily go adrift or sputter to a halt from lack of energy. As always, keep your focus on the questions driving the plot. Having raised them in act 1, you begin in act 2 to drive toward the answers.

The middle section requires a balancing act. On the one hand, you need to move the story steadily forward on a direct path toward a resolution. On the other, you must place barriers in the path to keep your detective from reaching the resolution too easily or too soon. The tension between these conflicting aims — progress versus impediment, gas pedal versus brakes — is what gives the middle of the story its energy and suspense.

These are your story objectives for the middle section:

(a) *Make your characters' lives difficult.* The events of the middle are referred to as complications, and for good reason. They should create at least as many problems for the detective or the secondary protagonist as they solve.

(b) *Raise the stakes.* With each complication, the overall situation should grow more serious, with a higher price to be paid should the detective fail.

(c) *Plant clues.* Act 1 sets up the problem to be investigated; most of the investigation occurs in act 2. One of your purposes in the middle section is to provide the detective and readers with much of the information needed to discern the hidden story.

(d) *Provide readers with a high point of tension.* To keep the tension line from flattening, boost it around the mid-point of the book with a complication that generates some excitement. For example, let your detective narrowly escape from a brush with danger. Make hearts pound a bit, both the detective's and the readers'. The trick here is make the incident integral to the plot, a genuine link in the chain of events.

(e) *Propel readers into act 3.* Conclude act 2 with another significant plot point. This one should provide a new problem and also turn the story toward the finale, setting the detective on a road that will lead inevitably to the confrontation with the villain.

The End: Solving the Mystery and Satisfying Readers

Act 3, according to Hollywood, is the resolution, but this final 25 percent of the movie includes more than the final wrap-up. This section is readers' payoff for sticking with your story. Finally, you bring the detective and the villain face to face and determine whether your detective will succeed or fail in reaching his or her goal. You answer all the questions you raised in act 1.

Make the end of your story worthy of its beginning. You probably know from your own reading experience that if anything frustrates readers, it's having a good story fall flat in the final pages. This usually happens for one of three reasons.

The first has to do with logic: For either the hidden story or the surface story, the author hasn't fully worked out the chain of events of the plot. The end seems tacked on or arbitrary rather than being the inevitable result of what has transpired in the story.

The second is a matter of misplaced compassion: To save the characters from pain or suffering, the author has let them off the hook, refusing to push them to their limits or create situations in which they face real fear or danger. As a result, the characters never really resolve the issues that the story set up.

Finally, the author may have simply taken the easy way out, possibly rushing through the last chapters. When the end is in sight, it's tempting to give the remaining chapters short shrift in order to have, at long last, the pleasure of writing "The End." Maybe the author lacks confidence or discipline, or was afraid of revealing too much about personal issues or feelings. For whatever reason, the author has not dealt with the hard work of devising a satisfying conclusion.

If you do a strong job of meeting the story objectives for the final section, you can successfully avoid all these problems. You'll leave your readers saying, "Wow! What a great mystery." In act 3 you want to:

(a) *Provide the remaining clues and complications.* Make sure that before the confrontation occurs, the detective (and readers) has all the information needed to solve the mystery.

(b) *Keep readers guessing about the story's outcome.* Sustain the suspense right up until the moment of the confrontation. The detective's role in solving the mystery and achieving his or her goal should not seem inevitable; readers should feel that the detective's fortunes could go either way.

(c) *Provide an all-is-lost moment.* At some point, either shortly before the confrontation or as it opens, make things very dark for your detective. Dangle the possibility of failure squarely before him or her. Your detective is trapped, in danger, or has jeopardized someone's life through errors in judgment — the choice is yours. The point here is to give your detective one last serious obstacle to overcome.

(d) *Stage a confrontation that's worth the wait.* This is the high point of the story, its strongest, most dramatic, most highly emotional moment. Everything in the story has been building to this point. Because of their power, the confrontation and the dark episode that precedes it can be frightening and filled with anguish, not only for the characters but also for the author.

This part of the book is challenging to write, and it can be tempting to hold back and to soften the blows. Don't do this. Bring the confrontation front and center, and rely on your detective's strength and resourcefulness to get you both through to the end.

(e) *Answer all the remaining questions.* All the questions you've raised in the story should be answered by the end. To keep the denouement short, the important explanations come as part of the confrontation, and lesser questions are often dealt with even before the climax occurs.

(f) *Don't just close; provide closure.* The final scene should provide a sense of completion. The chain of events has reached a final link, a logical conclusion. The characters' lives have been changed by the events of the mystery; what happens to them next is a new story.

Sample 4
Three-Act Chart

ACT 1 Setup	ACT 2 Development	ACT 3 Resolution

Plot point: Allen is arrested

Plot point: 2nd murder — who dies?

ACT 1	ACT 2	ACT 3
Jess meets her real father — he asks for help, wanted for murder	Have a scene with Allen in jail	
J. meets Kit Cormier	Talks to Brockway's accountant	Figures out meaning of C-Day
J. starts investigation, talks to:		
• Brockway	J. returns to boutique — finds 2nd necklace Which is real?	J. finds witness to D.'s murder?
• San Marco		
• Evan Krausgill	Uncle Jack tells her about Allen	
DEBORAH'S FUNERAL		
D.'s apt. — J. finds emerald ring	J. has run-in with cops (Gardino)	CONFRONTATION! Where? Boat? Theater?
Scene at office Intro Claudia, Tyler, O'Meara	Takes pictures to Hammer-wood Gallery	
Visits D.'s boutique	J. visits childhood home, stepfather	
Show J. in painting studio		
		Gallery opening — final scene?

Scene cards

Scene cards

Here's another clue from Hollywood: Try the screenwriter's system for figuring out the order of scenes using a stack of 3-by-5-inch or 4-by-6-inch index cards. On a separate card for each scene, write a key identifying word: where the scene takes place, which characters are there, what happens. Spread the cards on the floor or tack them to a wall to get an overview of your plot. You can now arrange and re-arrange the cards — and the scenes — until they're in the most logical and dramatic order. You'll also be able to spot missing scenes or holes in the story that need to be filled.

Managing Multiple Plot Lines

Every mystery has at least two plot lines. One is the hidden story, the other is the surface story (see chapter 3).

A short story may stick closely to the events of these two plot lines and venture no farther. In a novel, you may choose to add secondary plot lines to make the story richer and more complex. These subplots should relate to and impinge on the main plot in some way. For instance, if you center a subplot around a budding relationship between the detective and a potential love interest, this romance should have an impact on the investigation. Perhaps the romantic partner is connected to the case — a suspect, another investigator, or a relative of the victim or villain. Maybe the detective's pursuit of the investigation interferes with the new romance, or vice versa, so that the detective must make hard choices about his or her priorities.

Any relationship between two characters can be regarded as a miniplot, whether they are lovers, friends, enemies, or strangers who have an interchange on the bus. Each character brings to the relationship a particular set of hopes and fears, and an agenda that he or she wants to carry out. As one character does something and another character responds, a chain of actions and consequences results.

The main plot, the subplots, and the miniplots each create their own actions-and-consequences chain. All these chains weave together to form the web that is your story. Within this fabric, the main plot lines (the ones that define the hidden story and the surface story) should always be the strongest and most prominent. The subplots and miniplots must link to them in some way. The purpose of these smaller story lines is to increase the dramatic effect of the major ones, to keep the story moving forward, and to add additional insight to the questions raised and then answered by your plot.

Foul Play and Fair Play

Foul play is the raison d'être for a mystery. But while crime, violence, and murder provide its subject matter, the genre is imbued with a strong sense of fair play. This derives from its roots as a form of puzzle that challenged readers to beat the detective at his or her own game and come up with the solution first. If the game is to be fair, readers must have an equal chance to win.

S.S. Van Dine, a noted mystery writer during the 1920s, devised a list of 20 rules for writing detective stories. Most have been tossed overboard as mysteries have evolved from entertaining intellectual parlor games into fully developed stories that rely on characters as much as on plot. But three standards survive, and mystery fans expect authors to adhere to them. Not to do so is considered, well, foul play.

The Detective Solves the Crime

If readers are supposed to use their own wits to solve the crime, the detective must also. It's considered unfair to come to the detective's rescue by providing suspects who happily babble everything the detective wants to know before even being asked, or a deathbed letter of confession from a remorseful killer who has decided to take his own life, or a witness who returns home from out of town and says, "Oh, you've been wondering all this time who did it? Let me tell you. I saw the whole thing."

In other words, you must make the detective draw on the full extent of his or her strengths and resourcefulness to get the job done. If your detective does not figure out who the killer is, at the very least his or her endeavors should be directly responsible for forcing the villain to admit guilt or enabling a third person to nab the villain.

The Villain Plays a Part in the Story

To be a worthy opponent, the villain must be present in the story. The villain need not play a major role and certainly should not do anything that makes apparent his or her status as the perpetrator of the crime. But you should give the villain a sufficiently large role that both the detective and readers are fully aware of him or her. You should also provide enough of the villain's back story so that his or her actions will be understandable once the hidden story is revealed.

All the Clues Are Available

"What a surprise! Nobody else could have done it."

These are the reactions, contradictory though they may seem, that you want readers to have when the villain is unveiled.

Your task is to prevent readers from guessing the solution, while giving them all the information they need to figure it out. If readers were to reread the book, aware of the villain's identity and the details of the hidden story, they should be able to find that you have slipped in every necessary clue and foreshadowed the outcome of the investigation, so that the conclusion, while baffling, is also inevitable.

Just because you must provide the clues, though, doesn't mean you need to draw readers' attention to them with flashing neon arrows. You can use any number of techniques to hide them. For example:

> Your task as the author is to prevent readers from guessing the solution, while giving them all the information they need to figure it out.

- Tuck the important item among several irrelevant items presented at the same time. The detective opens a suspect's refrigerator and makes note of the contents: eggs, cheese, lettuce, beer. Which one, if any, is significant?

- Make the detective misinterpret a key piece of information.

- Drop the clue as a casual comment in a conversation about an entirely different topic.

- Show the clue while you are focusing the characters' and readers' attention on something that seems to be more significant.

- Provide the clue in one scene, but provide the reason for its significance at an earlier or later point in the book. The detective kicks a chocolate bar wrapper that is part of the trash littering the scene of the crime. Several chapters later, when the killer orders fudge cake for dessert and comments on his weakness for chocolate, the candy wrapper may well have been forgotten.

☛ If a personality trait of the villain is significant to the crime, be sure to show it. If she killed in a fit of rage, include a scene in which she displays her quick temper so it will be apparent that she has one. But make the object of her display of anger something unrelated to the crime.

Remember, too, that fair play requires only that you give readers the same information the detective has. It doesn't require you to make them aware of every aspect of the detective's thinking and analysis. Readers should do the figuring out for themselves. After all, if readers are matching wits with the detective, you want to give them a chance to show off their cleverness.

Keeping track of clues

Here's a good technique to try when you are in the third stage of planning, that is, when you have two-thirds of the book planned (and perhaps written) and are launching into act 3. By this time, you will have a good sense of the story. Begin by writing, "What [Detective's name] needs to know to solve the mystery" at the top of a sheet of paper. Jot down all the bits and pieces of information needed to figure out the hidden story and any other secret woven into your plot. On a separate sheet, list the scenes in your novel. Go down your list of required information, and note the scene in which that clue is revealed. If there is a clue you haven't included yet, use the list of scenes to figure out where to plant it. This way, you won't overlook any clues and you can be sure you've played fair.

From the Detective's Notebook 6
The Seven Basic Plots

It's been said that there are only seven plots. The seven basic plots are not plots in the sense of being fully developed sequences of actions; rather, they are categories into which story lines fall. Between its main plot and subplots, a mystery novel may incorporate several of them.

1. Revelation

Something is not what it appears to be, or someone's true identity is in question.

The key issue: What is the truth, or what is reality?

Example: *The Wizard of Oz* by L. Frank Baum.

2. Encounter

Boy meets girl. Good guy meets bad guy. Apprentice meets master. Ordinary person meets a deity. Ordinary person meets the devil.

The key issue: The interaction and its consequences.

Example: *The Silence of the Lambs* by Thomas Harris.

3. Chase

Two types: The hunt or quest (focusing on a character pursuing a prey or a prize), and the escape (focusing on a character fleeing from pursuit).

The key issue: Attainment of the object of the chase.

Example: *Les Miserables* by Victor Hugo.

4. Introspection

The character has a moral or ethical dilemma to resolve, and there is no one right or easy solution — it's damned if you do, damned if you don't. Heroic and villainous choice are embodied in one character.

The key issue: The ramifications of various choices.

Example: *Crime and Punishment* by Fyodor Dostoyevski.

From the Detective's Notebook 6 — Continued

5. Puzzle

Whodunit? Howdunit? Whydunit?

The key issue: Analysis of information to come up with a solution.

Examples: Almost anything by Agatha Christie or Sir Arthur Conan Doyle.

6. Retribution

Someone who has suffered a wrong or an offense seeks revenge against the perpetrator.

The key issue: Vengeance and punishment.

Example: *Hamlet* by William Shakespeare.

7. Transformation

A character is changed into something new by means of some external force or action, sometimes beneficial, sometimes not.

The key issue: Alteration and its results.

Example: The fairy tale "Cinderella."

The seven basic plots were first identified by Aristotle. Many thanks to novelist Chelsea Quinn Yarbro who provided the explanations included here.

7
Putting Your Story
in Its Place

The mysteries I like best are those firmly rooted in a place, so that I feel I'm right there — walking down those streets, gazing on that mountain vista, savoring the sea air, feeling the hot sun beating on my back or the winter wind whipping around my ears. They are books where the setting is integral to the story; the events described have happened because these people have come together at this time and in this place, and the combination has somehow proved volatile.

The setting of a mystery is far more than a pushpin on a map or a collection of street names. It is the entire fictional world you are creating for your readers, the context within which the characters operate and their drama unfolds. Your choice of a setting and the way you depict it will have a profound effect on your book.

In this Place, in this Time

The setting of a mystery locates the characters and the events of the story in both place and time.

Mysterious Places

In the mystery genre's earliest days, it seemed almost to be a rule: Mysteries had to be set in New York City, in California, or, if the author was British, in England. Of course this was never really true, and in recent decades the "rule," as useless as a 30-year-old train schedule, has been crumpled up and thrown out. Today, any place in the world is fair game for foul play.

In fact, the mystery genre lately has achieved renown for being a kind of regional literature, a form of storytelling in which a vibrantly depicted setting is almost as important as characters and plot in shaping the tale and defining readers' experience.

Tony Hillerman set the pace for this development with his stories about Joe Leaphorn and Jim Chee, Navajo tribal policemen in the Four Corners area of the American Southwest (where the borders of Utah, Colorado, New Mexico, and Arizona come together), which powerfully evoke the landscape and culture of that area. Other places you can visit, and some of the authors who take you there, include (and this is far from an exhaustive list):

> The development of vivid regional settings has turned mystery fans into armchair travelers.

- Alaska: Sue Henry, Dana Stabenow, John Straley
- Appalachian mountains: Sharyn McCrumb
- Berkeley, California: Susan Dunlap
- Boston, Massachusetts: Linda Barnes, Jeremiah Healy, Robert B. Parker, William Tapply
- British Columbia: L.R. Wright
- California's Gold Country: Penny Warner
- Cotswolds region, England: M.C. Beaton
- Hong Kong: William Marshall
- Kansas: Charlene Weir
- Kenya: Karin McQuillan
- Louisiana: James Lee Burke, Julie Smith (New Orleans)
- New Brunswick: Alisa Craig
- Oxford, England: Colin Dexter

- San Antonio, Texas: Rick Riordan
- Scotland: Ian Rankin
- Toronto: Alison Gordon, Eric Wright
- Yorkshire, England: Peter Robinson

Mysterious Times

When you're establishing a fictional world, the time when the story occurs is as important as the place where it occurs. By time, I don't mean six o'clock, or Saturday, or September, though the specific hour, day, or month can help readers follow the story and is often crucial to the plot. I'm referring to where your story is located in the continuum of history. Are you writing a contemporary tale, or one set at some point in the past or future?

Most mysteries occur in the present day. One reason is that mysteries are an excellent vehicle for considering the kinds of social, political, cultural, and personal issues that writers and readers grapple with in their own lives. Another reason, this one more practical than philosophical, is that we know, and to some extent understand, our own times. In other words, because we can write with confidence about the time in which we live, less research is required.

If you decide to write a present-day mystery, you can establish the temporal context of the story in either of two ways: You can set the story in some vague and indefinite "now," or you can tie it to a specific year, either by mentioning the date or by bringing in benchmarks associated with that time frame, such as news events, current fads, or popular songs and TV shows. Familiar references can heighten readers' identification. On the other hand, if you are less precise about the year, the story won't become dated so quickly. A few years from now, it will still seem fresh and current, while one tied to an earlier year might seem dated.

Of course, mysteries set in earlier years can be of great interest. The opportunity to journey back through time adds an exciting dimension to mystery lovers' armchair traveling, which is why historical mysteries are becoming more and more popular. Via mysteries, readers can time-travel to past eras in places like these (again, just a small sampling):

- Ancient Rome: Lindsey Davis, Steven Saylor

- China in the seventh century: Robert Van Gulik's *Judge Dee* mysteries
- Medieval England: Ellis Peters
- Victorian England: Anne Perry
- Victorian archaeological digs in Egypt: Elizabeth Peters
- Los Angeles in the 1940s and 1950s: Walter Mosley

Secrets of Creating a Great Setting

"A strong sense of place": these are words of high praise for a mystery novel. They mean that the setting is no mere backdrop to the action, no painted set behind the stage. It is a complete and fully developed story environment.

There are two secrets to creating a vivid setting with a strong sense of place: personality and interaction. By establishing the personality of a place, and showing how the place and the characters interact, you make the setting an active and vital presence in the story.

The concepts of personality and interaction may bring to mind people more than places; that's deliberate. In many ways, a great setting functions in a mystery much like a character does; it is an important member of the cast.

Whatever setting you choose, that place has a particular set of qualities and attributes that distinguish it from other places. In other words, it has its own character, and this will be a significant factor in defining the story situation, the nature of the crime to be solved, and the types of people who will become involved.

If you shift the locale of the story, for example, from an aristocratic manor house to a rough neighborhood's "mean streets," or from a southern seacoast city to a northern prairie town, the story will change too. Consider how drastically the group dynamic of a company of people is altered when you remove one member and add another. In a similar fashion, if you lift your characters and their situation out of one locale and drop them in a different one, the dynamic of the story will change and the plot will shift direction.

Clues to a Setting's Personality

Although its location makes a difference, the character of a place is more than a matter of geography. Like a person, a place has not only physical attributes but cultural and sociological ones as well; it has its own energy, rhythm, and style. By drawing on the qualities that define it and make it unique, you can depict your setting more vibrantly and make it an active player in your story.

Even better, you tap into a wellspring of ideas: characters, events, and situations that could exist only in this place and in this time. The keys described below will help you understand your setting and take advantage of the story material it contains.

Natural environment

Whatever we humans may have imposed on the landscape, places never lose the defining characteristics that Mother Nature gave them. These qualities include:

- *Geological features and type of terrain.* Is this place in the mountains, the hills, the prairie, the desert, the forest? Is it next to an ocean, a river, a lake? These factors shape a location's history and to a great extent determine its economic base.

- *Weather and climate.* Everyone has had experience with the weather. That makes it a good tool for hooking readers into your story world; they can empathize as your characters cope with heat, cold, rain, drought, wind, and storms, even if they are unfamiliar with the place where your story is set. You also can use extreme weather to provide the characters with challenging obstacles to overcome.

- *Plants and animals.* Consider not only what kinds of plants and animals are present but how they affect the place and the characters in the place. For example, redwood trees are valued by both loggers and environmentalists for conflicting reasons; bears in national parks pose a danger to incautious campers; rats lurk in urban alleys like the one in which your detective must hide while staking out the villain's apartment.

- *Natural disasters.* Okay, it's hard to consider a natural disaster an opportunity if you're faced with one. But they're a boon to writers, because floods, tornadoes, hurricanes, and earthquakes have great dramatic potential.

Humanmade environment

Humans have set their stamp, in one way or another, on just about every spot on earth. What effect have humans had on your setting? Whether you are dealing with a major city, a suburb, a small town, or a rural community, each has distinctive types of buildings and styles of architecture; a pattern of roads, traffic circulation, and (perhaps) public transport; and certain neighborhoods that are on "the right side of the tracks" while others are on the wrong side.

Populace

Next to the physical surroundings, the "people environment" of a place is probably the most significant factor in its personality. What are they like, the folks who live and work in or visit this place? What is the ethnic and cultural mix, the age and gender distribution, and the dominant socioeconomic status? This is the population from which you will draw your characters. Fill the roles in your book with characters you could logically expect to find in this place and who respond to it appropriately, whether locals or strangers.

History

If your mystery takes place in the past, having more than a nodding acquaintance with your chosen time period is essential. A brush-up on earlier times can enrich a contemporary mystery, too, because the history of a locality provides so many clues to its current physical, sociological, and psychological circumstances. The reasons and processes by which a place grew (and then perhaps faded) have an enduring influence on its personality, and certain persons and events will have left an indelible mark.

Economics

The economy of a place dictates the manner in which money flows through it. Important factors include the major industries; the available options for earning a living; and how, where, and to whom the wealth is distributed. Because money counts for so much in our culture, being one of the principal ways we measure a person's status, power, and success, economic factors offer mystery writers an abundant source of material.

Politics

Politics is the system that determines how things get done in a place. Consider the power structure of the community — not only the formal one embodied in the system of government, but also the informal one (which is sometimes more potent) of behind-the-scenes influence. This issue is closely allied to the previous one of economics, because politics and money often dance closely together.

Local issues

To learn a lot about a place, focus on its areas of controversy. Arguments within a community often stem directly from its local economic and political circumstances; frequently the perception is that one group is trying to gain a benefit to the detriment of another group, or that a few people want to profit at the expense of the community as a whole. The nature of the issues and the way in which each side conducts the fight can be very revealing — and provide excellent story ideas.

Local tastes

Many distinguishing features of a place can be found in the substance of everyday life. For example, think about the preferences its residents express about:

 Food. This is a famous variable. Reflect on all the places famous for their regional cuisine.

 Clothes. What is considered standard or appropriate dress varies greatly from place to place. In some major cities, wearing a three-piece suit to a business meeting is de rigueur, while in a north-coast lumber town or a prairie cattle-ranching community, businesspeople might be considered formally attired if their jeans have been mended and patched.

Vehicles. On a cross-country road trip, you'll notice that the mix of vehicles on the highway changes from place to place. In the locality of your book, what are the proportions of old automobiles to new, foreign to domestic, sports cars to sedans to pickup trucks?

Pets. Is this a pit bull or a poodle kind of place?

Arts, culture, and entertainment

How the people in this place express themselves, what they celebrate, how they have fun — these are great sources of local color. Think about the kinds of music, art, movies, and sports that are popular and the facilities and institutions available to support these activities. Most places have their own special occasions, with local celebrations such as festivals and parades that bring people together. In my short story "Dreaming of Dragons," I set the confrontation on a float in the Chinese New Year parade; San Francisco is one of the few cities that could offer this opportunity.

Prevailing beliefs, attitudes, and values

While divergent opinions exist anywhere, most places have a prevailing mindset about how the world does, or should, operate. Consider the local heroes of a community for clues in this regard. Residents of a given place may be characteristically liberal or conservative, tolerant or intolerant, trendsetting or out of fashion's loop. They may welcome strangers or be suspicious of them. A single religion may dominate, or many religions, or none at all.

If you're looking for a good source of conflict, think about what kinds of behavior the people in this place consider to be desirable, normal, or deviant, and how they reward or punish people who step outside certain behavioral boundaries.

Public image

The outward face of a place's personality is its reputation in its own eyes and those of outsiders. Which qualities do its residents take pride in and its supporters promote? Which do they despair at and downplay? What lures visitors, and what keeps them away? Examining these questions can provide insight into the character of a place, and might also reveal a potential for conflict that could trigger a story.

Crime

Crime is universal, but crime rates, types of offenses, and the legal apparatus that brings perpetrators to justice vary from place to place. It's obvious that you'd be more likely to run into cattle rustlers near Calgary than in Toronto, but some crime patterns are more perplexing. For example, for reasons that are unclear, the city of Boston was for a number of years the auto-theft capital of the United States.

For novels other than mysteries, the typical crimes of a certain place might not be an important issue. But for the mystery, they can be a crucial aspect of your setting; they can even provide story triggers or inspire developments for your plot.

No matter where it takes place, a mystery usually includes a murder, but it doesn't have to be just any murder. Part of the fun of committing crimes on the printed page is thinking of motives, methods, and opportunities that take advantage of your setting's unique personality.

Clues to a Setting's Interaction with Characters

Much of what we do as we go about our daily lives results from our interaction with our environment. It sets up conditions, and we respond. We wear boots to protect our feet from the cold and ice, or sandals to avoid scorching our soles on hot pavement. Trying to reach our destinations, we breathe exhaust fumes in freeway traffic jams, or trip over roots and rocks on a steep forest trail. What we eat depends on the variety of food our neighborhood market sells; how we earn a living is conditional on the types of jobs available in our community; who we meet and marry is determined by local courtship customs and the pool of eligible candidates.

Just as real people and events are shaped by their environment, so are fictional ones. The best way to establish a vibrant setting is through its impact on your story. Fling in your characters and set them in motion. Show what the place is doing to them, both physically and emotionally. Make the impact of the location vivid through details: the soreness of a character's sunburned shoulders, the homesickness from being in a strange environment, the anxiety of being trapped in traffic, the relaxation of stretching out on a tropical beach.

The keys to your characters' interaction with their settings can be framed as questions.

How does the place affect the character?

Readers experience the setting through the mind and senses of the detective or another viewpoint character. Is the environment familiar or foreign to the character? How does he or she feel in this place: comfortable, content, frightened, ill at ease? If the character's usual milieu is a funky apartment opening onto a trash-strewn alley, he or she might enjoy the luxuries of a posh penthouse as a welcome change of pace, or might feel totally out of his or her element.

How the character reacts to the setting helps determine both the mood of the story and the actions that he or she will take during its course.

What help does the place provide the character?

As the detective strives to solve the crime and achieve other goals, he or she can be helped by the environment. The help can come in many forms: the cover of darkness provided by nightfall, the improved visibility in daylight, a fortunate change in the weather, people nearby who can be called on for assistance, or handy objects from which to improvise tools or weapons.

What obstacles does the place impose on your character?

The environment can hinder your detective as easily as it helps, by limiting his or her options and erecting barriers that must be surmounted. Use the obstructions your setting offers to add excitement to your story. Daylight, darkness, and weather conditions can work against, rather than for, your detective. The people nearby might be hostile and uncooperative. A lack of resources, or the detective's inability (for whatever reason) to tap into them, can impede his or her progress.

Choosing Your Setting

Almost any place can make a good setting for a mystery if you understand it and use it wisely. To test the setting potential of the place you have in mind, ask yourself the following questions.

Will the Setting Support the Story?

Could the story in fact happen there? Does this place, given its personality and potential for interaction, provide you with the resources you need in the way of characters and opportunities for plot development? What kind of crime would occur in this place, and how would the locality affect the way that your detective goes about investigating and solving it?

How Well Do You Know the Setting?

While a map can help, nothing beats having an intimate knowledge of a place. This doesn't restrict you to using your hometown as the story's setting, though the place where you live might well make an excellent setting. But if you want to set your story in a place you're not familiar with, you have some research ahead of you. Not to worry. Research can be fun, and if you jump into it willingly, you can learn enough about almost any place, even a spot you've never visited, to be able to portray it in a fresh, lively, and accurate manner.

Consider writers of historical mysteries. Obviously, they have not physically journeyed to ancient Rome, Victorian England, or wherever else their stories might be set. They have no choice but to learn about their setting by scouring books and documents. A visit to the contemporary location might be fun and even enlightening, but most places retain their pasts only in monuments, occasional building facades or streetscapes, museums, and library archives. Today's Montreal doesn't look any more like the Montreal of 1750 than contemporary Toronto does.

Selecting a Mystery Setting: A Case History

When I started writing *A Relative Stranger*, I decided to set the book in San Francisco because I had recently moved there. Although I was a newcomer to the city, I made my protagonist, Jess Randolph, a Bay Area native. She grew up in Oakland and Berkeley, attended school at the San Francisco Art Institute, and now lived and worked in what locals call The City. What better guide could I have to help me get to know my new home?

The San Francisco in the book is Jess's city, seen through her eyes. An artist as well as a private investigator, she notices shapes and colors, light and shadow, and she made me aware of them too.

For instance, Washington, DC, my hometown, is a red and green city — the colors of its brick buildings and abundant trees. Downtown, the red shifts to the alabaster white of the Capitol, the White House, and the many memorials. Spring comes in two waves, first the yellow of daffodils and forsythia, followed by the azaleas' pale-to-deep pinks and reds. In the autumn, tree leaves take on the colors of flames.

By contrast, much of the year San Francisco is dressed in grays: the fog, the traditional paint schemes on the wooden Victorian houses, the chilly waters of the ocean and bay. Often the light is soft. But on sunny days, when the wind or recent rains have cleared out any haze, the light takes on a bright Mediterranean intensity that almost hurts your eyes.

In San Francisco, though, "colorful" doesn't just mean reds, yellows, greens, or blues. It refers to the city's rough-and-tumble Gold Rush history, the eccentricities of many current residents, the worldwide mix of cultures, the variety of lifestyles. Most residents are not natives of the city, and it has been said they come to San Francisco because they are running either from something or to something. Rudyard Kipling called it "a mad city — inhabited for the most part by perfectly insane people." What writer couldn't find great plots and characters in a place like that?

Settings Large to Small

Imagine a series of gift-wrapped boxes, one nested inside another. Tear the paper and ribbon from the outermost package, and you discover a smaller box tucked inside. That one in turn contains another that's even smaller. In a similar way, the setting of a book has multiple layers, starting on a grand scale with the overall locale of the book (a particular region or country, or the world at large) and working down to the smaller, more specific sites of individual scenes (a street corner, a building, a park). For example, *A Relative Stranger* takes place in northern California. In the first chapter, as readers move through the layers, they find that they are in San Francisco, on upper Sansome Street near Telegraph Hill, in a converted whiskey warehouse, in Jess Randolph's brick-walled office.

Each level influences what the next layer is like. Because the setting is San Francisco, the ambiance of Jess's office and its surroundings are different from what it would be if in Savannah, Georgia, or Sudbury, Ontario.

> Mysteries often sell best in the region where they are set, with their authors developing avid local fans.

Real versus Imaginary Settings

Most mystery authors, like those mentioned at the beginning of this chapter, set their books in places that are apparently real: locations that readers have visited or heard about, or at least can pinpoint on a map. Others enjoy the challenge of spinning new places out of thin air and infusing them with a reality that's all their own. St. Mary's Mead, where Miss Marple solves mysteries, existed only in the atlas of Agatha Christie's imagination, but her millions of fans came to know this little English village almost as well as the ones they lived in.

Real Places

When you set your mystery in an existing place, you have a ready-made milieu for your characters. Just drop them in, set the story rolling, and see how they react. Using a real place is like having a well-stocked theater-props cabinet at your disposal; you can rummage in it to find exactly what you need in the way of characters, story ideas, and details to make your mystery come alive.

Readers engage easily with stories set in places they may know. Being insiders, able to visualize the precise bridge over which the detective is driving, or to summon the tang of the ocean breeze on the beach where the villain and victim meet at dawn, adds a pleasurable dimension to reading. Because the characters' experiences touch directly on their own, readers can identify with them more strongly. This is one reason mysteries often sell best in the region where they are set, with their authors developing avid local fans.

Of course, many readers will have never visited the place in which your story is set. Quite often, a mystery appeals to its fans for that very reason; it gives readers an opportunity for a vicarious adventure in a new and intriguing locale. With the printed page as their transport, they can project themselves into an environment they have been curious about or longed to visit.

The flip side of using a real place as the story's setting is that your readers expect you to be accurate. Those who are knowledgeable will catch all your errors. The same readers who are delighted that your sleuth is solving a crime on their home territory take umbrage when you get the details wrong. Readers unfamiliar with your setting won't be aware of mistakes, but they *are* trusting you to give them an authentic picture, one that truly represents the place's spirit and ambiance.

> It helps to set up time lines for events and to keep running lists of characters and clues. At the first appearance of one in the story, jot down the key descriptive details. Keep the lists handy for reference as the story progresses.

Imaginary Places

An imaginary place setting gives you great freedom and flexibility. Because you invented the place, no one can challenge your accuracy. Readers can call your bluff, though, when it comes to consistency. If, at the start of the book, the marina is on the west side of town and the university campus is to the east, don't lose track and switch them around when you reach chapter 17.

Exploring your imaginary setting

If you're inventing a town to be the setting of your mystery, you want to make it as vivid to your readers as any real place would be. To do this, and to keep track of the details about your locale, you can use some of the same tools you would use if you were exploring or researching an actual city. The difference is that with an imaginary place you have the fun of devising them for yourself. Some examples:

☞ *Maps.* It's helpful to sketch out the physical layout of your town: where the streets run, where various neighborhoods and landmarks are located, and how the town relates to surrounding communities.

☞ *An encyclopedia entry.* Here is a place to assemble the basic facts and figures about your place, from the size of its population to the industries that support its residents to the name of its baseball team.

☞ *The chamber of commerce or tourist bureau brochure.* This lets you look at the town from the perspective of the people who live there. Now the personality of the place begins to shine through.

☞ *The local newspaper.* You don't have to write an entire newspaper; just jot down an index of the contents in a typical issue. What kinds of topics do the articles cover? Who are the local newsmakers? What are the hot issues? What is the editorial stance? What kinds of ads appear? A newspaper provides a valuable portrait of the community.

☞ *Photographs.* Although you can't take photos of an imaginary place, travel magazines or other sources might yield pictures of buildings, landscapes, or points of interest that resemble those in your town and can help to spark your creativity.

Just as with a real setting, it's essential to know your imagined place well, both its geographical layout and its personality. No research is required, of course (though you may want to research locations you think are parallel in some way to your imaginary setting), but give careful thought to the particulars so that you can convey the place in rich detail. Your goal is make your readers believe the place exists even though they know better. With a real setting, you can tap into the knowledge or impressions they've gained by living or visiting there, or simply by reading other works set in the same locale. An imaginary setting gives you no such advantage. You have to construct the place from scratch.

The Illusion of Reality

Some writers try to have it both ways, creating fictitious cities that parallel actual ones. Ed McBain's Isola, where the 87th precinct is located, closely mirrors New York City. Sue Grafton acknowledges that Santa Teresa, home of her private investigator Kinsey Millhone, is in fact Santa Barbara, California.

In a way, that's what all writers do. When we create imaginary places, we do so by borrowing features from existing counterparts. When we set stories in actual locations, we use those places as models on which to base our fictional worlds. Notice that at the beginning of this section, I said most mystery authors set their books in places that are apparently real. We are writing fiction, not travel guides, textbooks, or chamber of commerce brochures. While we strive for accuracy, we must remember that we are editing the truth. We pick and choose details, highlighting some facts about our chosen location and ignoring others, for the sake of the story.

Not long ago at an international conference of mystery writers and fans, I was one of half a dozen authors participating in a panel discussion on San Francisco mysteries. Each of us had set books there, but we had all approached it differently. While I enjoyed taking readers to some of the well-known spots that give the city its distinctive reputation — Haight-Ashbury, Golden Gate Park, the bayside marinas — another writer played against the tourist clichés, concentrating on industrial districts and marginal neighborhoods that visitors rarely discover. We all drew our characters from different segments of the population: the gay community, the Hispanic neighborhoods, the Nob Hill upper crust. Finally, one panelist commented, "Our books don't take place in the same city at all. We've each written about a different San Francisco." We each fabricated the place that would best serve the theme, mood, and tone of our own stories. Yet, if you knew the city, you'd would find that all six versions of San Francisco ring true.

Every book combines real and imaginary settings. The question is not whether you make up imaginary places, but at what level of the setting you do it. If you invent an imaginary town, you will probably place it within an actual region of an existing nation and strive to make it seem like the kind of town that might truly exist within this larger environment. If your city is a real one, you will no doubt construct imaginary buildings, furnish invented rooms, open make-believe businesses. You can take such liberties as long as you leave the landmarks, the physical layout, and the large identifying characteristics intact and accurately depict the keys to the city's personality.

Mind your own business

Speaking of businesses, be cautious about using real ones. Some owners delight in their association with a successful book; more than 60 years later, John's Grill in San Francisco takes such pride in being the place where Sam Spade dined on chops in *The Maltese Falcon* that it has walls covered with author Dashiell Hammett memorabilia and keeps the detective's supper on the menu (though not at the original price). But if you're going to have someone killed on private premises, it's best to invent the place. Most people are understandably skittish about having their businesses portrayed as the scene of a crime.

8
Bringing Your Story to Life

In the early days of TV, a program called *You Are There* transported viewers to the faraway site of a breaking news story. Through the magic of the camera, viewers became eyewitnesses to the dramatic event.

This sense of immediacy — the impression that the story is happening right here, right now — is one of the most engaging qualities of mysteries. For other types of fiction it might be less critical, but a mystery's pleasure and impact depends to a large extent on readers' involvement in the story.

The word "immediate" has been defined as "having nothing come in between." In fiction, it means readers experience the story directly, without having it filtered through the author's perspective. Readers participate in the story world, walking in the detective's shoes, peering through the detective's eyes, feeling a shudder crawl down their spines when they realize the killer is waiting just around the dark corner. The author steps out of the way and vanishes.

This is an illusion, of course. Immediacy is an effect that the writer artfully constructs to beguile readers into the fictional world. No matter how realistically you depict your setting or how closely it parallels an actual place, the story world exists only in your imagination. Immediacy is the bridge you build to link your mind with that of the readers. This chapter offers techniques you can use to bring readers into your imaginary world, persuade them to accept it as true, and make their journey there exciting and entertaining.

Show, Don't Tell

Show, don't tell. You've probably heard this before; it's fundamental writing advice. When you're writing a mystery, they're especially important words to which to pay heed. Showing, rather than telling, is the foundation on which immediacy is built.

So what does this sage counsel really mean? What is the difference between showing and telling? It has to do with how you give information to readers.

When you *tell,* your emphasis is on providing, explaining, and interpreting facts, even if, as in fiction, the "facts" have been made up. You are doling out information. In business writing, telling is the standard. Indeed, a precept of business writing is: "Tell them what you're going to tell them, tell them what you want them to know, tell them what you told them." When was the last time you picked up a corporate report to read for enjoyment? How often have you become so engrossed in an operations manual that you couldn't put it down?

When you *show,* on the other hand, you are doing far more than handing out data. You are creating an experience for readers. The difference is apparent in the following paragraphs, two versions of Jess's first encounter with her father, when they meet for drinks at his hotel:

Telling:

> *Allen Fraser was waiting in the lobby when I arrived at the hotel. He wore the promised flower on his jacket lapel, but he resembled me enough that I would have recognized him without it. About to meet him at last, I felt mixed emotions. I hoped I looked all right. I decided to pretend that this was just another meeting with a potential client.*

Showing:

> *The white carnation wasn't necessary. Allen Fraser was unmistakable. Tall and lean like me. Curly red hair like mine, though his was darker and thinner and good bit shorter, with a touch of*

gray at the temples. He stood by a marble pillar near the reception desk, wearing a dove-gray suit and a paisley tie in warm red.

I pushed at my hair and tugged at my blazer to straighten it, and then felt annoyed with myself — why should I worry about making a good impression on this man? In my court-going clothes I looked as cool and professional as he did. I could pretend this was just another meeting with a potential client.

Sure I could.

In fiction you have four options for acquainting readers with the story:

- *Action:* letting readers observe what the characters do

- *Dialogue:* letting readers listen in on what the characters say to each other or, in their thoughts, to themselves

- *Description:* itemizing the physical details of settings or characters

- *Exposition:* explaining or summarizing information readers need in order to understand the characters or story

When you use action and dialogue, you're showing. Notice two key phrases of these two options. First, "letting readers." Bring readers into the scene, then allow them to have the excitement and pleasure of discovering the story for themselves. Second, "what the characters do and say." Your characters are your emissaries. Through their thoughts, words, and deeds, they shoulder the responsibility for making sure readers know, and care about, what is going on.

Description and exposition could be either showing or telling, depending on how you handle them. An accomplished novelist I know rails against what she calls "expository lumps" — sections where the author pauses the story to provide explanations or background information. At these points, readers' involvement in the fictional world is disrupted, and the gripping sense of immediacy that's been so carefully fostered is lost. When the lumps occur too often or go on too long, the author has the thorny problem of igniting readers' interest all over again.

For example, the plot of a suspense novel I recently read centered around a scientific controversy, and its author had taken pains to explain both sides of the issue carefully so readers would understand the conflict. But that part of the book was boring, more like a textbook than a novel. It would have been more exciting if two characters had each taken a side of the question and engaged in a riproaring argument. Readers would still have learned the science, *and* would have gained more insight into the characters.

The trick is to integrate the information into the story so that it doesn't interrupt the flow or call attention to itself. The following techniques can help you accomplish this.

- *Keep the action going.* You can get away with a paragraph or two of description or exposition, but not much more. If you must write more, intersperse the passage with touchstone moments to remind readers where the characters are and what they're doing. For instance, if while driving, your detective is mentally reviewing information about the case, don't lose us completely in her thoughts. Show her passing the big rig or drumming her fingers on the steering wheel as she waits impatiently for the red light to change.

- *Let the characters describe and explain.* Frankly, in mysteries, readers don't care about the author's opinions. They want to hear from your characters, who are more interesting and reliable sources of information than you are. Give the viewpoint character the task of describing the people, places, and things in the story from his or her perspective. If you have a lot of information to impart, create a character who needs the information as much as readers do — for example, an employee starting a new job or a journalist researching a newspaper story — and let another character explain what he or she needs to know. Don't forget that a mystery is all about a detective's efforts to find out information and act on it; doing so is one of the detective's principal jobs.

- *Provide readers with something to visualize.* Try this test when you write: As you read over a finished paragraph, what picture appears on your mental screen? If it's hazy or blank, you've slipped into telling. Showing, true to its name, always gives readers something to see.

- *Use flashbacks to convey the back story.* Make the flashback a specific incident or memory. Don't simply refer to the fact that John has always had trouble dealing with his over-bearing uncle. Go back in time, and create a miniscene showing the moment John realized the relationship was hopeless.

When you write the first draft, you'll probably do a lot of telling, especially in early scenes. That's because you are still discovering the story: learning who the characters are, exploring the sites where scenes take place, and defining the questions the story will grapple with. As you continue to write and gain a stronger sense of what you are trying to accomplish, it will become easier to trust the characters to tell the story for you.

From the Detective's Notebook 7 discusses how to show your characters in more detail.

Dialogue: Giving Your Characters Their Say

Notice that two of the four methods for revealing characters mentioned in From the Detective's Notebook 7 involve dialogue. Another method listed, the viewpoint character's thoughts, is also a form of self-expression, because characters speak to themselves in a style similar to the way they speak to others.

With dialogue, your readers hear as well as see what's going on. Listening to dialogue appeals to the eavesdropper in all of us, triggering the guilty pleasure we take in listening to other people's conversations. Mysteries tend to include a goodly amount of dialogue, in part because the heart of an investigation is asking questions and obtaining answers, and in part because immediacy is reinforced when we hear things directly from the characters rather than from the author.

Writing dialogue that is clear and sounds natural is, in my opinion, one of the biggest challenges of fiction writing. Sometimes when you know your characters intimately, you hear their voices clearly in your head. Writing dialogue then becomes almost a matter of taking down their dictation. But often you will have to work hard to hear a character's voice and reproduce it on the page. When I write a first draft, I concentrate on capturing the content of what's being said. Later, in subsequent drafts, I work on fine-tuning the dialogue to give each person a distinctive and realistic voice. You can use the techniques presented here to make your own characters sound true.

> Writing dialogue that is clear and sounds natural is one of the biggest challenges of fiction writing.

Making Them Sound Individual

The body of a murder victim was discovered late Saturday night in the alley behind Mario's Pizza Palace. Using credit card slips, the detective

From the Detective's Notebook 7
Showing Your Characters

We don't select our friends on the basis of their résumés, nor do we have the advantage of seeing a biography in advance when we meet a new boss, a new love interest, or a rival for that lover's affections. We get to know them through what they tell us about themselves, what other people say about them, what we observe about their behavior. Your readers' relationships with your characters are formed in these same ways, with an added bonus: In the case of viewpoint characters, readers can listen to their thoughts.

Providing a background summary is the easiest but least effective way to give readers information about characters. What readers see and hear for themselves is far more powerful and convincing. It's like your blind date with your best friend's cousin; there's usually a big difference between your friend's description and the stranger who arrives on your doorstep. The following are the most revealing and accurate ways to show characters:

- *What the character does.* We learn a lot by watching a person in action. You don't need to tell us whether he or she is a wild, reckless driver or a cautious, meticulous one. Put the character behind the wheel and let us draw our own conclusions.

- *What the character thinks.* When we can read someone's mind, eavesdropping on his or her interior monologue, that person can keep few secrets. This is the basis of an intimate relationship with a viewpoint character.

- *What the character says.* The way a character expresses himself or herself to others, both in style and content, gives us information about that person well beyond the actual words spoken.

- *What other characters think and say.* Our attitude toward a character is influenced by the opinions expressed by other characters. We pay attention to how they treat that person, what they say to him or her directly, and how they discuss the character in his or her absence.

tracked down some of the customers who dined there that evening and asked whom they were with, what they ate, and whether they saw anything strange. Here are their responses:

Susan:

Yes, I ate at Mario's on Saturday. There were four of us: Mitchell, Todd, Jennifer, and me. We arrived at 8:37, split a large Mario's Magnifico special and a carafe of red wine, and left at 9:34. And no, we saw nothing out of the ordinary. Now excuse me, I'm busy.

Joey:

Mario's? Yeah, me and Skootch made the scene, man. Skootch is one cool dude. He got this double extra-large — say, you ever eaten at Mario's, man? They put stuff on pizza you wouldn't believe. Skootch's was covered with, well, I tell ya, that was the weirdest thing I saw the whole night.

Leon:

Ain't none of your business if I was at Mario's. But I'll tell you anyway on account of I'm a nice guy. I was there. I ate pizza with Moe and Frank. Anchovies. Moe always gets anchovies. We had three pitchers of beer, and after that I didn't see nothing.

Georgette:

Oh yes, I remember, Saturday night, Geoffrey and I went to that hole-in-the-wall pizza place, Mario's, is that what's it called? We were slumming a bit, I would have much preferred going to Café Vesuvio, they do a divine pasta primavera, everything fresh, but Geoffrey used to go to Mario's when he was a boy, and now and then he gets a craving for grease. I made him order the vegetarian special; it had broccoli and spinach, quite nutritious really. Geoffrey ruined the whole evening by complaining. He kept saying I fed him plenty of salad at home, he certainly didn't need to ruin a perfectly good pizza with all this green stuff. Now, did I see anything peculiar? Well, it depends on how you define peculiar, I suppose, but . . .

Each character is conveying similar information but doing so in his or her own personal style. Without knowing any more about them, you've probably formed impressions of Susan, Joey, Leon, and Georgette: their ages, their positions in life, their personalities, even what they look like.

How someone speaks is an important aspect of characterization. Your goal is to find each character's individual voice. Readers should be able to identify who is talking simply from the pattern of speech.

Many factors contribute to speech patterns: regional, cultural or socioeconomic background, profession or occupation, and education influence not only the words and phrasing used, but content and meaning. Gender is a big consideration; men and women use language in different ways and for different purposes, which creates misunderstandings and perpetuates the "war" between the sexes. (Linguist Deborah Tannen has written helpful books on differences in speech styles; see Appendix A.)

Giving characters distinctive voices is trickier when they have a lot in common. But even people of similar backgrounds and interests have their own habits and quirks when it comes to speaking. What are some of the things that make individuals sound different from one another? Here are some clues.

How someone speaks is an important aspect of characterization. Readers should be able to identify who is talking simply from the pattern of speech.

Vocabulary

Choice of words is one of the principal ways to distinguish one character from another. Variations include:

- *Basic vocabulary.* Is it expansive or limited; does the character favor long words or short?

- *Slang, professional jargon, and regional or ethnic expressions.* How formal or informal is the speech; how do word choices reflect the character's activities and background?

- *Pet phrases, habitual sayings, and favorite clichés.* What expressions does the character resort to frequently and automatically?

- *Profanity and curses.* Is the character vulgar or mild; which words does he or she use, how often, and in what circumstances?

Articulateness

People differ in their skill and comfort level when expressing themselves verbally. You can differentiate two characters in a dialogue by setting up contrasts:

- Glib versus tongue-tied

- Rambling versus direct and to-the-point
- Precise about grammar versus slipshod or unschooled
- Short, clipped sentences versus run-on sentences
- Complete sentences versus dropped words or broken thoughts

Volubility

Volubility refers to a character's inclination to talk. A taciturn person usually wastes few words and would be inclined to say less than the listener might deem necessary. A loquacious companion, by contrast, is a gushing fountain of speech, spewing words in abundance, often to little purpose.

Willingness to impart information

Have you ever listened to someone talk at length on a subject and then realized that very little was actually said? People vary in the amount and kinds of information that is typical of their speech. One person might enthusiastically volunteer intimate details about his or her own life or other people's business, while someone else will deflect any perceived invasion of privacy. That second person, though, might wax eloquent on some hobby or interest, boring listeners with footnotes and extraneous facts.

Making Them Sound Natural

If you've ever transcribed a tape recording of an interview or a casual conversation, you know one thing about writing good dialogue: replicating actual speech won't work. Real speech, when written, is a real bore, and confusing as well. Speakers wander off the point, repeat themselves, and load their thoughts with "uh," "ya know," and other useless filler words. They wander into sentences, get lost, and have trouble finding their way out again.

So, natural speech and speech that sounds natural are quite different. Dialogue is an artfully edited version of the real thing. Anything the characters in your mystery say should accomplish a purpose: illuminate a character, reveal information, escalate a conflict, or in some way move the story forward. The pleasantries; the idle chitchat; the Hello, how are you's?; the rehashing of a subject again and again — almost all of that can be left out.

Natural-sounding speech also differs from the rest of your prose. The spoken word is more casual than the written word, and this should be reflected in the dialogue. Let characters use contractions and drop the connective "that's" from their sentences (as in "I was so angry [that] I could have spit nails"); otherwise they'll sound stiff. You can bend strict punctuation rules in dialogue too. Author Chelsea Quinn Yarbro describes punctuation in dialogue as a form of musical notation, indicating the rhythm and pace of the speech, as in Georgette's monologue on her vegetarian evening at Mario's Pizza Palace.

Putting Their Words on the Page

In dialogue, your characters are speaking not only to each other but to readers as well. Your task is to bring readers into the conversation by making it clear who is speaking to whom, where they are, and what they're doing, and then to step out of the way and let the characters speak for themselves. There are, however, some conventions and guidelines to be aware of.

Give each person's speech its own paragraph

A new paragraph signals a change of speaker. It's confusing to encounter remarks by two people in one paragraph, or a single speech that carries on for two or three paragraphs.

Make the attributions clear and unobtrusive

An attribution is a tag line that identifies the speaker. Do this at the earliest opportunity: the first pause or breathing point in the speech. Unless the speech is very short, don't wait until the end to indicate who is speaking. The word "said" is frequently all you need to write, or occasionally a synonym that gives added information about how the words were spoken — whispered, muttered, yelled. I recommend skipping the adverbs and letting the character's own words convey the tone of voice:

> *"You despicable monster! Get out of here!" Sara yelled angrily.*

Sara's wrath is clear; the word "angrily" only hits readers over the head with the obvious.

The exception to this advice is when the character's tone is completely contrary to what his or her words would lead readers to expect:

"I'm going to break your neck," Derek said sweetly.

Use no more attributions than necessary

One attribution per paragraph is enough. When only two people are conversing, you can skip attributions altogether in most paragraphs; supply just enough that readers can keep track of who's talking. The advantage to this is that the scene will move at a much quicker pace.

Make the dialogue visual with "stage business"

"Stage business," a term borrowed from the theater, refers to the activity a character engages in while speaking: sipping coffee, doodling in a notebook, petting the cat, aiming a gun. When you substitute these small actions for attributions, you give readers something to "see" as well as "hear." Consider which of the following has more impact:

Berger said, "You go first."

Berger handed me the knife. "You go first."

Don't overexplain

Let your characters' words, not yours, convey what's going on. You're a reporter of their conversation, not a participant, and if you constantly interpret what they say, your intrusion will be obvious and distracting. The characters themselves are readers' best source of information; trust them to tell what needs to be told.

> Don't overexplain. Let the characters' words, not yours, convey what's going on.

Details, Details

If the concept of "Show, don't tell" is the foundation of the fictional world you're creating, details are the bricks you build it with. By carefully piling detail upon detail, you make your fictional world vivid and real. Here are some suggestions for using details effectively.

Be Specific

When you have a choice between a generality and specificity, choose specificity. When you tell us your detective is eating breakfast, you're imparting basic information. Mention that he is wolfing down coffee and toast, and our mental picture becomes sharp and clear. If she arrives at her office and sees it's been vandalized, we sympathize from a distance. When she discovers her prized painting has been slashed and papers that represent months of work have been burned to ash, we feel her distress more acutely.

Be Sensory

The "show" element of the concept "Show, don't tell" implies giving visual details, but it is really shorthand for providing sensory information of all kinds. Our senses — all five of them — connect us to the world we're in, whether that world is real or fictional. The descriptive details that will be most effective are those that create strong sensory impressions. Bring in colors, light and dark, sounds, smells, flavors, and textures. As the characters see, hear, smell, taste, and feel the various elements in their surroundings, readers will do so too. The more you trigger sensations from all five senses, the deeper and richer readers' experience becomes. Join my character in the following passage as she arrives at a marina late at night in search of a missing man. How many sensory impressions can you identify?

> Boats glistened like chunks of ice in the green-white glare of the security lights. Out in the black bay, a beacon pulsed, pulsed, pulsed at intervals, warning vessels away from the rocks of Alcatraz. The night had turned misty and cold. Fog blotted out most of the nearby Golden Gate Bridge. I got out of my car and pulled on the old fuzzy sweater I kept in the trunk. Salt was tangy in the air.
>
> The marina was full of eerie noises at 1 a.m. The security lights crackled and buzzed; the docks creaked and moaned as currents shifted them. Out on the boulevard, traffic still thrummed steadily. Music and faint laughter drifted across the dark water from a party on a distant yacht.
>
> A dozen or so cars were parked in the marina lot but hardly anyone was around. A man in stained, shabby jeans and cracked

shoes was sprawled on a bench, a tent of newspaper sheltering his face. There was a broken bottle under the bench; I caught a whiff of cheap wine, so sour I could almost taste it.

Far down the walkway a pair of silhouettes merged into one as a couple stopped strolling to embrace. What a lovely idea — I wished I had someone to hug at that moment, someone who would let me trade a little of my confusion and weariness for a morsel of calm and strength.

Be Moody

Details are not created equal. Some are warm, sweet, soft, luminous. Others are cold, bitter, hard, dark.

The details you select set a mood. Suppose your detective walks into a room lit by candles. If the candles are glowing steadily and you draw attention to their light, you create an ambiance of comfort, or perhaps romance. But suppose a draft in the room makes the flame jump and flicker, and you direct readers' awareness not to the candles but to the shadows dancing at the edges of the room. Readers will feel uneasy and won't be surprised when the detective draws a gun.

Contrast these two descriptions of the same house, the childhood home to which the narrator has returned after a long absence:

The house stood dark and silent in the encroaching dusk. It was smaller than I remembered, the yard weedier, the neighborhood more rundown. The walls had been tan when I lived there. Sometime in the intervening years — not recently — they'd been painted green, an unappetizing shade between lime and olive.

I stood outside a chain-link fence that hadn't been there before and surveyed the cottage and yard. The windows, dark and blank, stared back. I wished there was some sign of life about the place, something to keep it from looking abandoned and forlorn, to make it look like home — if not mine, then someone's. The rusty bike lying on the lawn was not enough.

* * *

The house was smaller than I remembered, but it looked cheerful and welcoming in the gathering dusk. When I lived there the walls were tan; now, freshly painted, they were springtime green, like the grass of the manicured lawn.

I stood outside the flowering hedge and surveyed the cottage and yard. Lace-curtained windows gleamed with lamplight. A new bike lay on the lawn, waiting for its young owner to dash out the front door and ride off to an adventure. I was glad to see the place looked like home — if not mine, then someone's.

Be Selective

Give your readers just enough details to create the desired effect.

The French writer Voltaire once said, "The secret of being boring is to tell everything." Rather, give your readers just enough details to create the desired effect. In creating a sense of immediacy — a you-are-there quality — your task is to bring readers into the scene not just physically but emotionally as well. Carefully selected details are one of your handiest tools for this purpose.

There is no need to provide an exhaustive list of the items your detective observes in a suspect's bedroom, or to describe your detective's every mood while zipping around town interviewing witnesses. Too much detail is overwhelming and dull. If you're not sure whether to include a particular detail, ask yourself:

- Does it help bring readers into the scene, clarifying which characters are present, what they are doing, or where and when the scene takes place?

- Does it sharpen the sensory impact?

- Does it intensify a mood or heighten the emotional impact?

- Does it help divert readers' attention from what would otherwise be a too-obvious clue?

- Does it interrupt the story or slow the pace?

Include only those details that rate a "yes" to any of the first four questions and a "no" to the last question. These are the details that will heighten the drama and enhance readers' understanding and enjoyment of the characters, setting, and plot. Leave the rest out.

Building Dramatic Scenes

The way to bring readers into the story is let the action unfold right in front of their eyes; in other words, to let them directly witness the scene.

A scene is a single link in the chain of your plot. It focuses on a unit of action: what transpires at a certain time, in a particular place. When you shift to a new location or jump to a different time, you're writing a new scene.

When you outline a mystery plot, you are already thinking in scenes: this happens, then this happens next, and then something else happens — three scenes. For this reason, planning your book is easier when you think in terms of scenes rather than chapters. Some scenes will fill an entire chapter. Others may require only a couple of pages, or perhaps just a few lines, which means some chapters may comprise several scenes. Once you know what the scenes should be, you can sort them into chapters.

A scene tells a small story of its own. It has a beginning, a middle, and an end. Depending on its length and importance, a scene will often contain conflict and a buildup of tension. In short, a scene gives you an opportunity to create a sense of drama. You do that by keeping in mind the same kinds of questions a journalist does when writing an article: Who? What? When? Where? Why?

Who, Where, When?

Orient your readers quickly at the opening of a scene so that they can create an accurate mental picture right away. Then they can easily follow the action, even if you choose to be mysterious about exactly what's going on and why. If readers realize halfway through the scene that their mental image is wrong, they end up distracted and confused. Early in the scene, make sure they know three things:

☛ *Who is in the scene?* Let readers know which characters are present. It's jarring to have Jake interrupt the conversation when for the past three pages, readers thought only Anna and Ted were in the room. Characters can enter or exit during the course of the scene, but readers should be made aware of this.

☞ *Where is the scene taking place?* Readers identify scenes according to their location: the scene in the dark alley where the body was found, the scene in the villain's mountain hideaway, the scene in the murder victim's apartment. This is pivotal information. I once read a suspense novel in which a key scene took place in a park; only at the last moment did I realize the park was in London, not in Paris, where the preceding chapters had taken place. The shift in location was crucial to the story, yet the author had neglected to make it clear.

☞ *When is the scene taking place?* Sometimes the time factor is obvious, especially if the scene follows immediately on another, or if it was set up in advance with a time attached. Suppose one character has earlier said to another: "Okay, then. It's settled. We'll meet at the cemetery at midnight." In that case, when you show them hiding behind a tombstone, we will assume that the steeple clock is striking 12 (though it never hurts to let readers hear it chime). Too often, though, the author knows how many hours or days have passed but fails to tell readers. Readers are still thinking that it's Sunday and the murder happened two days ago, when suddenly they realize that they somehow have been catapulted into next Wednesday afternoon. Time cues can be subtle, but they do need to be there.

It's hard to make readers clear about the time during which a scene occurs if you aren't clear yourself. In one detective novel I read, readers follow the private eye around all day Saturday in the first chapter, which concludes when he climbs into bed. At the start of chapter 2, the PI awakens, gets dressed, and visits a business executive at a corporate headquarters, and I realized it was Monday morning. Apparently, the PI slumbered for more than 30 hours and missed Sunday completely.

In another mystery I read — one fortunately still in manuscript format so the problem could be fixed — the murder took place in the morning and most of the investigation was completed by mid-afternoon, including the autopsy and the forensic lab reports. Impossible. The author had the time frame straight in her head but had neglected to work in appropriate time cues for readers.

In a mystery, time is truly of the essence. An understanding of when key events occur and how much time elapses between them can be vital to the success of a murder investigation. If you handle the time elements of your story logically and unequivocally, you'll help your detective solve the case and increase readers' appreciation of the story.

Chronology chart

The details of a mystery's time line — which suspect was where at critical moments, the order in which key events transpire — can be hard to keep track of if you're relying on your memory to do the job. Set up a chart to sort it out for you. Draw columns on a sheet of paper, or, if you prefer a larger scale, on a whiteboard on your wall. Head each one with a month, day, or hour (whichever is most appropriate for your story), and sort the scenes and key off-stage events in your story into their appropriate columns, according to when they occur. This overview of the story can help you nip time line difficulties in the bud.

Why Is this Scene Here? What Happens Next?

Every scene has one purpose: to move the story forward. If it fails to add momentum to your mystery, delete it from your story. To earn its keep, a scene should achieve one or more of these tasks:

- Introduce a character.
- Provide greater insight into a character.
- Establish, intensify, or resolve a complication in the plot.
- Set up a situation to which a character must respond.
- Raise the stakes for one or more characters.
- Reveal a clue.
- Present some other vital information.

Save that scene!

If one of the scenes that you need to cut happens to be the most brilliant thing you've ever written — as so often seems to be the case with extraneous scenes — file it. It might serve as a story trigger for another book.

> A scene is a minidrama, a little story of its own with a plot and a beginning, a middle, and an end.

Once you figure out which task you want the scene to accomplish, focus the action of the scene tightly on that goal. When the goal has been achieved, wrap up the scene quickly. Drop the curtain, and move on.

If nothing happens in the scene, if no specific action takes place, you don't have a scene — you have an expository lump. You're halting the story while you provide information. To build an effective scene, open with a line of dialogue or a peek at a character in action. Show your readers that something interesting is underway. Then stay focused on the action all the way through.

What if you need a scene that is not inherently active, one in which, for example, your purpose is best accomplished by having your detective mentally review the evidence related to the murder? Create some action by giving the detective something to do while thinking, for example, chopping onions for a stew. Let readers see the knife slash against the cutting board, smell the pungent odor, feel the onion tears well up. That way, neither readers nor the detective will become completely lost in the detective's thoughts.

Transitions

You have a couple of options for making the transition from one scene to the next.

The bridge

With a bridge, you provide a couple of lines, perhaps a paragraph or two, to transport the characters and readers from one time and place to another. A bridge summarizes the action that occurred between the scene readers have just left and the one that's about to begin. If your transition becomes paragraphs long, chances are you've created a whole new scene.

Here's a typical bridge:

> I left the photo studio with a heavy heart. Glancing at my watch, I realized I was late for my lunch date with Jack. On my way to his office, I stopped at Irma's Deli to pick up sandwiches. I gave myself a stern lecture on will power and self-discipline, then told Irma to put in two chocolate cookies, the ones with pecans.

When I arrived at the accounting firm, Jack's receptionist
said he was tied up in a meeting.

The line break

The line break is simple, fast, and effective. You end the scene, skip a line, and drop readers straight into the scene that follows. The white space you've inserted functions like a lowered curtain during a stage play. When the curtain rises again, the scene has changed. Or think of it in movie terms; the line break is like the camera's quick cut or dissolve.

The line break is also an effective means of indicating a shift in the point of view from one character to another, whether you're changing the scene or providing a new perspective on what's currently going on.

> The line break is a signal to readers: something is changing, the story's moving forward, let's go.

9
Building Suspense with Style

Suspense is used not only
to keep readers involved
until the end but to give
them a heart-pounding,
edge-of-the-seat ride
along the way.

Suspense and mystery. The two go hand in hand on bookstore shelves and in readers' minds.

All stories have an element of suspense. Without it, there is no uncertainty about what the ending will be. In mysteries, though, the element of suspense is much greater than in other kinds of fiction. Thrillers are carefully crafted to raise the level of suspense even more. Suspense is used not only to keep readers involved until the end but to give them a heart-pounding, edge-of-the-seat ride along the way.

What Is Suspense?

Suspense versus Surprise

Gary Driscoll, your protagonist, arrives at work on Monday morning. He enters the building, gives a cheery greeting to the receptionist, and ambles down the corridor until he reaches his private office. He pulls his key out of his pocket, inserts it in the lock.

Suddenly, an explosion blows up the door, slams Driscoll against the opposite wall, and ignites a blaze that soon engulfs the office.

A suspenseful moment? No.

Exciting, yes. Dramatic, certainly. But it was not suspenseful, because readers had no inkling it was coming. Until the explosion, there was no reason to be concerned about Driscoll's fate. The explosion was a shock; a surprise; a startling, unexpected event.

Suppose, though, that readers have been privy to a previous scene that took place the night before. Readers spied on a shadowy figure breaking into the building and followed a flashlight's beam down the darkened corridor to Driscoll's office. The mysterious intruder entered the office and fiddled with Driscoll's office lock.

Now, when Driscoll shows up on Monday, readers' awareness is heightened. Something is amiss, but what? Readers feel a tingle of anticipation.

Now imagine that readers have information that a bomb would be planted, somewhere, sometime. As Driscoll strolls down the corridor, readers begin to feel afraid for him. By the time he reaches his office, readers are all but yelling at him not to slide his key into the lock.

Readers are hooked, involved, caring about what happens. And you can be sure they will keep reading.

When you create suspense, you're asking readers to make a commitment to the characters and to the story. Their emotional investment gives readers a stake in the outcome of the story.

Surprise is a handy device, as Hollywood well knows (the shower scene in *Psycho* is one famous example). Surprise is dramatic, and it gets the blood pumping. While not suspenseful in itself, it is useful for establishing suspense because it provokes questions: What happened? What caused it to happen? What will be the consequences? For a bang-up start to your novel, or for plot points that twist the story in unforeseen directions, you can't beat a good surprise. But it is suspense that has the staying power to sustain readers' interest over the long haul.

Four Elements of Suspense

Suspense arises naturally out of the conflict you set up in your story. It is the tension between readers' hopes and doubts. Will the conflict be resolved happily or not? Will the main character accomplish his or her goal or not? In a mystery, you need to magnify this tension more than you might for a story in another genre, turning doubts into fears. You are dealing with life-and-death issues, making readers wonder not only whether the detective will achieve his or her goal but if the detective or other important characters will even survive.

Writing a mystery is like performing a magic trick. A stage magician once told me his profession's secret to handling audiences: "First you make them care, then you make them wait." You engage the interest and concern of your readers, then let them hang a while before revealing the fate of your characters. The interval between that moment of engagement and the eventual resolution is your opportunity to create suspense.

In fiction, suspense consists of four elements:

- *Interest.* Readers are curious and concerned about the characters, especially the detective, and are rooting for him or her to prevail.

- *Anticipation.* Readers expect that something is about to happen that will significantly affect the detective's fortunes or those of other characters, either for good or for ill.

- *Uncertainty.* Readers are in the dark about what the outcome will be. They cross their fingers for the detective's success, but worry that he or she might not achieve it. Yes, they can be reasonably sure that in the end the detective will survive this encounter with crime and solve the mystery. But how? And at what personal cost? The more uncertainty readers feel, the greater the suspense.

- *Emotion.* Suspense has a strong emotional component. In a mystery, that emotion is usually fear. Readers know the characters are at risk, and become afraid for their well-being, their safety, even their lives.

When you create suspense, you can tap into your readers' own fears. What do you think most people are afraid of? What frightens you most in your own life, either in fact or when you contemplate something that might someday happen? Throw your detective into that situation, and you'll be assured of suspense. The more readers care, and the more uncertainty and fear they feel, the greater their suspense will be.

Clues to Building Suspense

By now you have already laid the groundwork for a suspenseful mystery. Previous chapters have discussed the basic ingredients:

- Characters that readers care about
- A compelling goal for your detective beyond merely solving the crime
- A plot that focuses tightly on crime, conflict, and the questions raised by the story
- A sense of immediacy that makes readers feel like participants in the action

With this foundation laid, you can build, heighten, and sustain the suspense to can't-put-the-book-down levels. Here are some clues for going about it.

Make the Potential Outcome Dire

One reason mysteries are inherently suspenseful is that the conflict is a matter of life and death. In most mysteries, at least one character is murdered, and others may suffer violent deaths or wrenching upheavals in their lives before the story ends. For the detective, too, the consequences of failure should be serious and potentially destructive of his or her life, health, career, or happiness.

Keep Raising the Stakes

Remember, your job as a writer is to get your detective in trouble, and then in more trouble, then in worse trouble yet. Your watchword is "escalation." This especially applies when you are creating complications for your main character. As the story progresses, raise the level of risk he or she faces, the seriousness of the consequences, and the likelihood that disaster will occur. Make it increasingly difficult for your detective to avoid failure.

Make the Characters Feel Threatened

Both the characters and readers should always be aware of the menace lurking in the background of even the calmest scenes, whether or not they understand the nature and source of the threat. At any moment, violence should be a possibility. You can raise the suspense level by having threats to your characters emanate from more than one source and be of more than one type — psychological as well as physical.

The concept of threat is not limited to anonymous notes with the words constructed of letters cut from magazines, or warnings left on the detective's voicemail by snarling, unidentified voices. You can use those devices, certainly, but in this context I'm referring to the atmosphere of peril that permeates the story; the ongoing sense of uneasiness that both characters and readers feel because they believe something is about to go terribly wrong.

The threat, whatever its source, ultimately must prove to represent a genuine danger, and it must be explained by the time the mystery is resolved. Don't create worry to no purpose. If the detective is shot at by an unseen gunner, or chased down the road by a strange car, make sure the incident relates to your plot. One way to annoy readers is to insert an irrelevant event for the sole purpose of making their blood pound, then dismiss it as a triviality or a coincidence. From the Detective's Notebook 8 discusses how to handle violence in your writing.

Challenge Your Detective's Ingenuity

Force your detective to work hard to overcome the threats. Your detective should draw on all his or her strengths and capitalize on all his or her resources. Mystery readers do not consider it fair for writers to bring someone else to the rescue, at least not until after the detective already has the situation well in hand. It's fine to give your detective physical prowess or a gun for protection, but the story will be more suspenseful and satisfying if your detective relies on quick wits rather than brute strength or a weapon to get himself or herself, and others, out of a jam.

Let Your Detective Make Mistakes

To be believably human, your detective should err on occasion, or discover that his or her own efforts, however well meaning, have only made matters worse. You detective should encounter knotty predicaments and ethical dilemmas where the right course of action is not obvious, yet the wrong choice could have devastating consequences. A key factor in readers' engagement in a mystery is their interest in the personal issues and concerns of the main character. The problems that arise from within — from the detective's own flaws, misjudgments, and errors — place the resolution of these personal issues as well as the mystery in greater doubt. Internal conflicts raise the stakes for the detective and heighten the suspense.

Limit Your Detective's Options

Keep reducing the number of solutions that remain available to your character. As your detective tries each one, have it fail for some reason, until with the last possibility — success! (Or is it?) Suspense can come when you lead the characters, and readers, to believe a solution will work, then make it fail at the last minute.

> Suspense can come when you lead the characters, and readers, to believe a solution will work, then make it fail at the last minute.

Isolate Your Detective Physically

Trap your detective somewhere away from where he or she wants or needs to be. Put your detective into tight spots, literally:

- Lock your detective in a small space from which there is no apparent means of escape.

- Place your detective in a hostile environment, such as a dangerous neighborhood, late at night.

- Lose your detective in a wilderness with no maps, water, or idea of how to get back to civilization.

- Pack your detective off to an unfamiliar place where he or she doesn't know what help might be available or how to find it.

Isolate Your Detective Psychologically

Psychological isolation can be as harrowing as the physical kind. It is a devastating experience when the people around you, especially those you thought you could rely on, abandon you or cut you off. Having enemies is difficult enough, but being deserted by someone who you believe to be an ally can be worse.

There are several ways you can put your detective through this emotional wringer. Try having other characters:

- Be unable to understand what your detective is trying to communicate to them

- Refuse to believe your detective

- Deny your detective any assistance

- Prove treacherous or traitorous especially when your detective thought they merited his or her trust

Impose a Deadline

In a mystery, the "dead" in the word "deadline" has extra resonance: exceed the designated time limit, and someone might die. A time-honored technique for generating suspense is to set the characters racing against the ticking clock — or perhaps a ticking bomb.

Hollywood often does this literally. Think of all the movies where the bad guys thoughtfully provide a digital countdown so the heroes and the audience can count down how many seconds they have left to prevent the building, or the world, from being blown up.

Acting in the face of a known deadline is difficult and harrowing. A deadline that is unknown or uncertain can be worse. The detective must rescue the kidnapped child before she is killed, or find the murderer before he strikes again. But will that happen next week, or in the next hour?

Controlling Your Mystery's Pace

The word "pace" describes the tempo or rate of speed at which your story moves. The pace is closely allied to suspense. As the story moves faster, the tension winds tighter.

Pace: How a Story Flows

The late writer and teacher Jean Backus likened a story's pace to a river. In some stretches, the current flows gently and slowly. At other points, the water bounds over rocks and through rapids, and in places it plunges over cliffs, splashing and crashing as it cascades toward the bottom. Throughout its length, the water progresses inexorably toward the end.

The number and duration of these various stretches determines the pace of the book and perhaps even the kind of book that it is.

If you're writing a mainstream or literary novel, even one concerned with a crime, you have more leeway to float along leisurely. You can meander a bit; you can let the story sprawl across decades; you can wax philosophic or digress down interesting side streams. The result is that the pace will be slower and the suspense less intense.

A detective story is more like rafting through whitewater. The time frame is usually compressed: days or weeks rather than years, with a lot of action packed into a short time span. Although you may include brief flashbacks to weave in the back story, you move the story forward in a direct, linear way and focus attention on the events of the moment.

Some suspense novels provide an even wilder, more exciting ride, putting readers in a barrel and flinging them over Niagara Falls.

How to Pick Up the Pace

Pace is, to some extent, an issue to deal with in your second draft. Figure out the story first. Later on, you can fine tune its rhythm and flow, or decide where you'll let readers relax a bit and where you'll give them a thrill ride. When it's time to pick up the pace, here are some clues that might help you accomplish this:

 Tell the story through action and dialogue. Here's that maxim, "Show, don't tell," again. Action implies movement; exposition typically has little or no movement, which makes its pace slow indeed.

 Balance breakneck sections with slower ones. At some point, readers need a chance to catch their breaths. So do characters, for that matter. One of the functions of a subplot is to provide a welcome change of pace, since the action of the subplot generally moves at a different rate than does the action of the main plot.

 Provide miniclimaxes. Throughout your novel, you're constantly building toward its most electrifying moment, the confrontation between detective and villain. But that high point doesn't come until almost at the end, and it's hard to sustain the pace and excitement for 300 to 400 pages until you get there, without help.

One benefit of the three-act structure discussed earlier in the book is that it defines opportunities for incorporating smaller climaxes — intensely dramatic events that occur at strategic points in the story. These are the plot points or turning points that close acts 1 and 2. As described in chapter 6, a plot point significantly complicates the mystery: perhaps another victim is murdered, or the detective encounters an overwhelming setback, or a shocking clue is revealed. Having crises like these lets you aim the action and suspense toward targets that are nearer at hand than the far-off major climax that wraps up the mystery. Each plot point injects fresh energy into the story, giving it fuel to progress forward.

Concentrate on immediate events. As you move toward your climax, large or small, tighten your focus on what's happening at that instant; what the characters are doing, experiencing, and feeling; what their senses are aware of. Often, these are moments of peril or high emotional impact. Under the circumstances, your detective is not likely to be idly wondering what's for dinner, or recalling a funny incident from a high-school math class, or working out a philosophy of life. Nor should your readers be. To help you maintain a quick pace during these critical periods, save such speculation for other parts of the book.

Accelerate as you approach the high points. Shorten your scenes, paragraphs, and sentences when you want the pace to quicken. Make them punchy so that readers zip along. Readers quickly and easily absorb the content and become immersed in the mood. Because they are reading faster, the story itself seems to speed up.

Provide end-of-scene or end-of-chapter hooks. At the conclusion of each scene, readers make a decision: to keep reading or to put the book down. You want to provide every reader an incentive to continue. Conclude each scene or chapter on a high note, such as a dramatic discovery or a provocative line of dialogue. Toward the end of the scene, provide a tiny preview or hint of something that is to come.

Before they can set a novel aside, readers need to achieve a sense of closure. This technique denies them that. By impelling them to turn the page for "just one more chapter" before they stop reading, you pull them straight through the book.

From the Detective's Notebook 8
Handling Violence with Sensitivity

Murder is an act of violence; there is no way to get around violence as a subject of your book. Much of a mystery's suspense is built because at least some of the characters are in actual or potential danger.

The existence of violence in your story doesn't mean you must depict it in graphic, stomach-churning detail. How you present violence is a matter of your taste and sensibilities as well as the demands of the story, and it will help determine where your story falls on the continuum of cozy to hard-boiled.

One choice is to relegate the gruesome events to the backstage. A character may stumble on the body, but, for the most part, characters learn about and deal with the violence after the fact. This is the gentle, bloodless approach and one less disturbing to the writer and readers, if not to the characters, who still must cope with the impact of the murder on their lives. I think one reason poisoning is a preferred method of murder in mysteries, far greater than its actual prevalence as a cause of death in real-life homicide, is that it seems less gory than stabbing, shooting, or bludgeoning someone to death.

You could also depict the violence as it happens. By doing so, you heighten the drama and achieve a greater and more immediate emotional impact. You also impart a darker tone to your story.

Either approach can work well, as long as you handle violence with care and respect your readers' sensibilities. How much violence the story contains is not so much the issue, unless you reveal yourself to be psychopathically bloodthirsty. Where writers sometimes go awry is in the way they present the violence. You'll raise objections when:

🔫 *The violence is gratuitous.* Whether or not it's gratuitous is not determined by the quantity of blood spilled or the level of cruelty inflicted. Gratuitous violence means that the brutality serves no purpose to the story. Any act of violence must be essential to the plot, a sturdy link in the chain of actions and consequences. If it's included only to shock or titillate readers, it is probably gratuitous.

🔫 *The aftermath of the violence is unrealistic.* If your detective suffers a beating at the hands of the bad guys, brushes off the dust, and runs a marathon the next day, you may find readers questioning the sense of reality in your story. Violence generates pain, both physical and emotional, and even the toughest heroes require time to recover. People are affected profoundly by violence around them, even when they are not the direct targets.

From the Detective's Notebook 8 — Continued

Another easy way to lose your mystery's credibility is to have characters respond too casually, indifferently, or, worse, enthusiastically ("Oh, boy, we have our own murder mystery, right here in Plumfield! I've always wanted to play detective!"), especially if they are people with whom you want readers to sympathize.

☛ *The presentation of violence is out of synch with the mood and tone of the book, or out of character for the people perpetrating it.* This can work both ways: too much violence or too little. I read a detective novel in which the hero seems to be a peace-loving man who eschews violence for its own sake. The murders and other violent acts are tastefully and reasonably presented by the author. Until the end, when the detective finally confronts the villain and his henchmen. Suddenly, the story erupts into a bloodbath. Within just a couple of pages, the body count soars — unnecessarily, I think — from 2 to 20. The author failed to prepare me for such a leap into brutality, and I felt annoyed and dissatisfied with the way the book finished.

On the other hand, whenever you make a promise, you need to deliver on it. If a violent scene is crucial to your plot, don't get squeamish and back away from it. As a writing teacher, I've found that beginning writers are more likely to include too little violence than too much. They soften their blows in a way that poorly serves the characters and their stories.

10
Research:
Learning about Crimes
and How They Are Solved

Write what you know.

Like the maxim "Show, don't tell," this is classic writing advice. And, like many nuggets of good counsel, it's both right and wrong.

It's right in suggesting that your strongest stories will emanate in some way from your own experiences and passions, in part because you can enrich those tales with your perceptions and understanding.

Where this advice fails is that it can intimidate you into narrowing yourself too much and may curtail the sweep of your imagination. Many aspiring writers assume that what they know is too ordinary or dull, or their level of knowledge is too skimpy, to qualify them to write the kind of stories readers are interested in.

This is especially true when it comes to writing mysteries. Some authors have a professional background in law enforcement to draw on; the ranks of mystery writers include private investigators, lawyers, cops, and even a criminal or two. Most of us who specialize in this genre, though, have no such advantage. That means we must engage in an outward adventure as well as an inward one. Not only do we delve into our

> To write a mystery, you must engage in an outward adventure as well as an inward one.

imaginations to find stories, but we reach out to the real world to learn how to tell them with authenticity.

This expands the meaning of the phrase "Write what you know." Write what you know doesn't restrict you to what you knew when you made the decision to embark on your mystery. A better way of putting it might be: *Write what you're willing and able to find out.* Writing is a process of discovery. When you finish a novel, you will know far more than when you began. Part of your new knowledge will come from the insights you gain along the way. The rest you'll get through research.

Getting the Facts Straight

When writing, it is important to get your facts correct. The reason why is this: you will create a better story. Yes, you are writing fiction, but good fiction depends for its effect on a pact between author and reader, a mutual agreement that for the duration of the story you will both accept this imaginative invention as truth. To keep your side of the bargain, you must invest what you say with authority. If you make those parts of the fictional world that can be compared with the real ones as authentic as possible, readers will be more willing to suspend their disbelief of the rest of your created world.

Mystery fans are bright, knowledgeable, and well read. They can tell when authors know what they are doing. Mystery readers include professionals who will catch your errors in whatever happens to be their area of expertise. If you get the facts wrong, astute readers distrust the rest of what you have to say.

Knowledge helps you write with confidence. As you learn more about how crimes are investigated and solved, you will come to understand your characters better, both the ones who solve crimes professionally and the laypeople who interact with them. You'll have notions for new characters with interesting roles to play. You will construct more convincing plots, assured that your answers to What if? questions will strike readers as logical and appropriate. You'll be able to recognize problems with motivation and work them out more easily. You'll have a better sense of what clues your killer might leave behind and how the detective would uncover and interpret them. Moreover, among the techniques, tools, and procedures used by criminals and crime-fighters, you'll discover great story triggers and ideas.

What You Need to Know

Some of what you need to know as a mystery writer is the same as with any fiction. You need to know enough about psychology and human nature to create solid, individualistic characters; enough about the place and time period to make the setting vivid; and enough about the background elements of the story to render them lively and relevant.

As a mystery writer, you need to know much more. Verisimilitude, the appearance of being true, is vitally important in a crime story. Even though readers know the novel is fiction, the impression that a real crime is affecting real people is a critical factor in their becoming engaged in the story. Like immediacy (or the "you are there" quality), you achieve verisimilitude through the accumulation of telling, cogent, and accurate details; in this case, details about the murder, its causes, and its results. To a greater or lesser extent, depending on your story, you will need to become a miniexpert on subjects such as:

- Crimes and how they are committed

- Crime scene investigations, and how they are conducted

- Criminalistics and forensics: the science of crime-solving

- Criminology: the psychology of criminals, and the causes and effects of crime from a sociological or cultural perspective

- The bureaucracies of crime and crime-fighting: what agencies are involved, how they operate, and who does what

- Weapons: guns, knives, poisons, blunt instruments, ropes, fists, and more; how they are used and the kind of damage they inflict

Notice that I use the word "miniexpert." You don't need to acquire encyclopedic knowledge on these subjects. What you need is enough information to authoritatively present, develop, and sustain an accurate depiction for as long as necessary. That might mean the entire book. To write a police procedural, you need a solid understanding of how the police force is structured and operates in the place where the book is set.

But you could require a certain kind of information or expertise for a single scene — perhaps only a paragraph. Toward the end of *A Relative Stranger,* Jess and two other characters are involved in a struggle. Two of them have guns, which are flung around during the action and end up in hands other than their owners'. To keep this potentially confusing bit of detail straight, I decided to use guns of two different makes, so that I could refer to them by name. That way readers, and I, would have a better chance of keeping track of them. At the time, I knew little about guns, but I did enough research to assign a Colt and a Beretta to the characters in question with reasonable assurance that these were the weapons they'd choose for themselves.

Research is cumulative. You bring what you learn while writing your first mystery to subsequent ones. As you write a second book and a third, your interest and knowledge about crimes and crime solving will grow until the preface "mini" no longer limits your claim to expertise.

How to Find the Information You Need

Mystery writers generally obtain information from two kinds of sources: written materials or knowledgeable people. Appendix B will help you begin the pleasurable task of doing research using both of these types of resources. It lists organizations, Web sites, and books that can help you learn about crime and crime-fighting. These resources will give you a start toward developing your personal resource bank — a shelf of reference books, a clip file, and a Rolodex with telephone numbers of people you can call when you have a question to ask or a fact to check.

Read Books

Read lots of books. Haunt your public library and your local bookstore. In addition to reading mystery fiction, bone up on mystery fact. Try memoirs and profiles written by and about police officers, private investigators, prosecutors, defense lawyers, forensic specialists, criminal psychologists, and crooks.

Read true crime books; the quality of these books is uneven, but the good ones offer valuable insight into investigative procedures and the psychology of people on both sides of crime — the criminals as well as the police, the prosecutors, and others involved in bringing the perpetrators to justice.

Dip into police science textbooks and manuals written for professional investigators.

Want a quick overview of a subject? Head for the library's juvenile or young adult section. Nonfiction books written for young readers can provide a superb introduction: basic information that is not overly technical and that is presented in a clear, lively style.

Read Magazines and Newspapers

Your daily newspaper is an excellent resource for information on crime. Think about how often it addresses that topic, reporting on specific cases, the impact of politics on the police department, or the latest statistics on crime trends.

Magazines also run useful features. My clipping file contains material from news weeklies, regional publications, airline magazines, women's magazines, my insurance company's monthly, and general interest magazines. The articles I save for future reference include interviews with people in pertinent professions; in-depth features on specific crimes; analyses of social problems and trends, such as domestic violence, that are associated with crime; and self-protection tips to help readers avoid becoming crime victims; in short, anything that catches my interest as a possible source of background information or story trigger.

For more specific research, read trade and professional journals aimed at the occupations practiced by your detective or other characters. These magazines offer an intriguing insider's perspective on the practices, technologies, jargon, and issues related to a specific line of work. One place to look for names of journals you might find helpful is *Writer's Market*. This annual directory, produced by Writer's Digest Books, lists hundreds of book, magazine, and trade journal publishers. See Appendix A for more details about Writer's Digest Books.

When you come across a helpful article, clip it and save it. You'll build a double-duty file: a useful repository for reference material and a resource for story ideas. A flip through the clippings when you feel stuck will often start ideas flowing.

Some writers toss clippings into a box or stuff them into manila envelopes. I have a file cabinet full of them, sorted by topic in manila folders. Now and then I wonder what a stranger would think if he or she pulled open a drawer and read all my neatly lettered labels: Poisons, Guns, Crime and Criminals, Frauds and Con Games. I can only hope that person would be reassured upon reaching the ones labeled: Police Procedure or Criminal Justice System.

Consult Web Sites

The Internet is proving to be a great resource to writers who need to do research. It offers a wealth of information that you can obtain without leaving your desk. Web sites abound that are packed with fascinating details, and one good site often leads to another as you click on a link. Chat groups and bulletin boards allow you to post questions, obtain direct answers, discuss hot topics, and listen in on mystery gossip. The problem: The Internet can be almost too much of a good thing. It gives you so much information, you can scarcely sort through it all without consuming hours of your time.

Attend Conferences

A mystery conference can be a heady experience. After slogging away in isolation at your desk, with perhaps no one nearby who shares your excitement for your favored literary form, you're suddenly surrounded by several hundred mystery mavens — writers, booksellers, editors, fans. For a day or a weekend, you are immersed in a wonderful, mysterious world. You befriend people with like interests; talk shop; buy more books than will fit in your luggage; listen to readings, lectures and panel discussions; and go home exhausted but happy. The official programs of these conferences usually concentrate on literary concerns but often includes talks and demonstrations by police officers, private investigators, or forensic experts.

Mystery bookstores, magazines, Web sites, and organization newsletters are the best way to learn about upcoming conferences. Several occur annually; others are single or occasional events. The granddaddy of mystery conferences is Bouchercon, launched more than three decades ago as a memorial to the fiction writer and critic Anthony Boucher (the name is an acronym for Boucher Convention). Held every October in a different North American city, it attracts 1,200 to 1,500 people, the largest crowd of any mystery event.

Go to School

When a nearby university extension program offered a course in forensic science for laypeople, I jumped at the chance to enroll. On another occasion, I attended a weekend seminar, aimed at writers, on criminal investigation. During a career-opportunity program sponsored by a local open-education exchange, I took diligent notes as a veteran private investigator explained the tricks of his trade to a group of budding detectives.

Classes are invaluable to help you look, feel, and sound like a professional. Check out course catalogues of colleges and community centers for relevant classes. Writing courses and workshops are worthwhile for general writing skills, but you must push beyond these for your research on crime. Enroll in police-science or criminal-justice classes at your community college. Look for possibilities among the special-interest classes or evening lectures sponsored by adult education programs, education exchanges, public libraries, or bookstores.

Call the Cops

Contact your local police department to ask about the public-information programs it offers. In many communities, the police permit ride-alongs, where you can accompany police officers for an afternoon or evening as they respond to routine calls. Some cities sponsor Citizens Police Academies: courses that run for eight or ten sessions and inform members of the public about the basics of police operations. If your police department offers such a session, sign up right away; it's a priceless opportunity.

Ask an Expert

If you have questions, go straight to the source: a person who knows the answers. Consulting professionals in the field you're interested in is the best way to get the real inside scoop — not just theory, but the nitty-gritty, nuts-and-bolts details. Many professionals appreciate being sought out as experts; they enjoy expounding to someone who will listen seriously. They will tell you what reference books won't: anecdotes, war stories, the day-to-day workings of their jobs. You will learn about the rewards, challenges, costs, and frustrations of being in a particular profession. You can test out story ideas or plot developments and find out if they make sense or ring true.

> Consulting professionals in the field you're interested in is the best way to get the real inside scoop.

I spent one fascinating morning at the San Francisco Hall of Justice interviewing two homicide inspectors who generously gave me their time to answer questions. Sitting in an interrogation room, we turned the tables: I got to give them the third degree. They explained how they would handle the case in my book, answered all my questions, demonstrated their computer system, and gave me a tour of part of the jail. *A Relative Stranger* benefited tremendously from this inside view.

How do you find experts? Chances are, you know some already, or you're acquainted with someone who does. Pull out your list from chapter 2 of people you know and their areas of expertise.

Look to the experts that your newspaper quotes as sources of information and use your detective skills to track those people down. Or call the appropriate department of your local university; faculty members might well be willing to help. The department of police science or criminal justice is an obvious start. The psychology or sociology department might have a professor who has examined criminal behavior or the impact of crime on society. If you need technical information for your plot, contact the departments of, for example, biology, chemistry, or computer science.

If you live in a city that has a chapter of Mystery Writers of America or Sisters in Crime (or both), attend these organizations' meetings. Experts in pertinent fields are frequently scheduled as speakers. Take advantage of the question-and-answer session that follows the talk. Afterward, ask the expert for a business card and permission to call him or her.

Ask other writers who their sources are. Most will be happy to pass along a name or introduce you.

When you do contact an expert, be respectful and appreciative of his or her time and effort. Plan your questions in advance, be organized, show up on time, and don't overstay your welcome. Send a thank you note afterward, and refrain from making a pest of yourself with follow-up calls. When your book is published, send the expert a copy.

How Much Research Should You Do?

How much research do you need to do? Just enough. Research offers twin temptations, opposite sides of the same coin.

One snare is doing too much. Research can be fascinating enough to distract you from your main purpose, which is to write. Also, since knowledge helps you write with confidence, if you lack confidence, it's easy to conclude that the problem is that you don't know enough. More digging into books, or more classes, or more talks with experts are required to bolster your nerve.

The trick is to recognize when you've moved from productive research to procrastination. Research can be an excellent way to avoid writing, to put off having to face the blank page until tomorrow, which of course never comes. You gain a satisfying glow of accomplishment without having to actually sit down and write. But you are not doing yourself a favor if you hide behind your research efforts. Eventually, your pride shifts to frustration as you realize that you're making no real progress on your mystery.

At some point, the information you're collecting reaches a critical mass and starts sparking story ideas. You can feel that your characters are excited and ready to move. When that happy moment comes, set aside your research for a while, even if you feel it's incomplete. Start writing. Go back later to fill in details. Remember, most of the time, miniexpertise is all you need. If you hit a snag, do just enough additional research to get you through that the scene and into the next one. Here's a secret: Quite a few writers do a significant amount of their research after they've finished the first draft. By the time they're done, they've figured out exactly what they need to learn to make the story work, and the story itself is well underway.

The flip side, of course, is doing too little research. Writers succumb to this temptation for a number of reasons. If you're impatient, you may be tempted to dash through the research or skip it altogether in order to jump into the writing. If you're guilt-prone, with a strong work ethic, you might give research short shrift on the grounds that you think "real work" is not being accomplished; after all, finished pages are not piling on the desk. Or you may have the mistaken notion that research is not fun; it reminds you of the homework you did, or avoided doing, for school.

Consider research to be part of your professional education as a mystery writer. Be curious, adventurous, and willing to learn. Your mystery will be better for it.

However, research is a fundamental and necessary part of the mystery writer's job. With just enough research, neither too much nor too little, you make the formidable task of writing a mystery easier. Even better, you ensure that the result of your work — your finished mystery — is a stronger, more compelling, more authoritative book.

11
Helping Yourself Through the Rough Spots

At some point in the middle of writing your mystery, you're going to say to yourself, "This is absolutely the worst drivel ever written in the history of humankind. It's boring, it's stupid, it's hopeless, it's irredeemable. I can't believe I ever thought I was planning to ask a publisher to kill trees to print this abomination."

It might help to know that every author has similar thoughts at least once in the course of every story.

Writing a mystery, especially one that is book-length, is a long, sometimes tedious, process. No matter how excited you are at the outset, no matter how much you believe in yourself and in your story, no matter how eager you are to write, there will be mornings when you can't face the idea of dragging yourself to your desk. There will be afternoons when you sit there ready and willing, but your characters fold their arms, turn their backs on you, and stomp off to sulk. There will be evenings when you realize deep in your soul what's meant by the saying "Writing is a lonely occupation." The aim of this chapter is help you keep those times to a minimum.

Overcoming Writer's Block

From time to time, you may feel stymied. No matter how diligent you are about showing up for your date with the muse, nothing happens. The words refuse to flow. The ideas have dried up and blown away, as irretrievable as dust in the wind. You are suffering from a case of the dreaded writer's block.

Be assured that this affliction is not fatal and can be overcome with a little effort. Writer's block occurs when something falters — your body and spirit, your vision for the story, or your nerve.

Problems with body and spirit are often not writing-related at all. Perhaps some other issue has arisen in your life that is diverting your mental energy, and you may need to deal with it before you feel free to write again. The predicament can stem from something as basic as fatigue. Take time off for a good night's sleep or take a vacation at the beach. Once you're refreshed, the writing will be rolling again.

While losing your vision for a story can be frightening, it's in some ways the easiest problem to solve. Quit writing for a while. Try freshening up with some What if? scenarios. Work on a completely different writing project. Often the problem is that you've followed along as the plot took a wrong turn or you've assigned a role to a character who's not right for the job; the section below, called Getting Your Story Back on Track, will give you some clues about where to start looking.

At some point in your efforts, the breakthrough will come, the "aha!" moment when you realize what the problem is and can begin to work out a solution. Be prepared; this moment is likely to occur when you least expect it and are thinking about something else entirely. When the bolt of lightning strikes, write your new ideas down. (Remember the Brilliant Idea Syndrome I told you about in chapter 3?)

A faltering of nerve can be trickier to deal with. Fear, when it strikes, is likely to masquerade as something else. Practicality and common sense are among its frequent disguises, and it can be hard to figure out whether it's fear or reason that is actually calling the shots. If you have the dream and ambition to write but find yourself regularly avoiding your desk, try to look behind the scenes and see if fear isn't lurking.

Summon up your courage. Writing requires it, and your reserves are probably deeper than you think. Revisit the commitment you made to yourself when you began working on your mystery. Copy your commitment in big, bold letters, and post it in a prominent place. Read it over until you believe you can accomplish it. Then set yourself down to work. You may never vanquish the fear completely, but you can banish it to a corner and ignore it when it tries to grab your attention again.

Getting Your Story Back on Track

Your story has wandered astray. Or it's lying lifeless on the page. It's sagging, and so are your spirits. What do you do?

Although every story is different, there are some common reasons for getting into a muddle in the middle or, for that matter, at the beginning or end. If you're feeling stuck, some of the solutions listed here might apply to your book:

> *Do some more research.* One frequent reason for writer's block is that the writer doesn't have enough knowledge of a particular subject. Stuck in the chapter where the police are examining the location where your detective discovered the body? The snag may be that you're unsure of how a crime-scene investigation is conducted. When you find out, you'll approach the chapter with fresh confidence and enthusiasm.

> *Work on the hidden story.* Problems with the surface story can arise because you are confused about elements of the hidden story. If you write out the hidden story in some detail, it will become clearer to you how the surface story must unfold if the detective is to solve the mystery that the hidden story poses.

> *Keep the primary question in mind.* The primary question is the central issue of the story, the main question you're exploring in the writing of the mystery. Also, don't ignore the other questions that drive the plot, the ones concerning your detective's goals. When the story stumbles, it's often because the author

has lost sight of these questions, or never figured them out in the first place.

 Know your characters well. Again, many story problems are a direct result of not fully understanding who the characters are, what they want, and what they would do in a given situation.

 Let the characters do what comes naturally to them. No matter how brilliantly conceived a plot may be, the characters will balk or rebel if you try to force or manipulate them to do things contrary to their natures or circumstances.

Consulting your characters

If you're having trouble overcoming a hurdle, ask your characters for insight by using the stream-of-consciousness technique. At the top of a page (either on paper or a computer screen), write a direct question, addressing the character by name: Aldrich, what are you going to do next? Bethany, why did you make such a fool of yourself? Clifford, why are you so angry? Davina, what are you doing in this story, anyway? Eldon, why do you want Ferguson dead? Or even: Zachary, what's gone wrong here and how can I fix it? Then let the character respond. Speaking through your characters, your subconscious mind will often give you the help you need.

 Jettison a character if need be. The problem may be that you have a wonderful character who's wandering around lost in the wrong story. Don't hesitate to give that character the boot if he or she isn't working out. Chances are, the character will pop back into your mind later, toting a story idea more suitable to his or her talents.

 Follow the chain of actions and consequences. Make sure the actions in the story arise as a result of previous actions. Don't forget, the choices that characters make will have ramifications that change their situation. When the new situation presents itself, the characters face new choices about what to do next. If you follow this chain of events, of actions and consequences, it often leads you directly to the story's end.

 Keep the risk and payoff in balance. Believability problems can occur when what a character stands to gain from a course of action is not worth the risk it entails. As you place obstacles in your detective's path and raise the stakes involved, you must increase not only the degree of risk your detective faces but also the payoff that will come with success. Otherwise, any sensible character would cut his or her losses and walk away. Be alert for the opposite problem too. If the complications you set up never really threaten your detective's goal, readers won't worry that it won't be achieved.

When the risk and payoff are out of balance, the outcome of the course of action is no longer in doubt. If the risk is too great, readers assume the detective will fail. If it's too slight, they take for granted that the detective will succeed. The suspense vanishes, and so does readers' concern.

What is the proper balance? That depends on the situation and the character. Suppose your detective must face an angry, armed villain to plead for the safe return of a kidnap victim. There is a good chance that the villain will kill your detective. Is the payoff worth the risk? If the detective is the mother of the kidnap victim and there is no other way to save her son, her action is highly believable. It might be tougher to convince readers she'd risk her own life for a total stranger, unless you have established the character solidly as someone who would behave this way.

☛ *Stick to the point.* Keep the story moving forward. Avoid slowing the pace by loading in too much of the back story, digressing into philosophical discussions, inserting unnecessary scenes, or interjecting authorial asides that pull readers out of the story world.

☛ *Don't pull back from the conflict.* Uncomfortable though it may be, you must allow the characters to wrestle with the forces that oppose them, even if doing so causes them some pain. A big reason that stories don't succeed is because their authors set up significant issues and then excuse the characters from dealing with them, so that a satisfying resolution is never achieved. Don't spare your characters the anguish. You may feel you are saving them from suffering, but you are hurting your story in the process.

Working backward

If you can't make the story move forward, try putting its gear in reverse. Start from the confrontation where the murderer is revealed, and follow the chain of actions and consequences back to the start: "If this was the result, then this must have been what caused it." Shifting direction in this way can sometimes make an unclear sequence of events fall neatly into place.

Joining a Writers' Group

One difficulty of being a writer is working in the dark. Not in literal darkness, of course, but working without having the advantage of helpful interaction with colleagues that could shed light on your story and make you feel less alone in your endeavors.

This is why many writers seek out a writers' group, especially in the early stages of their careers. A writers' group is a small, informal band of like-minded writers who read each other's works-in-progress and offer comments and suggestions to improve the developing story.

A writers' group provides a sounding board for participants; you can share information, test ideas, ask for advice, complain when the going gets rough, and celebrate success.

What You Can Gain

Both you and your work can benefit when you join a writers' group. A good group provides you with:

> *Helpful criticism of your own work.* As the group reads and discusses your chapters at regular intervals, the members come to understand what you are trying to accomplish, and your aims become clearer to you as well. Your fellow members will tell you where you've succeeded, and, if you haven't, they can suggest how you might better hit your target. Their comments on your opening chapters can help you better plan the later ones. Remember, though, that no matter how certain they sound, the other members of the group are not necessarily right. Listen to and assess what they have to say, and take action on those issues that make sense to you.

- *Sharpened writing skills.* As you read and evaluate the writing of other members, you hone your own critical skills, learning not only *what* does or doesn't work in a story, but *why* it does or doesn't work. You can then bring this enhanced proficiency back to your own mystery.

- *Fellowship of other writers.* It's invigorating to have a regular opportunity to meet with colleagues who share your passion for writing. As I mentioned above, it helps dispel the isolation that is inherent in the occupation of writer.

- *A deadline, and an incentive to meet it.* It's hard to make room in your life for writing when you're writing strictly for yourself. Other demands keep getting pushed to higher priority, and your mystery can languish. But each meeting of your writers' group imposes a deadline for finishing your next scene or chapter. When you make a commitment to the group, you accept the obligation to do your part to make it function well, and that means contributing your work. It is embarrassing to show up at meetings without some pages in hand.

How a Writers' Group Works

I belong to two writers' groups, and describing them is the best way to explain how such groups may work. One group comprises four mystery writers, three of whom have been published and one who is currently unpublished (although we are confident she won't be for long). We meet every two to three weeks for a session that lasts two to three hours. Each member mails the chapters to be discussed to the others in advance. We read them at our leisure and mark them up with corrections, questions, and suggestions. At the meeting, we go through each person's work page by page, with every member offering comments.

The other group, with seven members, is also a mix of published and unpublished writers, working in a wide range of fiction genres. This group meets monthly for an entire day. Rather than sending out material to other members to read in advance, we each bring two copies of the chapters we want critiqued. We pass the copies around the circle; as each member completes a page, he or she hands it on to the next person. While we read, we jot questions and comments in our own notepads. When everyone has finished reading, each member offers an evaluation in turn. Since there are two copies of the material, the person critiquing and the author each have one to refer to during the evaluation.

Members of both groups prefer to read the chapters themselves, silently, as this replicates the experience most readers of our stories will have. Some writers' groups, though, have participants read their work aloud at the meetings. Hearing the words gives both author and listener a better sense of the rhythm and flow of the language and reveals confused or clunky phrasing. Both approaches have merit.

Writers' groups sometimes have an official leader or moderator who directs the meetings. Neither of the groups I belong to has felt the need to assign leadership positions since our numbers are small.

Finding or Forming Your Own Group

How do you locate a writers' group? Ask your friends. Contact a local writers' organization. Attend a writing class. You might recruit fellow students to join you in a continuing group.

In my experience, four to seven members seems to be the ideal number of participants in a writers' group. With a larger group, it's difficult to give each participant a fair share of attention in a reasonable time. With a smaller group, it's not possible to hold a productive meeting unless all members can attend, and the members' busy schedules can make that hard to arrange.

Experiment a bit to come up with workable operating procedures: how often you'll meet, the number of pages a participant may bring each time, the ground rules for offering criticism. The basics are simple: be positive, be constructive, and don't interrupt during someone else's turn.

What counts most is the chemistry of the participants. You want people who are congenial yet businesslike, who take their own writing and yours seriously. You don't need members who are domineering, who are out to make points at someone else's expense, or whose fragile ego falls apart when any word of their prose is challenged. Ideally, each member will have a talent for both insightful criticism and encouragement, so that you and your fellow members will each receive constructive help, friendly support, and a better sense of your strengths as a mystery writer.

> Hearing the words spoken out loud gives both author and listener a good sense of the rhythm and flow of the language and reveals confused or clunky phrasing.

Rewarding Yourself for a Job Well Done

Be certain to reward yourself along the way. This is vitally important. Don't hold off until your book is published, or you sell it to a publisher, or an agent accepts you as a client. Don't even wait until you finally type "The End" on the final page of the manuscript.

Honor your small successes. Whenever you accomplish a mini-goal — a scene or a chapter completed, a particular number of pages written, a week or month in which you faithfully kept your writing appointments — celebrate a bit. Treat yourself to a movie, a new book you've been wanting to read, a bubble bath, a glass of wine.

Small indulgences like these help you mark and acknowledge your progress. When you can validate that you're making headway, it's much easier to keep up your writing momentum.

12
Writing, Rewriting, and Revising

It's been said there is no good writing, only good rewriting. It is useful to keep this in mind as you're struggling over your first draft. You don't need to make your writing beautiful and perfect — certainly not at this stage. This burgeoning pile of pages is not yet the novel that you hope will appear someday on bookstore shelves; nor is it supposed to be. It is simply a draft, one phase in the evolution of what ultimately will become that book.

New writers frequently ask more experienced writers how many drafts they write. It's a hard question to answer. What exactly is a draft? Particularly if you use a computer, the process of revising is constant. Technology makes it easy to continually play around with thoughts, tinker with wording, and rearrange paragraphs. You can delete a sentence or a scene with just a keystroke. Also, different parts of the book make their own demands. You might struggle with chapter 8, rewriting it five times before it finally feels right; yet chapter 10 may flow so smoothly that it feels as if you're just taking dictation; when you sit down to revise it, you find all it needs is a couple of commas added.

For our discussion here, I'm not referring to minor fixes, the little adjustments you make as you write, or the extra attention you might give one individual scene. By a "draft," I mean a version of your entire mystery, complete from beginning to end.

Using the 1-2-3 Approach

Good things come in threes, according to an old saying, and there are several sets of three that I associate with mystery writing. First come the three starting points for a story: characters, a conflict, and a crime. Then there's the three-stage outline system described in chapter 3 that I use to plan a story. Those three stages correspond neatly to the three-act structure of a plot.

Here's another set of three: While the creative process works differently for each writer, a mystery typically goes through three phases of development and refinement as it evolves from a few ideas in the author's mind to a completed manuscript, ready to be presented to agents, publishers, and, ultimately, readers. As you write your novel, you draw on your powers of inspiration and analysis. Inspiration bubbles with ideas; analysis lets you evaluate the ideas and impose order on them. The three phases are distinguished by the extent to which inspiration or analysis is the primary force at work.

My working pattern is to write three drafts, one that corresponds with each phase. This is not a hard-and-fast rule that I would advocate for every writer or every story. You'll need to determine what works best for you. A few seasoned professionals claim to write only a single draft: their first version is the final one. Usually, these are authors who plan a novel extensively before they jump into the writing.

> Few writers couldn't improve their stories by reviewing them a second or third time with a critical eye and a sharp pencil.

Few writers couldn't improve their stories by reviewing them a second or third time with a critical eye and a sharp pencil. Indeed, many writers go through the entire book a fourth or fifth time, or even more. The right number of drafts is the number that it takes for you to feel that the story is fully developed and compellingly told.

Thinking in terms of three drafts, though, makes the mystery writing process easier to understand. Let's consider the issues and the work to be accomplished in each one.

The First Draft: Discovering the Story

Your goal while writing the first draft is to figure out what the story is. You are getting to know the characters, envisioning the various locations that your setting consists of, discovering what's going on. No matter how much figuring out you do in advance, or how careful and detailed your planning is, you will have surprises in store once you start writing: A minor character demands a starring role. A player you thought was key to the plot walks away in chapter 5, never to be seen again. The plot twists and turns until suddenly you're in uncharted territory.

For the first draft, your inspirational powers are in charge. Give them unfettered rein. Resist the urge to be too analytical, to start evaluating and criticizing either your ideas or the way you are expressing them. There will be plenty of opportunity for that later. The point now is to capture your ideas on paper, to bring the characters to life, to begin expressing your vision of a mysterious fictional world.

The result will probably be a sprawling, undisciplined, chaotic mess. Good. That means your creative process is working. My advice is to let the story roll. Don't go back and revise any part of it until you've completed the first draft of the entire manuscript. There are several reasons for this.

First, if you continue to rework chapter 2 before you launch into chapter 3, you create an ideal opportunity for your analytical impulses to elbow their way in, and this is much too soon. At this point, analysis can turn into negative self-criticism. It undermines your confidence and makes you obsess over perfection. In your quest for the flawless page or chapter, you lose sight of the larger goal: to write a book. You place yourself in danger of losing momentum and never finishing at all. Trust me, when you reach the end of the entire first draft, no matter how rough and awkward it is, the exhilaration you feel far exceeds any momentary satisfaction you might gain from achieving just a single well-honed chapter.

Turning yourself from creator to critic during the first draft also creates extra work for you. No matter how magnificently you craft that early chapter, you'll need to make changes to it. The discoveries you make as you proceed through the story will affect the parts you've already written.

For instance, in chapter 12, your detective is sitting in her parked car at midnight, staking out an abandoned warehouse where she suspects the stolen computer equipment is hidden. A vintage red Thunderbird pulls up, the driver gets out, and, using a key, enters the warehouse. In the darkness, the driver is just a shadow, but the detective recognizes the car as belonging to the brother-in-law of the recently murdered computer-firm president. At that point, a key issue occurs to you: your detective has no way of knowing what kind of car the brother-in-law drives unless she saw the Thunderbird or discussed it with him when they encountered each other in chapter 3. So it's back to chapter 3.

Another example: About halfway through the book, you realize Jack and Elizabeth are not the loving husband and wife you had thought they were. Instead, each harbors a seething hostility toward the other, and they are no longer willing to keep it submerged. You'll need to revisit the earlier scenes where the couple appear to make sure the anger smolders beneath the surface, thus setting up the moment when it erupts into violence.

Suddenly your perfect chapter 3 is perfect no longer. Not only that: because you've honed and polished it so thoroughly, it's harder than it might have been to figure out how to work in the new information.

Writing the first draft should be like making castles in mud puddles — have fun, feel free, let your imagination soar, and don't worry if things get sloppy. The mess is an important part of the creative process.

The Second Draft: Expressing Your Vision of the Story

Now that you know the whole story, it's time to transform it from a mud castle into a book. For the second draft, your inspirational and analytical powers collaborate. Working together, they help you bring your mystery under control, give it coherence, and make sure it expresses your intentions and vision in the strongest, most compelling way.

For me, the first draft is akin to a very long outline. I'm both relieved and excited when I finally have a thick stack of pages to ponder over and scribble on. The mystery has stopped being mysterious to me, because I've worked out the main points. Now that I understand the story, I can concentrate in the second draft on how best to tell it.

Prepare to do substantial work. You'll be writing new material, restructuring and rearranging scenes, sharpening your presentation of the characters, intensifying the mood, heightening the suspense, wrapping up loose ends, and cutting out entire sections that seemed important when you wrote them but proved not to belong in the story. Your analytical side now has important contributions to make as you begin to evaluate the presentation of your mystery. Does it stand up logically? Are you using language to the best effect?

But the second draft entails more than editing. Rewriting means "writing again"; you are still engaged in a creative process. That's why you continue to need inspiration — to help the story gain clarity both on the page and in your mind. As you write and rewrite, you'll come up with fresh insights and understanding about your characters, your plot, and the issues dealt with in your story. Your second draft may turn into a series of drafts as you work to bring all the elements into play.

The Third Draft: Polishing Your Presentation

Finally the story is complete, the puzzle is solved, the questions are answered, and the characters have wandered off to a well-deserved rest. You may feel as if your mystery is done. While it's true you've finished the creative part of the work, it pays to read carefully through the manuscript one more time.

The third draft is the time to make a calm, analytical assessment of your book. By now, the elements of the story should all be in place; what you are concentrating on is its presentation. Have you told the story in the way that will make the strongest dramatic impact? If your goals include seeing your work published, now is the time to make it market-ready.

If you encounter a problem with the story itself, for instance, a scene in which the sequence of action is unclear, or a character whose motivation remains murky, you definitely want to fix that problem. By this time, you probably will have remedied most difficulties like this, but you should make certain.

Your other task in the third draft is line editing; that is, going through the manuscript line by line to ensure that the manuscript is polished and professional. Test each word and sentence to make sure it is accurate, necessary, and strong — the most powerful way to say what you want to say. Trim whatever is unessential. Correct any errors in grammar and spelling; catch factual mistakes; repair glitches of all kinds.

> When you are working on the third draft, double-check all the facts of which you were unsure.

Burnish your novel to a gem-like gleam, so that when you present it to agents and editors, it will outshine every other manuscript in their read-me-buy-me pile.

Being an Effective Self-Editor

Once you finish writing the first draft, set your manuscript aside for a few days or weeks, and give yourself a treat to celebrate. Setting the manuscript aside will allow you to put some distance between yourself and your story, as well as refresh your brain for the next round of work. The trick to successful rewriting and revising is to separate yourself from the story and become as objective as possible.

Reading with Fresh Eyes

A few days (or, even better, a couple of weeks) after you have completed your first draft, read the manuscript all the way through. If possible, read a clean, unmarked copy. Try to forget that you've seen this manuscript before; that you know anything about it. Pretend you're a mystery fan who is picking it up for the first time.

Mark typos if you like, but don't do any serious editing or revising. Just read attentively. Try to get a sense of the how the story flows, how all the bits and pieces fit together, what works, what doesn't. In the long course of writing the first draft, you necessarily focused on one paragraph, one scene, one character at a time. Now it's time to examine the big picture, to pause in the process of growing trees and take a good look at the forest. If you jump straight into rewriting, you'll miss out on this valuable overall perspective.

While half your brain is reading, the other half will brim with thoughts about changes you want to make. If you set up a planning notebook like the one I described in chapter 3, keep it close at hand: this is one of the times it proves its worth. As you read a scene, the notebook will remind you about the revisions you've already planned to incorporate. In addition, it will give you a convenient place to jot down new insights and necessary fixes as they occur to you. You will be able to capture your ideas without distracting yourself too much from your reading.

Chances are, you'll recognize that there's a lot of work to be done. But you'll be amazed, impressed, and delighted by the quality of what you've accomplished so far.

Looking at Story and Style

Now it's time to rewrite. In the second draft and beyond, you'll need to deal with two kinds of issues: those that concern the story and those that relate to style.

Story issues are matters of content: characters, plot, setting, and suspense. Make sure that all the story elements are clear, logical, and accurate and that you've presented them as dramatically as possible. Did you play fair with readers? Did you wrap up all the loose ends? Did you fully reveal the hidden story? Do the characters come across as real, well-rounded individuals who behave in believable ways? Did you maintain the tension and control the pace?

Style issues concern the way the story is told: how you use language, point of view, details, and sensory impressions to engage readers in your story world. Be conscious and purposeful about what you are doing when it comes to style. When you are finished writing, you want your storytelling to be tight and vigorous. Every word, phrase, and paragraph should earn its keep. Cut out everything that is unnecessary. Ask yourself: "Can I say this in fewer words and still retain the flavor, the color, the mood, and the information essential to the story?" This doesn't mean you must opt for a bare-bones style. You can be as detailed and can lavish in your language as you wish. Just be sure that each word makes a real contribution to the story, and that the story is continually rolling forward.

From the Detective's Notebook 9 is a checklist of story and style issues to think about as you tackle your second draft.

Capturing that Elusive Quality Called Voice

As you progress through the various drafts of your book, you'll find that your distinctive writer's voice emerges. Each writer has a natural and personal mode of expression.

A narrative voice is a difficult quality to define because it is so individual. Your voice is the product of the decisions you make about the story issues and style issues of your book, the manner in which you combine ideas and language to create a dramatic effect or elicit a response from your readers. It has do with how the book sounds — its music and rhythm, the vocabulary used, whether the tone is formal or casual. But

From the Detective's Notebook 9
A Self-Editing Checklist

Story Issues

The Detective or Protagonist

❏ Is your detective a believable individual whom readers can identify with and root for?

❏ Is your detective presented fully and completely, without holding back feelings and emotions, so that an intimate relationship with readers can be established?

❏ Are your detective's goals and personal issues clear? Are they sufficient to compel his or her actions in this story?

❏ Does your detective solve the mystery fairly and squarely, without reliance on coincidences or last-minute manipulations by you, the author?

Other Characters

❏ Does every character play a significant role in the story, whether that role is major or minor?

❏ Are the villain's motivations strong enough for the criminal act?

❏ Is each character a believable individual? Do the character's actions stem naturally from motivations, experiences, backgrounds, and personalities?

❏ Does each character sound natural, with a personal style of expression?

Plot and Structure

❏ Does the story hook readers right at the start, by jumping into the action, establishing conflict, and raising questions that demand answers?

❏ Is the primary question of the plot clear, and does it guide the way the plot is developed?

❏ Do the main plot and subplots develop as chains of actions and consequences, with each event happening as a result of a previous one?

❏ Are there plot points at appropriate intervals to keep the story energized?

❏ Does each scene serve a specific purpose in moving the story forward?

❏ Is the time line of the story realistic and accurate?

From the Detective's Notebook 9 — Continued

- [ ] Do readers have adequate cues to know when the story, and each scene, is taking place: the day, month, and season of the year?

- [ ] Are you accurate in your depiction of police operations, the criminal justice system, and forensic science?

- [ ] Are the loose ends tied up? Are all the characters accounted for, all the situations dealt with, and all the questions answered?

- [ ] Did you force the characters, especially the detective, to confront and deal with their issues and conflicts?

Setting

- [ ] Is the location where the book takes place established at an early point (preferably in chapter 1)?

- [ ] Is the setting depicted in such a way that it has real personality? Did you make it vivid through a careful choice of details?

- [ ] Does the setting have an impact on the story through the ways that the characters and the setting interact?

- [ ] If the setting is real, is it portrayed accurately?

- [ ] If the setting is imaginary, is it portrayed consistently and authentically, so that readers will believe in it?

Suspense

- [ ] Does your detective have something significant at stake that will be affected by his or her participation in the investigation?

- [ ] Is a palpable sense of threat made apparent quickly and sustained throughout the book?

- [ ] Does the line of tension rise steadily toward the climax?

- [ ] Did you present your detective with increasingly difficult complications to overcome? Did you avoid getting him or her out of jams too easily?

- [ ] Did you raise the stakes for your detective during the course of the story?

- [ ] Are the risk and payoff kept in balance?

- [ ] Did you provide a hook at the end of each scene or chapter to draw readers into the next one?

From the Detective's Notebook 9 — Continued

- ❏ Did you provide a hook at the end of each scene or chapter to draw readers into the next one?

- ❏ Did you control the pace well? Does the story continually move forward? Did you quicken the pace when building up to moments of high excitement? Did you provide slower scenes to allow readers and characters to catch their breaths?

- ❏ Is your depiction of violence respectful of the sensibilities of your readers and appropriate to the story you are telling?

The Hidden Story and the Surface Story

- ❏ Is the hidden story fully comprehensible by the end of the book? Are the questions of Whodunit?, Howdunit?, and Whydunit? answered? Could readers now reconstruct the crime?

- ❏ Do the events of the surface story grow logically out of the events of the hidden story?

- ❏ Did you play fair with readers? Are all the clues and information necessary to solve the crime presented in the story?

Style Issues

Point of View

- ❏ Is each scene presented from a specific character's point of view?

- ❏ Is the point of view within each scene consistent, with no jarring shifts into a different character's head (or the author's)?

- ❏ Are the thoughts, observations, and actions of the viewpoint character in keeping with that character's personality, feelings, and background? Do they reflect the philosophy, passions, and perspectives of a distinctive character?

Showing and Telling

- ❏ Have you relied as much as possible on action and dialogue to tell the story?

- ❏ Have you smoothed out expository lumps?

- ❏ Does each scene present a strong visual picture?

- ❏ Does each scene include other sensory details: sounds, smells, textures, tastes?

- ❏ Are the details specific and vivid?

- ❏ Have you provided readers with a "you are there" experience?

From the Detective's Notebook 9 — Continued

Language

❑ Is the language lively and active, with strong verbs and colorful modifiers?

❑ Do sentences and paragraphs flow smoothly, without sounding awkward or confusing? (Read them aloud to help answer this question.)

❑ Are words carefully chosen and correctly used, with attention to their connotations or implied meanings as well as to their literal meanings?

❑ Is the wording tight, with each word making a real contribution?

❑ Are specialized or arcane terms explained or made clear from the context?

❑ Is the grammar correct?

❑ Is the spelling correct?

it goes beyond that. Voice is also the way you flavor the story with your singular perspectives, insights, and attitudes.

Authors' voices vary in much the same way characters' voices do, ranging from terse to garrulous, straightforward to oblique, serious to comic. In a story written using the first-person point of view, the narrative voice should belong to your character; one of the interesting challenges of writing with an "I" character is setting aside your natural voice in favor of the character's.

The best way to understand voice is to read mysteries by many authors and see how they compare. The mysteries of Walter Mosley and Elizabeth George are good works to start with. Mosley's Easy Rawlins stories, set in the Los Angeles of the 1940s and 1950s, are recounted by an African-American man who has learned through hard experience to be wary. His voice is spare, laconic, and reserved. By contrast, George's novels, set in England and featuring the upper-crust Sir Thomas Linley and the proletariat Barbara Havers as investigators, are dense with details and rich in emotions. Yet, in their way, George's novels are as tightly written as Mosley's.

> Your writer's voice is a combination of the way you use language, your storytelling style, and your unique outlook and opinions.

When you embark on your first draft, your voice is likely to sound tentative, unsure, and ordinary. As you keep writing and your skills and confidence grow, your narrative voice will develop too, becoming stronger, fresher, and more original.

Your writer's voice is a combination of the way you use language, your storytelling style, and your unique outlook and opinions. Here are a few tips to help you make your voice more powerful and assured.

- *Learn to use language as a precision instrument.* Pay attention to the meanings of words; not only their literal meanings, but their connotations, their emotional color and weight, the visual images they conjure in the mind. Brush up on grammar if you are unsure of it. Develop a sense of the sound and rhythm of your sentences and paragraphs. Reading aloud is a good exercise for training your ear. Read your own work and that of writers you admire, including a bit of poetry.

- *Let the story reflect the narrator's insights, philosophy, and worldview, whether the narrator is you, the author, or a character.* Of course, a mystery should never become a philosophical treatise. But readers' pleasure is enhanced by the sense that they are in the company of someone with distinctive personality traits, passions, and perspectives.

- *Try the storytelling techniques and suggestions in this book.* As you strengthen your storytelling skills, your natural voice will grow more powerful as a natural corollary.

- *Be willing to experiment.* Approach your writing with a sense of fun. One of the joys of writing a mystery is the opportunity to play on paper, to try out ideas, to dabble with plots, to frolic with characters, to get away with things you never could in real life. Especially when writing the first draft, keep in mind that there is no right way or wrong way to be creative. Here is the only real test: Does what you are trying help you express your vision more clearly and powerfully? Does it help you build a solid bridge to connect your imagination to that of your readers?

- *Keep writing.* Experience counts. The more you write, the more dynamic and individual your narrative voice will become.

Getting Feedback

At some point, you'll want to share your mystery with other people to find out how well you've succeeded in accomplishing your aims. A good time to do this is once you've completed a second draft. At that point, both the story and style will be in good shape. Then, when you tackle the third draft, you can incorporate the worthwhile suggestions you receive from the readers.

Obtaining reader responses and reactions to your manuscript can be invaluable. Because you're so close to the story and the characters, it's hard to judge for yourself how well you've succeeded in expressing your vision in the way you intended. A discerning reader can give you a fresh perspective on your story and help pinpoint flaws that may have crept in: action that's hard to follow, a description that's imprecise, a clue that's too obvious, a character who is too unsympathetic or wooden or insufficiently motivated, a lag in the tension, an awkward phrase, or a point of key information that's clear in your mind but somehow never made it onto the page.

> A discerning reader can give you a fresh perspective on your story and help pinpoint flaws that may have crept in.

Naturally, what you hope to hear is that your mystery is brilliantly conceived and written, with wonderfully drawn characters, an enthralling plot, suspense that won't quit, and a writing style that elevates the standards for prose writing to a new and glorious peak. What you need to hear are thoughtful comments from someone who encourages you in your writing and can provide well-considered suggestions that will help you improve the book.

Qualifications of a Suitable Reader

Whom should you ask to read your mystery? First, choose a reader who enjoys and respects mysteries. If your reader understands what constitutes a good mystery, he or she will be able to evaluate yours in a way you'll find beneficial.

Second, pick someone who supports your efforts in this endeavor. You need bolstering and reassurance as well as criticism. You'll benefit from hearing what's right as well as what's wrong.

Third, select someone who'll be honest as well as supportive. You want to assign this important task to a person who is willing to give well-considered, constructive suggestions, not just massage your ego.

Finally, you need a skilled critic. It isn't enough to say yes, this is good, or no, I don't like that. Your reader should be able to back up an opinion, whether positive or negative, with reasons why he or she responded that particular way. Your reader should also be able to point out where problems exist, and suggest how you might fix them.

Finding Readers

Who is the paragon who will fill this admittedly big role? Look among the following groups.

Other writers and writers' groups

Another writer, especially another mystery writer, can make an ideal reader. Better than anyone, that writer understands how stories are structured, how characters function, and how dramatic effects are achieved. The writer has grappled with the same issues you have and has experience in devising solutions.

If one writer can provide helpful feedback, a group of writers can assess your work even better. I discuss the merits of these groups at length in chapter 11.

The experts you consulted

If you consulted an expert during your research, ask if he or she will be willing to review your manuscript when it's completed, with an eye as to whether or not you have your facts straight, your crime-solving procedures depicted accurately, and so forth.

Nonwriting mystery fans

If one of your friends is a nonwriting mystery fan, ask him or her to read your mystery strictly for the story's sake. Don't ask for corrections of typos or comments on style, but simply this: Does the story hang together? What questions does the reader still have at the end? Where does he or she become confused? Are there scenes where the reader has trouble following the action? Is anything puzzling left unexplained? Does the reader beat the detective in solving the mystery? At what point in the story does the reader figure out who the perpetrator of the crime is?

Spouses, partners, and friends

The people closest to you might make admirable critics. Then again, they might not. They often have a vested interest in not hurting your feelings. Moreover, it may be difficult for them to separate their regard for you from their assessment of your book, and this can hamper them from giving you an objective evaluation. Let them read your work if you feel good about doing so, but you'll probably find it helpful to seek out other opinions too.

Paying for Feedback

You may be tempted to hire a professional such as an independent editor to evaluate or edit your manuscript. This might be a great idea or a terrible one, depending on whom you choose. Some editors insist on a hefty fee but provide little help; others charge a fair rate and give you specific, detailed comments that you could find extremely useful.

The best way to find the right person is to have a writer you know recommend someone. Otherwise, before you sign on as a client, ask the editor to give you references, and then check them out. Since you can assume that you'll be given the names of only satisfied customers, ask probing questions: What did the evaluation consist of? How did the writer put the suggestions to use? What claims or promises did the editor make, and did he or she live up to them? Was the cost reasonable? Did the editor use the critique as a lead-in to push more expensive services? Would the writer use the same editor's services for another manuscript?

Talk in depth to the editor to be sure you understand the precise nature of the service to be provided and the approach you can expect the editor to take. And by all means, get your agreement in writing.

Be cautious of evaluation services suggested by literary agencies, especially if the agency makes using the service a condition of taking you on as a client. No doubt there are legitimate agents who have excellent working relationships with credible independent editors. But there have been cases of unscrupulous operators who solicit for manuscripts by representing themselves as agents, but whose real objective is to peddle critique services that are both expensive and superficial.

> When you are considering paying to have your manuscript evaluated, remember: "caveat scriptor" — let the writer beware.

Assessing the Evaluation

When the feedback you've asked for comes in, try to keep it in perspective. It's difficult to take criticism, even when it's gentle, well-intentioned, and constructive, about a book into which you've poured so much of yourself.

Remember, just because one of your readers recommends that you change something, that doesn't mean you must agree. If everyone who reads your novel points out the same problem or makes similar suggestions, consider that they might have pinpointed a genuine flaw, and revise your story accordingly. Otherwise, bear in mind that individual preferences and prejudices come into play in an evaluation. Pay attention to the suggestions that feel right and ignore the rest. I belong to two writers' groups, and I tend to ignore about half of what my fellow members say. The other 50 percent, though, proves invaluable. Some of the advice concerns minor points that are easy to fix, such as changing or cutting a word. At other times, they raise significant issues: questioning a character's motivation perhaps, or suggesting a plot point that works better than the one I'd planned. In that case, I may rethink, and rewrite, a good part of the book. Having a better story is worth the extra work.

Even when you agree that something could be improved, it's likely that you'll find better solutions than your readers did, ones that are more true to the story you have in mind. After all, it's your book. No one knows your characters, your plot, or your goals and intentions better than you do. How the story should be told is ultimately your decision.

Knowing When Your Book Is Finished

With every creative work, you reach the point when it's time to declare it finished. Ask yourself, are you still making your mystery better, or are you simply afraid to let it go? Some writers, fearful of the response their book might receive if they sent it out into the marketplace, use its lack of perfection as an excuse. After all, there's no point in sending it out if there's still work that might be done, if it's not yet stellar.

The problem, of course, is that perfection is impossible. No mystery achieves it. Your novel, though it might be excellent, won't quite fulfill the wondrous vision you had for it when you began. But it will have helped you reach positive goals — the completion of a significant and satisfying project, and greater proficiency in the art and craft of mystery writing.

Chances are, as a result of all your planning and writing and re-thinking and rewriting, you have produced a strong, compelling story. You have created believable characters, an intriguing plot, a "you are there" setting, and suspense that will keep your readers turning pages. Your book is ready to go out into the wide world to seek its fortune. Whatever happens in the marketplace, you have written a mystery. Congratulations. This is a real achievement, one in which you can take great pride.

PART 3
Clues to Selling Your Mystery

13
From Writer to Reader: An Overview of the Publishing Process

What you have is a manuscript. What you desire is a book between covers with your name on the front and the spine. You want a spot on the bookstore shelves, royalty checks, avid fans, your name up in lights.

Selling your mystery, which I'll discuss in the next chapter, becomes a little easier when you learn about the business side of writing: what the marketplace for mysteries is like, how the publishing industry works, and how to put yourself forward as a real professional. The more you understand the publishing process, the better prepared you'll be to weather the uncertainties, overcome the disappointments, and savor the triumphs.

How does your mystery travel from your word processor into the hands of readers? It's a long but interesting expedition, with various stations along the way. A number of people play their part to help your book along.

Every mystery's journey is a bit different. Some authors are represented by literary agents and others sell their work themselves, approaching publishers directly. Publishing houses have their own policies and practices, so the process of transforming a manuscript to a book differs somewhat from one house to another. While your own experience no doubt will vary in some of the particulars, this chapter tracks a typical route.

The Writer's or Agent's Role: Selling the Manuscript

Your first marketing step involves a crucial decision: Should you submit your manuscript directly to publishers or should you start by trying to find a literary agent to handle the submissions for you? Writers have been successful in using both approaches, and both have their strong advocates.

> A good agent can be your ally, advocate, and best asset in dealing with the world of commercial publishing.

The advice of the editors to first-time writers in From the Detective's Notebook 11 later in this chapter includes obtaining an agent's services if possible. It could take some searching to find an agent who will take on an unpublished writer, but many authors find that the result is worth the effort. A good agent can be your ally, advocate, and best asset in dealing with the world of commercial publishing.

The author and agent work as a business team. While you are busy writing, creating the product to be sold, the agent represents you and your work in the marketplace.

While writers often find the publishing world to be strange, baffling, and sometimes frustrating, it is the agent's natural milieu. A good agent keeps abreast of literary trends and business developments in what is a tumultuous industry. Knowing which publishing houses favor mysteries and which editors enjoy certain types of books, the agent can determine the most likely homes for your novel.

Once an agent accepts you as a client, he or she will provide editorial advice, handle submissions of the manuscript, negotiate with publishers to secure for you the best possible financial deal and contract terms, act as a liaison (and when necessary, a buffer) between you and the publisher, help to resolve problems, market subsidiary rights not covered by the original contract, collect moneys owed you, and offer counsel on the development of your mystery writing career. Valuable services indeed.

Not every author needs or wants an agent's services. Writers of short stories almost never use agents. An author who wants to work with a small or regional publisher might find no advantage to having one. Most

From the Detective's Notebook 10
Finding a Literary Agent

When to Begin Looking

Begin looking for an agent after you have completed, revised, and polished your mystery. When an agent expresses interest, you want an excellent manuscript ready to show.

How to Find an Agent

There are various ways to find an agent:

- *Mystery conferences and other writers' conferences.* Agents frequently speak at these events, giving you a chance to hear them talk about their work and perhaps to introduce yourself.

- *Referrals from fellow writers.* Your colleagues will share recommendations and might be willing to let you use their names, which can be helpful in getting an agent's attention.

- Publishers Weekly, *the industry's news magazine.* Features on agents and items describing successful deals will give you clues about agents who could be worthwhile to approach.

- *Writers' organizations.* Some maintain lists of agents who handle books in particular genres. Newsletters frequently feature interviews with agents or notices about agents who are seeking clients.

- *The Association of Authors' Representatives.* (See Appendix A for contact information.) This is the principal professional association for literary agents. The Web site includes a listing of members with contact information, the organization's code of ethics, advice on finding an agent, and other helpful information.

- Literary Market Place, *the annual directory of persons and organizations in the publishing industry.* It also includes listings of literary agencies. You can see it in your public library or on the Internet at http://www.bookwire.com. The Web site includes agents' names and addresses; you must be a subscriber to access more detailed information.

- *Acknowledgments in books that you like or are similar to yours.* Authors often will thank their agents.

What to Find Out Before Signing On

Not all agents are alike. To help you determine whether a particular agent is suitable for you, ask the agent these questions:

- What kinds of books do you favor? Do you specialize in particular genres or categories? What is your experience in marketing mysteries?

From the Detective's Notebook 10 — Continued

🔫 What is your background and experience in the publishing industry? What kind of publishing houses do you work with most? What connections do you have for selling subsidiary rights such as movie and foreign sales?

🔫 How many clients do you represent? What are some key names? What successes have you achieved for these clients? (Note that bigger is not necessarily better. An agent who represents a large client list or superstar talent may not have enough time and energy to devote to a new author's needs.)

🔫 Will you provide client references? (If yes, check them out. You can learn a great deal of valuable information from talking to writers about their experiences and satisfaction with particular agents.)

🔫 How do you handle submissions and rejections? Will I be kept informed about which editors and publishing houses have received my book? Will I be sent copies of rejection letters? (While it is nice to lift the burden of sending out manuscripts and getting them back to other shoulders, you want to be able to track the submission process.)

🔫 How do you handle the business relationship with your clients? Will I have a formal contract or a handshake arrangement?

In your discussions with an agent, clarify the expectations on both sides. And be sure to determine whether the agent is courteous and responsive, and has a professional attitude. This is something of a judgment call, based on your intuition. But if you don't like the way the agent treats you from the beginning, your red warning flag should go up.

Commissions and Fees

For standard book sales most agents today charge a commission of 15 percent. The commission may vary according to the type of rights sold. You should not expect to pay an agent a fee to read your work. Required reading fees are considered unethical according to the covenant of the Association of Authors' Representatives. While some legitimate agents do charge fees to help offset the serious investment of time that reading a manuscript entails, beware of "agents" whose primary business is not really selling manuscripts but reading them for a price. There is an exception: when unpublished authors pay a fee to consult with an agent at a writers' conference. In that case, the money does not go to the agent but helps to defray the cost of the conference.

Submissions

Some agents prefer that you approach them by way of a query letter before sending any additional material. (Chapter 14 discusses query letters in more detail.) Others want to receive a synopsis and sample chapters as well. A few would like you to send the whole manuscript. Agents often have a

From the Detective's Notebook 10 — Continued

brochure or flyer stating their preferences, which they'll provide to you on request. If in doubt about the best way to approach an agent, send a query letter.

Multiple submissions, that is, sending your manuscript or book proposal to more than one agent at once, used to be frowned on by agents. However, more and more, multiple submissions are becoming the standard. If you plan to contact a number of agents at once, use a query letter. An agent who's interested may ask to see the manuscript on an exclusive basis. In that case, try to determine when you can expect a reply so that you don't have forestall other interested agents for too long. Usually, you can expect a reply on a submitted synopsis or manuscript within a couple of months. If the wait drags out much longer than that, a polite inquiry to the agent about the status of your submission is in order.

Always include an SASE (self-addressed, stamped envelope) with sufficient postage when you communicate with an agent. If you are contacting an agent outside your own country, purchase international reply coupons (IRCs) at your post office to include in your mailing.

See chapter 14 for detailed information on preparing your submission materials.

publishers of mysteries will welcome the submission of an exciting, superbly crafted book no matter who brings it to their attention.

If you understand the publishing industry, or you're willing to do some research, you can determine which editors and publishing houses are likely to be receptive to your work. A good place to start is your local bookstore. Study the books in the mystery section to see which publishing house is publishing novels similar to yours. In your library, search out the issues of *Publishers Weekly* that focus on the mystery; there are one or two each year. The genre profiles provide an overview of the current marketplace and the names of editors who specialize in mysteries. Attend mystery conferences; you'll learn a lot about the publishing world, pick up helpful marketing tips from other writers, and have the opportunity to make worthwhile contacts with agents and editors.

The Editor's Role, Part 1: Acquiring the Book

The editor at a publishing house wears two main hats: the chapeau of acquisitions and the green eyeshade of production. In other words, the editor's job is first to acquire works that can be reasonably expected to make money for the publisher, and then to shepherd these projects through the process of turning them from manuscripts into finished books.

What the acquisitions editor rarely gets to do any more is edit, at least in the old-fashioned sense of the term. Gone, alas, are the days when editors like the legendary Maxwell Perkins had the luxury of time to work with a promising young author like Thomas Wolfe to turn an unruly manuscript into a work of art. The reality of today's publishing world is that to be seriously considered for publication, a manuscript must be polished and professional from the start.

The Acquisitions Process

For the editor, the acquisitions process involves reading a lot of manuscripts, knowing the pulse of the book market, and determining whether and where a particular book will fit into the publisher's overall list.

Once the editor decides that your manuscript has the potential the publisher is looking for, he or she will consider making an offer on the book. At some publishing houses, the editor makes that decision alone. At others, it's a committee decision. The editor presents your book and others of interest at a conference attended by other editors and sales or marketing staff. After lengthy and occasionally heated discussion in which advocates of various books state their cases, the group jointly decides which manuscript to acquire.

When your novel receives a positive nod, the editor contacts you or your agent with the good news: The publisher wishes to make an offer. If you do not yet have an agent, now is the time to find one. An author with a publishing offer in hand is a highly desirable client. The agent, consulting with you, will negotiate with the publisher to come up with contract terms agreeable to all. As an novice author, you are wise not to undertake these negotiations without assistance. Someone familiar with publishing contracts and with the standards, practices, and trends in the industry can help you obtain the best possible deal.

The Publishing Contract

The terms and conditions of your agreement with a publishing house are formalized in a contract that is signed by you and an authorized representative of the publisher. The contract establishes the responsibilities and expectations of both parties. What does it include? The specific details can vary greatly from publisher to publisher and from book to book, but your contract is likely to have clauses that cover the following areas:

> *Rights being acquired.* Writers speak of publishers buying their books, but that's misleading. The publisher is actually licensing the right to produce and distribute the work in certain formats and circumstances; other rights to the work remain yours. Your contract specifies which rights are whose to deal with. Typically, at a minimum, a book contract gives the publisher the right to issue a hardback or paperback edition (sometimes both) in a given language and distribute it in specified countries.
>
> Lately, the issue of electronic rights has been much discussed in the publishing industry. Because electronic rights are so potentially lucrative, publishers increasingly are trying to acquire these rights, using terminology in their contracts such as "all electronic media that now exist or will be invented in the future." You and your agent should negotiate to obtain clauses in your contract that work to your advantage.
>
> Rights pertaining to film versions of the book and foreign editions are also among those that may be negotiated. The contract may use the term "subsidiary rights." This refers to any production of the work other than its first publication in book form. Subsidiary rights could, for example, be sold to a magazine or newspaper to reprint a chapter of the book. This reprinting often generates further interest in the book.

> *Copyright.* Generally for a work of fiction, the author retains copyright and the publisher agrees to imprint the legally required copyright notice to that effect in each copy of the book.

> *Content, preparation, and delivery of the manuscript.* These clauses indicate when the publisher expects to receive the completed manuscript for the book, describe what happens if the manuscript turns out be unacceptable, and provide for editing and revisions.

> *Financial terms.* Authors are usually paid a royalty, a specified percentage of the price of each book sold. An author may also receive a payment (or series of payments) called an "advance on royalties." These are payments that an author receives before

From the Detective's Notebook 11
Advice from the Editors

What Editors Look for in a Mystery

What commands an editor's attention? How do you make your mystery stand out from the competition? In my interviews with editors, they cited five qualities that are shared by manuscripts that excite them:

Superb Writing

First and foremost, editors want a well-told story. If your book keeps them turning the pages, it's three-quarters of the way to being sold. Of course, it goes without saying that to impress an editor, your style should be strong, your use of language appealing and accurate, and your grammar impeccable.

Strong Characters

"A wonderful protagonist," as one editor puts it, is the best way to distinguish yourself in a crowded field. Editors are looking for three-dimensional characters who come across as real people; individuals who, as one editor describes it, "have texture in their lives." Editors respond to characters with whom they enjoy spending time. (Book time, that is. Many of us savor reading about people whom we might not care to encounter at night on a dark street.)

"I will put up with a less than wonderful mystery plot for a great character," another editor notes. "Relationships interest me; how people solve problems interests me."

A Vivid Regional Setting

Like many readers, editors are armchair travelers, and they applaud the mystery's development into a form of regional literature. They look to books to transport them beyond the bounds of their homes or offices into a new environment, rendered in vibrant detail. It matters less whether the setting of the book is exotic or familiar, so long as it brings readers squarely on scene inside a specific milieu. What matters, one editor says, is having "characters who are firmly rooted in a place" and a book that conveys a strong sense of the community in which the detective operates.

An Interesting Background

Editors, and presumably readers, like to learn something while they read. They relish getting the inside scoop on an interesting subject or having experiences that push them beyond the patterns

From the Detective's Notebook 11 — Continued

of their day-to-day lives. The novelist Arthur Hailey, although not a mystery writer, was a master of this approach. He turned readers on with behind-the-scenes looks at the inner workings of familiar institutions such as airports *(Airport)* and hotels *(Hotel)*.

This become-an-insider element is one reason why forensic procedurals, with their intriguing close-ups on the science of crime-solving, have become popular. It's also part of the appeal of remote settings and protagonists with offbeat professions.

Examples abound of mystery authors who ably fit this bill. Three that come quickly to mind are —

 Jonathan Gash, whose Lovejoy novels divulge tricks of the antiques trade

 John Dunning, who reveals the world of rare books and their collectors in his Cliff Janeway mysteries

 Penny Warner, whose deaf heroine, Connor Westphal, helps readers better understand persons who are hearing impaired

A Distinctive Voice

None of the editors I spoke with could define precisely what a distinctive voice is, but they claimed to recognize it when they read it. They all cited it as a key element in books that grab them. Check back to chapter 12 for some clues about what they're referring to.

Editors' Advice to First-Timer Writers

Asked to offer their counsel to aspiring writers, this is what the editors I interviewed had to say:

Do Your Own Thing, and Do it Well

Editors want fresh ideas and polished writing. Don't imitate other authors, not even the ones you admire. Hone your work; make sure the writing is as good as it possibly can be.

One editor quoted a remark made by the 18th-century British critic and essayist Samuel Johnson to a fellow writer: "Sir, your book is both good and original. Unfortunately, the part that is good is not original, and the part that is original is not good." Make sure your manuscript is both good and original.

Do Your Homework

Earlier in this book, I discussed the advice to write what you know or be prepared to find out what you need to know. This means doing research to be able to present your characters, your setting,

From the Detective's Notebook 10 — Continued

Do Your Homework

Earlier in this book, I discussed the advice to write what you know or be prepared to find out what you need to know. This means doing research to be able to present your characters, your setting, your background, and the events of your plot with authority and confidence. One editor says about the books she chooses to publish: "Every element feels right. They distinguish themselves by their utter authenticity."

Write Something with Series Potential

Editors like series; fans like series. If your novel could launch a series, it will be easier to sell to a publisher. Once readers discover a series they enjoy, they seek out the subsequent books by that author. With each new volume, additional fans discover the series and the author's audience builds. This pays off for everyone — the publisher earns profits, the fans have greater reading pleasure, and the writer enjoys both financial and artistic rewards.

Get an Agent

On this subject, the editors' voices rise in a chorus: "Get an agent." "Get a good agent who knows mysteries."

While editors may read manuscripts that are submitted directly by their authors, most admitted to paying a little more attention, and responding a little more quickly, to a manuscript from an agent, especially an agent they know and respect.

Get to Know Other Writers and People in the Field

Make your professional network as large as possible. Join organizations such as Mystery Writers of America, Crime Writers of Canada, and Sisters in Crime. (See Appendix A for contact information about these organizations.) If you are close to a local chapter, take part in its activities. Attend mystery conferences and make contacts. (However, a conference is not a time to thrust your manuscript on anyone.)

the book has been published. When your book is published, a certain number of copies must be sold before you earn out the advance, in other words, before the amount you are due, based on your percopy percentage, adds up to the amount you have already been paid. Once this advance has been paid out, you will then be paid royalties based on additional books sold.

The contract specifies the amount of the advance, the royalty percentage, and the schedule of royalty payments. At regular intervals, typically every six months, the publisher sends a royalty statement indicating the number of books sold and the money you've earned during that period. If you are owed a payment, a check will be enclosed.

☞ *Warranties and permissions.* In signing the contract, you are certifying that the material is your original work, that no one else has any legal claim to it, and that you have not entered into any prior agreements that would affect the publisher's rights under the contract. If you have included in your mystery any quotations from a copyrighted source — a song lyric or a poem, perhaps — you must obtain written permission from the copyright owner and provide it to the publisher.

☞ *Author's copies.* Usually, the publisher agrees to provide the author with a certain number of free copies of the published book. Often, the publisher also will sell you additional copies for your personal use at a discounted price.

☞ *Out of print.* The contract specifies what will happen should your book go out of print, which occurs when the publisher decides to discontinue publication and sale of the book. Frequently, the author is offered the opportunity to buy at a discount any remaining copies.

☞ *Right of first refusal on next manuscript.* Sometimes the contract includes a clause that gives the publisher the right to see and make a decision on whether it would like to publish your next manuscript before you submit it to other publishers.

A word of advice: Read the contract carefully before signing it. Overcome your natural resistance to wading through pages and pages of tiny print and legal language. Review its terms line by line with your agent and have your lawyer (if you have one) read it as well. Your contract is a legal document and you will be bound by it, so make sure you can live with the terms and conditions. Neophyte authors, eager but naive, sometimes sign away rights they later regret losing.

A publisher's contract is written with the publishing house's best interests in mind, not the author's. One of your agent's jobs is to know the potential problem areas, negotiate the terms of the contract, and push to have detrimental clauses rephrased to your better advantage.

The Editor's Role, Part 2: Producing the Book

Once the publishing contract has been signed, the editor's work as production manager begins. The process of producing a book from a manuscript is very complicated. You can expect to hear from the editor or an editorial assistant at certain key points in the process.

Revisions

Most likely, the editor will suggest you write revisions to improve the manuscript. Accept these suggestions gracefully and gratefully. The editor isn't out to ruin your book. His or her goal is the same as yours: to market a mystery that is strong, powerful, and irresistible to mystery fans. You needn't go along with all the suggestions, but consider each one carefully: What problem is it intended to address? On reflection, you may agree with the proposed change, or you may come up with an even better solution.

Copy Editing

Once the editor has reviewed and approved the revised manuscript, the editor sends it to a copy editor, often a freelancer who works with the publishing house on a book-by-book basis. The qualifications for the job include a keen understanding of the correct structure and use of language, a fondness for delving in reference books, a memory that can retain the most minute points of a story, and a nit-picking attention to detail. These are the copy editor's tasks:

 Fix mistakes in grammar, punctuation, and spelling.

 Make sure the facts are right.

☞ Catch inconsistencies. For example, in *A Relative Stranger,* a jeweled ring plays a part in the story. In two early chapters, I described the ring as having an emerald set off-center, with three small diamonds to the side. One hundred pages later, I transformed it to an off-center diamond accompanied by three small emeralds. It's easy to lose track of such details over the long weeks and months you spend writing a book. The copy editor makes sure that in the published book, you haven't switched your diamonds and emeralds, or turned the blond suspect on page 63 into a brunette on page 217, or had your detective go to bed on Saturday night and wake up Monday morning. (See chapter 7 for tips on how to avoid such problems in the first place.)

☞ Make sure the manuscript conforms to house style, that is, to the publisher's standards, preferences, and general rules regarding punctuation, spelling, capitalization, abbreviations, word usage, and similar issues. An example is the question of numbers: Are they presented as numerals or written out as words? Or does the publisher favor British or American spelling?

☞ Mark the text with instructions to the typesetter.

Once the manuscript has been copy edited, your editor will send it back to you. Your beautiful manuscript is no longer pristine. It has scribbles all over it, showing where corrections have been made. Yellow sticky notes will flutter from the pages, indicating points where the copy editor caught a factual error, noted an inconsistency, or has a question or suggestion. Your job is to review the manuscript, make sure you agree with changes, and address the issues that have been raised. This is your last opportunity to have any second thoughts: to choose a more cogent word, to clarify a passage that, when reading it for the first time in months, sounds awkward or murky.

It is in your best interest to give the copy editor as little work as possible. Make your original manuscript as close to perfect as you can. Most copy editors are conscientious and hard-working, and their goal is to bring out the best in your manuscript. A few are overzealous about rules of grammar and style; they might try, for instance, to force proper diction on characters whose dialogue would naturally be ungrammatical, casual, or error-prone. Occasionally, you encounter one who is a frustrated author and seems to be trying to write his or her own book on top of yours. Remember, no matter how authoritative the copy editor may seem, it is your book. As the author, you are entitled to make any final decision.

Galleys or Page Proofs

The next time you see the book-in-progress is when the galleys, which are also called "page proofs," arrive at your door. At last your novel is beginning to resemble a real book. The galleys are photocopies of the pages that have been set into type, looking just as they will in the printed volume. Back at the publishing house, the copy-edited manuscript, with your corrections and changes, was sent to a typesetter or designer, who designed the book, deciding on the typeface and any graphic elements.

Your assignment at this stage is to proofread the pages carefully. This is your final chance to catch errors. This task will be done at the publishing house as well. With more than one pair of eyes doing the hunting, it's more likely that any problems will be found and corrected.

Scan the pages to make sure no typographical glitches have snuck in, no glaring mistakes have been overlooked. A good way to do this: Take a ruler and slide it down the page line by line, checking each one as you go. This method slows you down enough that you'll pay attention and notice any problems. If you try to read it like a book, straight through, your eyes will fool you. Because you already know what is supposed to be on the page, that's exactly what you'll see.

It's too late at this point to reconsider the killer's motivation or decide that the big confrontation should take place in Quebec instead of Calgary. Major changes now are very expensive and will almost certainly threaten the publishing schedule for your book.

The Book's Cover

Once the book's cover has been designed, the editor sends you a copy. You won't like it; that's almost guaranteed. I read a statistic somewhere that 95 percent of mystery writers are not happy with the covers of their books.

In part that's because the cover almost always comes as a shock. This is your first chance to see how someone else might visualize your story, and an outsider's mental picture almost never coincides with your own.

Sometimes it's not a matter of a divergent vision; the cover art is simply wrong. For example, on one mystery where significant events occurred in a large stone barn, the artwork instead showed a snug red wooden structure straight from a child's storybook. Covers of a paperback series starring a detective from an eastern Canadian First Nations tribe were decorated with totem poles from the Pacific Northwest, an entirely different culture.

If something similar happens to the cover of your book, it might help to remember that the purpose of the cover is not to illustrate the story but serve as a billboard to grab a bookstore customer's attention. A well-designed cover catches the eye. The book's title and the author's name are easy to read. The colors and graphics accurately reflect the mood and style of the mystery. A blurb or quote on either the front or back cover sells potential buyers on the book's merit.

While a prominent author might negotiate the right to approve the book cover, most book contracts don't include such a provision. But if you have real concerns, bring them to your editor's attention.

The purpose of the cover is to serve as a billboard to grab a bookstore customer's attention.

Publication Day

One exciting day — several months or even a year after you signed the contract — your doorbell rings. A courier delivers a package. You open the box and find . . . books. Real books. The first, fresh, hot-off-the-press copies of your mystery. Your author's copies have arrived from the publisher.

Call your friends, pop the champagne cork, and celebrate.

The Publisher's Role: Distributing and Marketing the Book

The campaign to place your novel in the hands of eager mystery readers begins at the acquisitions meeting and continues through that long period of anticipation between the signing of the contract and publication day. Once you receive your copies, you'll also find your book on the shelves of your favorite bookstore.

The publishing house includes your novel in its catalogue. Most publishing houses issue catalogues twice a year; spring and fall are the typical publishing seasons. A team of marketing representatives visits bookstores to generate excitement about the upcoming books and persuade the store managers and buyers to stock them.

Meanwhile the publicist is hard at work, mapping out a marketing strategy for your book. Shortly after you sign the contract, the publicist may send you a questionnaire asking you to describe yourself and your novel and to provide the names of contacts you may have among journalists, booksellers, and others who could help bring your mystery to the attention of readers.

The publicist sends review copies to the publications he or she determines are most likely to review your book: the major publishing trade magazines, such as *Publishers Weekly, Quill and Quire, Booklist,* and *Library Journal;* newspapers in your home region and the region where the mystery is set; and publications that focus on mysteries. If your book would be of interest to any groups with special interests, review copies might go to publications for those audiences.

If review copies are sent out well in advance of the official publication day, they usually take the form of bound galleys, the page proofs assembled into a paper binding. Sometimes the packaging includes the cover art; more often it displays only the title and author's name.

If you've been hoping for book tours and TV appearances, such enticingly glamorous occasions will most likely remain a dream. With limited budgets for promotion, publishers don't usually give first-time mystery authors the biggest push. Keep writing, and these opportunities may await you in the future.

The Bookstore's Role: Selling the Book

The bookstore is the place where your book and its readers meet. It's a thrill to go into your local bookstore and spot your novel on the shelf, tucked in among those of your favorite mystery authors. While you're there, introduce yourself to the bookstore's proprietor. Offer to sign copies of your book.

Booksellers can be a new author's best supporters and allies.

Booksellers, especially those in independent and mystery bookstores, can be a new author's best supporters and allies. If they think highly of your book, they may make a point of recommending it to customers and mentioning it in their newsletters. This process of hand-selling — putting the book directly in customers' hands — has helped launch many first-time authors.

The Writer's Role: Promoting Your Current Book and Writing the Next

You'd think that writing a marvelous book would be enough. But a fact of publishing life is that you need to get out there and promote yourself and your book. While you're waiting impatiently for your mystery to come out, a productive way to spend the time is to develop a marketing strategy of your own.

It's easiest to focus your attention locally, at least at first. Work on building your sales and your reputation in your home territory, and in your protagonist's home territory (the place where your book is set) if that's a different place than where you live. Readers and booksellers enjoy books with a hometown connection, and publishers pay attention to regional sales figures. The following are a few of the things you can do:

- *Send announcements.* Design an attractive card or flyer and mail it out to local bookstores, mystery bookstores, your family, your friends, your dentist, your college alumni association, and anyone else you can think of.

- *Set up bookstore events.* Arrange with local bookstores to do readings from your work. If another mystery writer in your area has a book being published around the same time as yours, see if he or she is willing to do bookstore appearances in tandem. Two writers often pull a larger audience than one, and if no one shows up, you'll each have one friendly person to talk to.

- *Participate in mystery conferences.* Just as these events can fire you with enthusiasm while you're writing your mystery, they give you opportunities to increase your visibility and make valuable contacts with other writers, booksellers, and, best of all, fans. It's a great thrill to meet a stranger who says, "What a great book!" and realize that she's talking about the one you wrote.

- ☞ *Take advantage of mystery organizations.* The networking and resources offered by these groups is immensely helpful. Other mystery writers have walked this road before. You can benefit from their experience.

- ☞ *Keep the publicist at your publisher's office informed.* Let the publicist know about the promotional activities you undertake, and send him or her copies of any materials you produce. If you coordinate your efforts, you can work as a team for the best results.

- ☞ *Start writing your next book.* This is very important. A mystery-writing career is not built on a single book. You want to be ready when your agent, your publisher, and your fans follow "What a great book!" with, "Where is the next one?"

An even more significant reason to keep writing is this: As exciting as publication is, most writers find the satisfaction of the writing itself is even greater.

14
Presenting Your Work to Agents and Editors

Now that you have crafted a compelling story, now that you have honed it and polished it as best you possibly can, and now that you understand, to some extent, the publishing process, you're ready to take the next big step: submitting your manuscript for publication.

This can be a daunting prospect. It's not easy to send your creation, your precious child, into the big wide world to seek its fortune. After all, you have put a lot of yourself into this mystery — your hopes, dreams, fears, and deepest thoughts.

The best approach to take is to treat the process the way you would a job search (after all, if you're like many mystery writers, your ultimate goal is a career switch: to quit your day job and write full time).

Remember your first job interview? The nervous flutter in your stomach, the sweaty palms? You may experience some of the same sensations when the moment arrives for you to begin approaching agents and editors. The materials you submit to an agent or editor — the query letter, the synopsis, the manuscript itself — are your application, showing off your credentials.

First impressions count. Career counselors report that when prospective employers meet you, they decide within 15 seconds whether you are a candidate they'll consider further. In that flicker of time, they assess:

225

☞ *Appearance.* Are you dressed appropriately for the job?

☞ *Communication skill.* Do you communicate clearly and understand the jargon of the profession? Do you sound as though you know what you're doing?

☞ *Professionalism.* Do you present yourself with confidence, and with respect for yourself and the other person?

A literary agent or editor who receives your submission materials or meets you at a mystery conference makes a similar judgment. The all-important initial assessment comes from the look of your manuscript or query; the way it reads (grammar, spelling, and style); and the way you handle your dealings with other professionals.

> Remember the wise saying: You never get a second chance to make a good first impression.

Your Submission Package

Your first step in approaching an agent or editor is to send a carefully prepared submission package. Think of it as the résumé or portfolio you would show that prospective employer. Your goal is to sell the recipient on the potential of your mystery, to tantalize him or her enough to want to read the entire novel.

Before you begin knocking on doors, you need to have your mystery finished. Established authors can sometimes sell a novel by providing a proposal or a few sample chapters, but an agent or editor will rarely commit to a new writer on that basis alone; both will want to see the entire book as reassurance that you can sustain a well-crafted narrative for 300 pages or more. When your submission materials intrigue and the agent or editor requests the complete manuscript, you want to be ready to fire it off right away.

Your submission package should consist of:

☞ a query or cover letter,

☞ a synopsis, and

☞ the first 50 pages of the manuscript.

Establishing a working relationship with an agent or editor is a two- or three-step process. Some agents and editors prefer the author's initial contact to consist of the query letter alone; others would just as soon receive the whole package. Unless you know the agent or editor's preferences, start with a letter; it's easier and less expensive, especially if you're making multiple submissions. If the agent or editor likes your preliminary material, he or she will ask to see a synopsis and sample pages.

The Query Letter

The query letter is your handshake, the moment when you introduce yourself and your book to the agent or editor. In a single eloquent page, you want to:

(a) *Spark interest.* Write a strong lead paragraph to hook readers of your letter just as you would in your book to hook readers. Make your mystery sound exciting. To get an idea of the approach to take, visit a bookstore's paperback mystery section and read the copy that publishers put on the back covers to lure buyers.

(b) *Sell the story.* Mention anything about the book that is particularly fresh, distinctive, or timely: the detective's special qualities, an unusual setting or background, or a tie-in to events in the news.

(c) *Give the manuscript's vital statistics.* Indicate the number of words it contains, the mystery subgenre it falls into, and the fact that you have the complete manuscript ready to submit.

(d) *Briefly describe yourself and your background if it is relevant.* For example, if your sleuth is a lawyer, refer to your 12 years of experience working as a paralegal, or if your plot concerns the health care system, mention that you're a hospice volunteer.

(e) *List any pertinent writing credits you have.* Present yourself in a positive, upbeat way. Don't apologize if you lack applicable experience or haven't previously been published; don't even mention it. In that case, just leave this paragraph out.

Sample 5 illustrates a typical query letter.

The Synopsis

The synopsis is your manuscript's résumé, its curriculum vitae, its sales brochure. It describes the story and what you've accomplished in telling it.

Sample 5
Query Letter

Dear _____ [name of agent or editor]:

Beautiful, scandalous Deborah Collington has been found murdered in a seedy Tenderloin alley after an arts-benefit ball. Her valuable diamond-and-emerald necklace is missing.

The case comes to private investigator Jess Randolph. When the father who abandoned her as a child turns out to be the prime suspect, she's faced with more than a homicide case; she must solve the mystery of her own past.

Jess's search to find the truth about the murder — and her family's secrets — takes her into a world of art galleries, theaters, and exotic gems. And before long, she finds herself in a conflict that threatens her career and, ultimately, her life.

An artist as well as an investigator, Jess finds no contradiction in her two professions. Both are ways to search for truth. Jess lives and paints in San Francisco's colorful Haight-Ashbury district and works for the small (three people and one dog) detective firm of Parks and O'Meara. Thirtyish, red-haired, and independent, she is learning what it is like to put her emotions and her life on the line.

The story is told in A Relative Stranger, an 85,000-word mystery novel in the tradition of Marcia Muller and Sue Grafton. In writing this novel, I drew on my background in the arts and my experience in writing scripts for several mystery weekend events. I've also published more than 50 feature articles and reviews.

The manuscript is complete. Can I interest you in reading it? I am happy to send a synopsis and sample chapters if you prefer.

Thank you. I look forward to your response.

Sincerely,

Margaret Lucke

How long is your manuscript?

There are two ways to find out the number of words in your manuscript.

Ask Your Computer

If you're writing on a personal computer, counting words is easy. A simple command in your word-processing program will accomplish the task for you. Look in the help index or program manual for details.

Do a Manual Count

If you don't have a machine that will do it for you and must count the words yourself, here's a simple way to obtain a reasonably accurate total:

(a) Choose three full pages (not partial pages like those at the beginning or end of chapters).

(b) Count all the words on each page, including short words and articles such as "and," "a," or "the."

(c) Add the totals of the three pages together, then divide by three to obtain the average number of words per page.

(d) Multiply that average by the number of pages in your manuscript, and you have a good approximation of the total number of words in your manuscript.

Some authors maintain that a synopsis is harder to write than a novel. It's best to tackle this task after your book is complete. Until you've written the book, you can't know exactly what the story is; novels have a fascinating and sometimes frustrating way of reinventing themselves a number of times as they are being written.

In a synopsis, you retell the story, this time in just a few pages. Some agents and editors, as Linda Mead indicates in From the Detective's Notebook 13 at the end of this chapter, suggest that you keep your synopsis to one single-spaced page. Others give you more latitude on length, but five to ten pages would be tops. If you contact the publishing house or agency in advance for the submission guidelines, it will likely indicate its preference.

Otherwise, the choice is yours; you may even want to prepare two versions. The advantage of a one-pager is that its brevity encourages the recipient to read it. With a longer synopsis, on the other hand, it may be easier to do your mystery justice.

The synopsis establishes the who-what-when-where-why of your mystery, summarizes the plot, and clarifies the main issues dealt with in the story. In introducing your detective, provide enough information that readers can sense her as an individual: who she is, why this case makes a difference to her, and what distinguishes her from other mystery sleuths.

Go ahead and give away the ending. The synopsis should reveal the hidden story as well as the surface story. That way, the agent or editor can be certain you have brought the events to a logical and satisfying conclusion. Don't abruptly halt the narrative to announce: "If you want to find out what happened, read the manuscript." Whatever interest you have generated will just as abruptly evaporate.

> The synopsis establishes the who-what-when-where-why of your mystery, summarizes the plot, and clarifies the main issues dealt with in the story.

Sample Chapters

To accompany your synopsis, send the chapters that constitute approximately the first 50 pages of the manuscript; if chapter 3 ends on page 46 or page 52, stop there. Put the pages into proper manuscript form, described in the next section, and make sure they are as compelling, polished, and well crafted as you can make them.

Making a Good Impression

I once heard an editor tell a tale about addressing participants of a workshop at a writers' conference. The conference brochure had listed this editor's topic as "What Editors Look for in a Manuscript," and the room was packed with eager aspiring writers. Yet, as he spoke, discussing the importance of strong characters and well-constructed plots, the audience members seemed restless and inattentive. Finally, a woman toward the back of the room raised her hand. "Excuse me," she said, "but you're not addressing the advertised topic. Tell us, what do editors want in a manuscript? How wide should we make the margins?" The question was like a jolt of electricity in the room. Everyone sat up straight, ready and eager to take notes.

From the Detective's Notebook 12
Writing a Selling Synopsis

Penny Warner, the award-winning author of *Dead Body Language, Sign of Foul Play*, and other mysteries, offers these hints on writing a synopsis to students in the mystery-writing classes she teaches:

1. A synopsis (sometimes called an outline) is a heavily condensed narrative of your book's plot. The focus is on showing the Big Picture.

2. Emphasize the plot rather than the theme, settings, or characters. These other elements can be revealed through your telling of the plot.

3. Introduce the characters as they appear in the book, with colorful entrances, brief lines of dialogue, or anecdotes. Avoid simply listing the character's traits. If you like, you may include a cast of characters with one-line descriptions.

4. Show the events of the story as they occur, moment by moment. Use examples, anecdotes, and action to build and sustain interest.

5. Make the beginning and ending read like the beginning and ending of a story. In other words, hook readers at the start by jumping into the action. Then, finish by bringing the narrative to a logical and satisfying resolution.

6. Be sure to include the complete ending, revealing the solution to the mystery. Do not leave it out in the hope that the suspense of not knowing will lure the editor or agent into reading the entire manuscript.

7. Write the synopsis in the present tense, using the third-person point of view. Make sure that your writing is clear, concise, and engaging.

8. You may break the synopsis into the book's chapter divisions, or let the story flow from start to finish without chapter breaks.

9. You may begin your synopsis where your sample chapters leave off, or relate the entire plot from the beginning.

10. Your synopsis should be five to ten pages long.

Frankly, adequate margins won't sell your manuscript. For that, you must rely on the power of your writing and the strength of your story. But if your manuscript doesn't show both the book and its author to best advantage — in other words, if you don't make a good first impression — you can "unsell" it before the agent or editor gets to page 2.

Dress Your Manuscript in Proper Business Attire

The publishing equivalent of dressing appropriately for the job interview is to format your manuscript correctly.

If you're accustomed to preparing or reading business letters, memos, or reports, a fiction manuscript may look odd at first. In the corporate world, documents are usually single spaced, with a line skipped between the block-style (unindented) paragraphs. That doesn't apply in publishing, because a manuscript isn't a finished product but a working tool. The standard format for a manuscript is really a matter of common sense. It makes the pages easier to read and provides room for the editor to make corrections, suggest minor revisions, and provide instructions to typesetters and book designers. Follow these guidelines in preparing your sample pages and your final manuscript:

- *Paper.* Use white 8½-by-11-inch, 20-pound paper (the kind of paper used for photocopiers and laser printers). This standard size and weight is easy to handle. Type or print on one side only.

- *Type color.* Use black ink. Black ink on white paper provides the best contrast, which makes it easy on the eyes.

- *Typeface.* A standard typewriter font like Courier is fine. If you're printing out your manuscript from your computer, choose a basic serif font like Times Roman or New Century Schoolbook. Avoid script styles, like Zapf Chancery or any font that resembles handwriting, and sans serif typefaces like Helvetica; studies have shown that in long passages of text, these types of fonts are difficult to read. (Serifs are the cross strokes at the tops and bottoms of letters. "Sans serif," from the French, means "without serifs.")

- *Line spacing.* Always double space your text. Experiment to see what looks good; with some printers, two-and-a-half spaces between lines is a more comfortable interval. Remember, the idea is to have room for editing notations as well as to provide a comfortable amount of white space on the page.

- *Margins.* Here is the answer to that infamous question from the writers' conference: Leave at least one inch all the way around.

- *Paragraph format.* Indent the first line of each paragraph one-half inch, and don't skip lines between paragraphs.

- *Paragraph alignment.* Align the paragraphs to the left margin, leaving the right margin ragged. With a computer, you have the tempting option to justify the text so that the lines are all the same length and both sides are in perfect, ruler-straight alignment. In theory, this should make your manuscript look more like a printed book. But often, when printed, it creates awkward spacing between letters or words, which can drive readers' eyes crazy. Many publishers request the straight-left, ragged-right alignment in their publishing guidelines.

- *Page numbers.* Number the pages consecutively in the upper right-hand corner. Page numbers are crucial. An experience I had with a friend's mystery manuscript explains why. I was carrying it downstairs from my upstairs office so I could curl up on the living-room sofa for a good read. At the top of the staircase I tripped and dropped it. Pages sailed down the stairs and flew over the banister, scattering every which way. As I gathered them, I discovered the pages were not numbered. I spent my evening reassembling the manuscript as if it were a monster jigsaw puzzle, matching sentence fragments at the top and bottom of the pages until finally I came up with a meaningful sequence. Fortunately, I had read an earlier version of the book, so I had some idea of the orde of the scenes. The friendship survived, but an agent or editor may not be as forgiving as I was.

- *Manuscript identification.* In the upper left-hand corner, on the same line as the page number, put an identifying tag — your last name, a slash, and key words from the title (for example, "Lucke/Writing Mysteries").

- *Chapter openers.* Writers have different preferences for chapter openers. I like to start a new chapter about one-third of the way down the page. I center a head reading "Chapter ___" (inserting the appropriate number), then skip a line or two and begin typing the text. The result is neat, professional-looking, and easy to read.

- *Title page.* Include a title page with your name and contact information (address, telephone number, fax number, e-mail address) in the upper left-hand corner, and the word count of the manuscript in the upper right-hand corner. Just above midpage, center the book title and, underneath it, the author's name or pseudonym as you want it to appear on the published book.

- *Assembly.* No paper clips, staples, or binders are needed. Lay the loose pages in a sturdy box, enclose a cover letter and a self-addressed, stamped business envelope for a reply, and send it on its way. (If you want the whole manuscript returned if it's not accepted by the editor, enclose sufficient postage. In the days of typewriters and carbon paper, this was standard; that way a writer could send the same manuscript to the next agent or editor on the list rather than having to retype a new one. Now that word processors and photocopiers have improved writers' lives, it's usually easier to send each recipient a fresh copy.)

- *Short story manuscripts.* You don't need a title page. On page one, put your name and contact information in the upper left-hand corner, the word count in the upper right-hand. Center the title and author's name about halfway down the page, skip a line, and start the story.

Show Off Your Communication Skills

Good communication skills are important to almost any job, but when you write for publication, they're essential: communication is your business. Your whole purpose is to transmit to readers the knowledge, insights, and ideas contained in your story, while at the same time keeping them enthralled and entertained.

Words, grammar, and spelling are the tools of your trade. Professional artists and craftspeople respect their tools, take excellent care of them, and keep them sharp. You want agents and editors to tell on their first cursory glance at a page that you are a pro.

Everyone makes an occasional mistake, but misspellings, grammatical errors, or slipshod language will undercut your credibility. You can't communicate clearly if the words are wrong, the sentences are badly structured, and the language is muddled. If you haven't paid attention to the basics, editors will assume that you also didn't spend much time on plot, characters, or style.

Some writers say: "Hey, it's not my job. I'm the creative person. The editor is supposed to take care of the boring stuff like spelling and grammar. Why should I worry about that?" This attitude reveals a misunderstanding of both the writer's job and the editor's. From the editor's perspective, your job is simple: it's to make his or her job as simple as possible. You do this by writing a fascinating story that will be irresistible to readers and by submitting a manuscript that requires a minimum amount of additional work.

Present Yourself as a Professional

Starting with your first submission of your first mystery, present yourself as a consummate professional. This image results not just from an impeccably prepared manuscript but also from the way you conduct your relationships with agents and editors. Act with confidence, treat yourself and others with respect, and as much as possible, assume the best. Optimism and a willingness to give the benefit of the doubt can serve you well in the publishing world.

Here's a hint for acting like a pro: Don't fax your manuscript to an editor or an agent.

When an agent or editor invites you to send in your manuscript, zip it off by mail or courier or another delivery service. Then be patient. If a couple of months go by without your hearing anything, a polite telephone call is in order. If you don't get the courtesy of a response, consider withdrawing your book and sending it elsewhere. You aren't the only one who should behave like a pro; agents and editors should too.

Once your book is sold, your network of professional relationships expands to include the editor at your publishing house. Although the publishing industry sometimes works in baffling ways, and not always to the writer's advantage, you should assume the editor is on your side unless he or she proves otherwise.

In your dealings with both agents and editors, be businesslike: meet deadlines, honor commitments, alert them to problems, be responsive when they try to get hold of you, respect their time. Expect similar treatment in return. Know what your rights are and stand up for them. And be prepared for frustration and exhilaration during the publishing process; you are sure to encounter both.

From the Detective's Notebook 13
A Literary Agent's Submission Guidelines

Linda Mead, a literary agent in the San Francisco Bay Area, has kindly agreed to let me reproduce the submission guidelines she sends to mystery writers who inquire about becoming her clients.

Cover Letter

 Keep it short — no longer than one to two pages.

 State that the work is fiction, as well as its (sub)category in the genre of mystery (e.g., cozy, police procedural, historical).

Be persuasive without being pedantic.

Is the manuscript complete? What is its length in words or pages?

Title

Make it snappy and seductive. The title offers the first look at the book's focus.

Synopsis

 A good, tight one-page synopsis is important. Start with a few-line opening that reads like advertisement copy or cover copy — something that holds readers' attention.

The synopsis should present the manuscript's focus, purpose, and a summary of the plot.

Include a list of characters with a blurb about each.

Marketing

Be persuasive. How is your mystery different? What is the hook for your book or series? (E.g., Jaqueline Girdner's humorous New Age mysteries; Mary Wings's lesbian PI.) With the plethora of mysteries in the market, does your book fill any voids? Is it a fresh new approach that is both timely and marketable? These are important selling points and may also be addressed in your letter.

Sample Material

 Include a couple of well-written consecutive chapters (approximately the first 50 pages). Since the opening of a mystery is crucial, it should be strong, a grabber. These sample pages introduce the characters and plot, show the author's style of writing and ability to craft a mystery.

From the Detective's Notebook 13 — Continued

Information about the Author

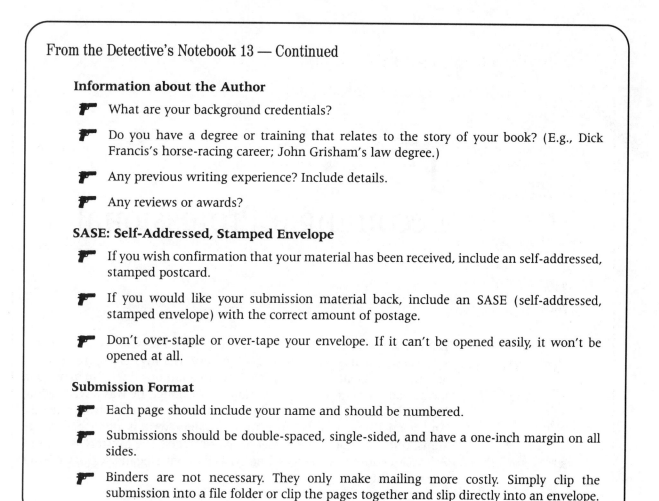

- What are your background credentials?

- Do you have a degree or training that relates to the story of your book? (E.g., Dick Francis's horse-racing career; John Grisham's law degree.)

- Any previous writing experience? Include details.

- Any reviews or awards?

SASE: Self-Addressed, Stamped Envelope

- If you wish confirmation that your material has been received, include an self-addressed, stamped postcard.

- If you would like your submission material back, include an SASE (self-addressed, stamped envelope) with the correct amount of postage.

- Don't over-staple or over-tape your envelope. If it can't be opened easily, it won't be opened at all.

Submission Format

- Each page should include your name and should be numbered.

- Submissions should be double-spaced, single-sided, and have a one-inch margin on all sides.

- Binders are not necessary. They only make mailing more costly. Simply clip the submission into a file folder or clip the pages together and slip directly into an envelope.

15
Becoming a Professional

A professional is usually defined as being someone who is paid for his or her work, which is one worthy goal to have as a mystery writer. Samuel Johnson, the great British essayist, said in a famous line, "No man but a blockhead ever wrote except for money." Although he was a wise fellow, he was wrong in this, for writing offers many other kinds of rewards. And good thing, too, because most mystery writers don't earn huge sums, certainly not at the outset of their careers. The Mystery Writers of America counters Johnson's line with its own slogan: "Crime doesn't pay — enough."

Being a pro in the mystery field is a broader concept. The term denotes someone who understands and appreciates the genre, who is congenial and courteous in dealings with others, and who takes seriously his or her own work and that of fellow writers.

The Business of Mystery Writing

As a mystery writer, you are an entrepreneur. Your writing endeavors constitute a small business, of which you are the sole and very busy employee. You are the chief executive officer, creative director, production manager, head bean counter, chief clerk, and bottle washer. Creative director is the role to concentrate on until you've finished writing your book, but it helps to keep the other responsibilities in mind. You'll accomplish more and do so more easily if you approach your new enterprise in a businesslike way.

Setting Up Shop

It's easier to show up for your appointments with the muse when you meet in supportive surroundings. If at all possible, create an office — tuck a desk, a comfortable work chair, and a good lamp into a corner that you can dedicate to your mysterious efforts. If you must clear a corner of the kitchen table every time you want to write, or have to trek to the public library to find peace and quiet, that's not conducive to producing your best work. The desk, chair, and lamp are your first three equipment essentials. The fourth is some kind of storage system: a file cabinet, stacking desk trays, or even a capacious cardboard box. Writing generates piles of paper in astounding profusion — early drafts, scribbled ideas, magazine articles, newspaper cuttings, research notes. You'll need a way to keep it all tamed.

A computer of your own is ideal, but not absolutely necessary. A couple of writers I know, with 40 books to their credit between them, still pound out their novels on old IBM Selectric typewriters, and a third, equally prolific, writes the entire first draft of each book on yellow legal pads. Still, a computer is a worthwhile tool. It allows you to keep track of multiple drafts and speeds up the revision process. It also connects you to the Internet, which is invaluable not only for research but for keeping you in touch with other mystery writers, helping you become part of a professional community.

Keeping Records

If you pride yourself on being a free-spirited creative artist, the notion of keeping records probably strikes terror in your soul, but being a pro demands it. The records you need are of three types.

Financial records

Okay, it may be a while before you have to put on your financial-manager hat to count all the money you're making. But it's a good idea to set up a notebook, calendar, or spreadsheet on which to record any revenues you might receive as well as all the money you spend in your mystery-writing business. Keeping track of your expenses is a good habit to get into if you're hopeful of someday generating an income, and the records will come in handy at tax time. Types of business expenses worth recording include money spent on things such as:

- Office supplies

- Costs incurred in doing research (long-distance telephone calls, books, the lunch you bought for the firearms expert you consulted)

- Postage for mailing queries and manuscripts

- Registration fees for writers' conferences or classes that contribute to your professional education as a mystery writer

- Subscriptions to publications that relate to your writing career

- Membership dues for mystery writers' organizations

Tax laws are complex and constantly changing, and individual situations vary. So you will need to consult with your financial adviser to determine what you should report to the taxing authorities and what expenses you are legally entitled to claim as deductions. Be sure to keep the receipts for your business expenses as part of your records.

Submission records

Time becomes strangely warped in the publishing business. After you send a query letter or a submission to an agent or editor, the time you spend waiting to receive a reply may seem like aeons. Without a system to keep track, you can grow impatient too soon or else forget the submission altogether. While it's possible to set up something elaborate on the computer, I find that simple works best. For short story submissions, for instance, I set up an index card with the name of the story written at the top. Each time I mail the story out, I make note of the date sent and the destination. When the response arrives, I pull out the card and jot down the date of the return. Low-tech and easy. If I don't receive a response within two months, the blank spot on the card reminds me to contact the publication to which I sent the story and follow up.

You might also keep a submissions calendar. Pick a calendar that has a page for each month and a box for each day. When you send material to an editor or an agent, mark the date block with a couple of key words indicating what you sent and to whom. Then enter that information again on a date about two months later. When the later date arrives, you'll know it's time to make inquiries if you haven't heard anything. You can also mark the date on the calendar when you receive the response.

Color coding the calendar entries can help you keep track at a glance. Choose the coding system you'll find most useful:

- ☞ *By submission and response dates.* Enter information on outgoing material in blue, expected responses in green, and actual responses in red.

- ☞ *By destination.* If you send similar queries to more than one agent or editor, use a different color to track each query.

- ☞ *By title.* If you are prolific enough to be circulating queries or manuscripts for more than one mystery, use a different color to track each work.

Networking records

That expert on poisons someone referred you to — where did you put her name? The agent you met at the conference who liked the premise of your novel — you know his business card must be around someplace. Keep at it, and writing mysteries is sure to expand your circle of professional relationships in wondrous and fascinating ways. It's easiest to set up your contact file — an address book, a Rolodex, a data base on your computer, those handy index cards again — in the early stages when you have just a few names to record. If you wait, the business cards and the torn pieces of paper with telephone numbers written on them will pile up and entering all the data becomes a real project.

An advantage of using your computer to set up your contact file is that you can code and sort the entries according to topic as well as by name. This makes pinning down the poison expert much simpler.

Surviving Rejection

When I first began writing in earnest, I was greatly heartened to read in a biography of F. Scott Fitzgerald that this revered writer collected something like 287 rejection slips before he ever sold a word. If one could be rejected that often and still go on to become an icon of American literature, perhaps there was hope for me yet.

Being rejected is a fact of life in the writing business. What winnows the pros from the wannabes is not that they never are flattened by rejection but that after it happens, they pick themselves up, dust themselves off, and try again.

One rejection slip, quoted by Lawrence Block in one of his *Writer's Digest* columns on fiction writing (but certainly not one that Block, recipient of a Mystery Writers of America Grand Master award, received personally), was less than kind: "I regret that I must return the enclosed shipment of paper as unsatisfactory. Someone has spoiled it by typing gibberish on every single sheet."

Clearly there are hierarchies of rejection, with the one Block cited on the bottom rung. Fortunately, that kind is rare. The most common sort of rejection, the form letter, occupies the next step. Next, and slightly more encouraging, is the form letter embellished with a personal comment, perhaps just a "Thanks" or "Good luck," suggesting someone actually read the manuscript. Ranking above that is the regretful turndown that invites you to submit something else. At the top of the list, there's the personal letter that's so glowing and complimentary you have to read it twice to realize you've been turned down.

There are two things to remember when you receive a rejection letter of whatever sort. The first is this: Don't take it personally. It's hard, when you've put so much of yourself into your book, to recognize that the publishing world has not rejected you, but that one editor on one occasion has declined to purchase one particular manuscript. Moreover, why that editor did so may have nothing to do with the quality of your work; editors pass on excellent books. Some possible reasons yours was one: It didn't suit the editor's personal taste or fit with the publisher's marketing goals. The editor purchased a similar book last week. The editor had a pounding headache, had just received a parking ticket, had had a fight with the boss, and was in the mood to stamp NO on every piece of paper that crossed his or her desk. The editor suffered from a lapse of judgment.

Which brings us to the other thing you should remember: Editors can be wrong. Consider the one who declined John le Carré's early novel *The Spy Who Came in from the Cold* with the words, "You are welcome to le Carré, he hasn't got any future." Or the one who, on rejecting Tony Hillerman's first book, *The Blessing Way*, advised the author to, "Get rid of all that Indian stuff." Publishing annals are filled with tales of books that were rejected multiple times and went on — to the chagrin, one hopes, of the shortsighted editors who turned them down — to become bestsellers and even literary classics.

Your success as a writer is not determined by whether you suffer rejection. You will; it's inevitable, and you will be in excellent company. I know several mystery writers, big names today (though I won't embarrass them by telling you those names), who wrote three, six, as many as eight novels before seeing one published. Almost every author has a failed manuscript or two stuffed at the back of a closet or buried in the backyard.

What successful authors have in common, besides talent, is tenacity. Both qualities are good to have, but if you must pick only one, choose the latter. A writer without talent who persists is far more likely to succeed than a talented writer who gives up.

Celebrating Success

The mystery is solved. Whodunit? You did. You made the commitment to write a mystery. Perhaps you have already begun. The adventure is underway.

Howdunit? By applying to the task all the clues you've discovered in this book and elsewhere about mystery writing: its delights, its demands, and the tricks of the trade.

Whydunit? Because you love a good story well told. Because you relish the challenge of devising a baffling but logical puzzle. Because you enjoy the thrill of creating a fictional world and having characters come to life in your imagination and on the page.

If you persevere, the day will come when you celebrate the publication of your first mystery (and please invite me to the party so I can raise a glass in your honor).

But even if that never happens, you should count your mystery as a success. You will have benefited greatly from writing it. The information you've learned, the insights you've gained, and the friendships you've formed in the world of mystery are worth celebrating. So is the satisfaction that comes from committing yourself to an ambitious project and seeing it through. Published or prepublished, at that point you can consider yourself a pro.

Whoever said that the journey is as important as the destination could well have been talking about mystery writing. Enjoy your journey, and don't forget to reward yourself for the steps you accomplish along the way. I wish you good speed and good fortune.

Appendix A
Information and Resources on Mystery Writing and Publishing

Contact information listed in this appendix is as complete as possible. Some organizations, especially those run by volunteer groups of dedicated mystery writers and fans, may not maintain phone and fax numbers. You can reach these organizations by mail or e-mail or, in some instances, by accessing their Web sites.

Organizations

American Crime Writers League
18645 Farmington Avenue #255
Aloha, OR 97007
E-mail: sharan@hevanet.com
Web site: http://members.aol.com/theACWL

An advocacy organization and information exchange open to professional mystery and crime writers. You are eligible for membership if you have published one full-length work of fiction, three short stories, or three nonfiction crime articles.

Association of Authors' Representatives
10 Astor Place, 3rd Floor
New York, NY 10003
Phone: (212) 353-3709
Web site: http://www.bookwire.com/aar

The principal professional association for literary agents, and a good place to start your search for representation.

Canadian Authors Association
PO Box 419
Campbellford, ON K0L 1L0
Phone: (705) 653-0323
Fax: (705) 653-0593
E-mail: canauth@redden.on.ca
Web site: http://www.canauthors.org

A major organization dedicated to the support and development of Canadian writing. Its slogan is "Writers helping writers." In addition to the national organization, there are 15 branches across Canada. It has an associate membership category for aspiring writers.

Crime Writers' Association
Thistles, Little Addington, Kettering
Northants NN14 4AX, UK
Phone: 44 (0) 01833-650973
E-mail: russell.james@dial.pipex.com
Web site: http://www.twbooks.co.uk/cwa/cwa.html

The British association for professional writers of crime fiction and nonfiction.

Crime Writers of Canada
3007 Kingston Road, PO Box 113
Scarborough, ON M1M 1P1
E-mail: ap113@freenet.toronto.on.ca
Web site: http://www.swifty.com/cwc/org

The national association for professional practitioners of the crime-writing genre in Canada. Has membership categories for published writers, publishing professionals, and prepublished writers and fans.

International Association of Crime Writers/ North America
PO Box 8674
New York, NY 10116
E-mail: mfrisque@aol.com

The North American branch of an international organization; open to published writers of mystery and crime fiction and nonfiction, and to other professionals in the field.

Mystery Readers International
PO Box 8116
Berkeley, CA 94707
E-mail: whodunit@murderonthemenu.net
Web site: http://www.murderonthemenu.com/mystery

For fans, friends, and writers of the mystery genre. Publishes the quarterly *Mystery Readers Journal*.

Mystery Writers of America
17 East 47th Street, 6th Floor
New York, NY 10017
Phone: (212) 888-8171
Fax: (212) 758-8107
E-mail: mwa_org@earthlink.net
Web site: http://www.mysterynet.com/mwa/

One of the oldest and largest mystery writers' organizations. It has an international membership, with membership categories for published mystery writers; editors, booksellers, and writers in other fields; and pre-published writers who can demonstrate (via copies of query letters, rejection slips, verification of enrollment in courses) that they are serious about their work. Ten regional chapters sponsor local activities and events.

Private Eye Writers of America
4342 Forest Deville Drive
St. Louis, MO 63129
E-mail: rrandisi@aol.com

For writers (published and aspiring) of books featuring detectives who sleuth for pay. Contact the membership chair at the address above for membership information.

Sisters in Crime
PO Box 442124
Lawrence, KS 66044-8933
Phone: (785) 842-1325
Fax: (785) 842-1034
E-mail: sistersincrime@juno.com
Web site:http://www.books.com/sinc/

Open to anyone (men and women) interested in advancing the mystery field and women's participation in it. Members include mystery readers, authors, agents, editors, and booksellers. There are local chapters in the United States and Canada, and an Internet chapter. Excellent services and information for writers.

Conferences

This listing includes annual mystery conferences that have been held for several years. Some of them change their locations, organizing committees, and contact information every year. In addition, a number of one-time-only mystery conferences and workshops are held each year. For current information, check with your local mystery bookstore, an organization like Mystery Writers of America or Sisters in Crime, the Clue Lass Web site, or The Deadly Directory. (All but the bookstores are included in these listings.)

Book Passage Mystery Writers' Conference
Book Passage
51 Tamal Vista Boulevard
Corte Madera, CA 94925
Phone (toll free): 1-800-999-7909
Fax: (415) 924-3838
E-mail: messages@bookpassage.com
Web site: http://www.bookpassage.com

Held annually in July, in Corte Madera, California (near San Francisco), this weekend-long conference is sponsored by an independent bookseller and *Writer's Digest* magazine. It features presentations by mystery writers, editors, publishers, police professionals, forensic specialists, and private investigators.

Bouchercon World Mystery Convention

Held annually in October. Location varies. This is the world's largest mystery gathering; now in its fourth decade. For information, consult mystery publications, contact your local mystery bookstore, or check the Clue Lass Web site at http://www.cluelass.com.

The CAA Annual Conference
Canadian Authors Association
PO Box 419
Campbellford, ON K0L 1L0
Phone: (705) 653-0323
Fax: (705) 653-0593
E-mail: canauth@redden.on.ca
Web site: http://www.canauthors.org

Held annually in June. Location varies among sites in Canada. The Canadian Authors Association has been sponsoring its annual conference since the organization was founded in 1921. Presentations, workshops, and readings covering topics of interest to writers of any genre.

Left Coast Crime

Held annually in February or early March. Location varies among cities in the western United States. Emphasis on writers and books from the western United States, though it attracts people from all over the country. For information, consult mystery publications, contact your local mystery bookstore, or check the Clue Lass Web site at http://www.cluelass.com.

Magna cum Murder

E.B. Ball Center
Ball State University
Muncie, IN 47306
Phone: (765) 285-8975
Fax: (765) 285-9566
Web site: http://www.parlorcity.com/secop/murder.html

Held annually in the fall, usually in Muncie, Indiana.

Malice Domestic

PO Box 31137
Bethesda, MD 20824-1137
Fax: (301) 208-1555
E-mail: malice@erols.com
Web site: http://www.erols.com/malice

Held annually in late April or early May, in Washington, DC. Focuses on the cozy or traditional mystery. Generally, a very well-run conference. Enrollment limited; fills up fast.

Mystery Writers of America Events

17 East 47th Street, 6th Floor
New York, NY 10017
Phone: (212) 888-8171
Fax: (212) 888-8107
E-mail: mwa_org@earthlink.net
Web site: http://www.mysterynet.com/mwa/

Varying dates and locations. The national Mystery Writers of America (MWA) and some of its regional chapters sponsor annual conferences and events, a one-day conference, and other events in New York in late April during the week of its annual Edgar Allan Poe Awards dinner. Several of the regional chapters also sponsor conferences for writers and fans:

Edgar Week

Sponsored by the MWA national organization. Held in late April, in New York City. A one-day symposium and other events culminating in the presentation banquet for the Edgar Allan Poe Awards for outstanding mysteries.

Mystery Writers Conference

Held in the fall, in the San Francisco Bay Area. Sponsored by the Northern California chapter.

Of Dark and Stormy Nights

Held in May or June, in Chicago. Writers' conference sponsored by the Midwest chapter.

Sleuth Fest

Held in March, in varying Florida cities. Writers' conference sponsored by the Florida chapter.

No Crime Unpublished

Sisters in Crime, Los Angeles Chapter
PO Box 251646
Los Angeles, CA 90025
Phone/program information: (213) 694-2972
E-mail: sincla@email.com
Web site: http://www.sistersincrimela.com

A one-day conference for published and prepublished mystery writers to "gather, learn, share, and have fun."

Web Sites and Internet Resources

In addition to Web sites included in the listings in other sections, these sites are gateways to a wealth of information. There are many more interesting mystery-related Web sites than the ones listed here, but these link you to them. The Internet is in a constant state of flux, with sites constantly appearing, disappearing, and shifting from one address to another; the addresses listed here are current as of the publication of this book.

Blue Murder

Web site: http://www.bluemurder.com

An electronic mystery magazine with fiction, helpful articles (e.g., a regular column on police procedure), and reviews.

Bookwire

Web site: http://www.bookwire.com

The Internet home of *Publishers Weekly*, *Literary Market Place*, the Association of Authors' Representatives, and other publishing-industry resources.

The Clue Lass Home Page:
A Mystery Lover's Notebook

Web site: http://www.cluelass.com

Under the direction of webmaster Kate Derie, this site is a must-visit for anyone interested in mysteries. Jam-packed with information on new books, awards, events, magazines, organizations, publishers, bookstores, and other resources. Lots of helpful links.

DorothyL

E-mail: listserv@kentvm.kent.edu

A mailing list for mystery lovers, with postings by writers, librarians, booksellers, fans, and generally knowledgeable people. Named in honor of Dorothy L. Sayers, creator of the character Lord Peter Wimsey. To subscribe, send an e-mail message to the e-mail address above. The message should read:

subscribe dorothyl firstname lastname

Substitute your own name (not your e-mail address), and don't include anything else in the message. Leave the subject line blank or insert a quote mark if your Internet service provider won't accept a blank subject line.

A Guide to Classic Mystery and Detection

Web site: http://members.aol.com/mg4273/classics.htm

An educational site, created by Michael E. Grost, that contains reading lists and essays on great mysteries, mainly, although not exclusively, of the pre-1960 era. A good way to explore the history and development of the mystery genre.

Inkspot: The Writer's Resource

Web site: http://www.inkspot.com

A very helpful site for writers of all types, genres, and levels of experience, with information on markets, networking opportunities, and the craft of writing. Produces a free biweekly electronic newsletter called *Inklings*.

Mysterious Home Page

Web site: http://www.webfic.com/mysthome

A comprehensive listing of links that will connect you to a vast array of international mystery resources on the Internet.

MysteryNet.Com: The On-Line Mystery Network

Web site: http://www.mysterynet.com

Mystery news, discussion groups, resource listings, and links, as well as the chance to play detective by solving the daily mini-mystery.

Mystery Pages

Web site: http://www.mysterypages.com

A site shared by three prominent mystery magazines: *Alfred Hitchcock's Mystery Magazine*, *Ellery Queen's Mystery Magazine*, and *Mystery Scene*.

Mystery Writers of America: NorCal Chapter

Web site: http://members.aol.com/mwanorcal/index.html

The site of the northern California chapter of MWA. Has an extensive list of helpfully categorized links to other sites providing information on mysteries, writing in general, and crime and forensics.

Writer's Way

Web site: http://www.angelfire.com/in/dpbimrose/writersway.html

A collection of links to Web sites that provide a variety of information of interest to writers, including sites for agents, publishers, writers' organizations, copyright information, writing how-to's, and more.

Magazines

The Mystery Genre

Alfred Hitchcock's Mystery Magazine
Ellery Queen's Mystery Magazine
c/o Dell Magazines
475 Park Avenue South, 11th Floor
New York, NY 10016
Phone: (212) 698-1313 or (212) 698-1198
Subscriptions: 1-800-333-3311 (toll free in the United States); (303) 678-8747 (elsewhere)
Web site: http://www.mysterypages.com

These mainstays of the mystery magazine genre share an emphasis on short fiction, a digest-size format, a corporate owner, and their contact information. However, they are editorially independent, and each has its own flavor.

Cozy Detective Mystery Magazine
686 Jakes Court
McMinnville, OR 97128
Phone: (503) 435-1212
Fax: (503) 472-4896

A small magazine that specializes in, as you might guess, the cozy, or traditional, detective fiction.

The Drood Review of Mystery
PO Box 50267
Kalamazoo, MI 49005
E-mail: jimhuang@ameritech.net

Reviews, previews, and commentary covering all types of mystery fiction.

Gila Queen's Guide to Markets
PO Box 97
Newton, NJ 07860
Phone: (973) 579-1537
Fax: (973) 579-6441
E-mail: GilaQueen@aol.com
Web site: http://members.xoom.com/GilaQueen

A quirky, informal, desktop-published magazine in which editor Kathryn Ptacek provides news, updates, and writers' guidelines for fiction and nonfiction markets. Approximately one issue each year is devoted to mystery and suspense.

Mary Higgins Clark Mystery Magazine
Gruner and Jahr USA Publishing
375 Lexington Avenue, 8th Floor
New York, NY 10017-5514
Phone: (212) 499-2000
Fax: (212) 499-1987

A bright, slick magazine with lots of short mystery stories and some informative tidbits about the mystery field.

Mayhem, the Mystery and Suspense Magazine
c/o MSI, PO Box 827
Clifton Park, NY 12065
Phone: (518) 664-3478
E-mail: mayhem@mediasi.com
Web site:http://www.mediasi.com/chantingmonks/mayhem/

A magazine that publishes interviews and features focusing on mystery authors and their work, reviews of books and Web sites, and fiction.

Murderous Intent Mystery Magazine
Madison Publishing Company
PO Box 5947
Vancouver, WA 98668-5947
Phone: (360) 695-9004
Fax: (360) 693-3354
E-mail: madison@teleport.com
Web site: http://www.teleport.com/~madison

A quarterly magazine with fiction and nonfiction "targeted to readers and writers of mystery/suspense who want not only to be entertained but challenged."

Mystery Buff Magazine
304 Lover's Lane
Townsend, TN 37882
Phone: (973) 579-1537
Fax: (973) 579-6441
E-mail: editor@mysterybuff.com
Web site: http://www.mysterybuff.com

Mystery news, reviews, interviews, short stories — "anything designed to entertain fans of mystery fiction."

Mystery News
Black Raven Press
262 Hawthorne Village Common, Suite 152
Vernon Hills, IL 60061

A periodical in newspaper format with mystery news, reviews, previews, and interviews.

Mystery Readers Journal
PO Box 8116
Berkeley, CA 94707
E-mail: whodunit@murderonthemenu.net
Web site: http://www.murderonthemenu.com/mystery

A quarterly journal with articles themed to a particular topic (e.g., literary mysteries, historical mysteries, culinary mysteries) and information about happenings in the mystery world.

The Mystery Review
PO Box 233
Colborne, ON K0K 1S0
Phone: (613) 475-4440
Fax: (613) 475-3400
or
PO Box 488
Wellesley Island, NY 13640-0488
E-mail: mystrev@connect.reach.net
Web site: http://www.inline-online.com/mystery/

A Canadian publication that covers mysteries ranging "from domestic malice to the mean streets." Articles, interviews, reviews, and puzzles.

Mystery Scene
PO Box 669
Cedar Rapids, IA 52406-0669
Phone: (319) 363-7850
Web site: http://www.mysterypages.com/MysSc.html

The "news magazine" of the mystery field. Information on resources, publishers, trends; interviews with authors; reviews and announcements of upcoming books; and lively discussions.

New Mystery
The Flatiron Building
175 Fifth Avenue, Suite 2001
New York, NY 10010-7703
Phone: (212) 353-1582
Fax (subscriptions): (212) 353-3495
E-mail: newmyste@erols.com
Web site: http://www.newmystery.com

A magazine that publishes what it bills as "the world's best mystery, crime, and suspense stories."

Over My Dead Body! The Mystery Magazine
PO Box 1778
Auburn, WA 98071-1778
E-mail: OMDB@aol.com
Web site: http://www.ruidomain.com/omdb/index2.htm

Fiction and nonfiction about the mystery genre.

Sleuthhound
Whispering Willows Ltd.
PO Box 890294
Oklahoma City, OK 73189-0294
Phone: (405) 239-2531
Fax: (405) 232-3848
E-mail: wwillows@telepath.com
Web site:http://members.tripod.com/~wwmm/main.html

A mystery-focused magazine for writers that includes interviews, tips on writing, and short stories.

The Strand Magazine
PO Box 1418
Birmingham, MI 48012-1418
Phone (toll free): 1-800-300-6652
Fax: (248) 874-1046
E-mail: strandmag@worldnet.att.net

A revival of *The Strand,* the magazine that published the first Sherlock Holmes book and featured the work of many other British mystery greats until 1950. The new version is striving "to uphold the tradition of exceptional mystery fiction for which *The Strand* was known."

Writing and Publishing

ByLine
PO Box 130596
Edmond, OK 73013-0001
Phone: (405) 348-5591
E-mail: bylinemp@aol.com
Web site: http://bylinemag.com

This publication, which features fiction as well as nonfiction concerned with writing and selling, describes itself as "a magazine aimed toward helping writers succeed."

Publishers Weekly
245 West 17th Street
New York, NY 10011
Phone (subscriptions): 1-800-278-2991 (toll free in the United States); (310) 978-6916 (elsewhere)
Fax: (310) 978-6901
Web site: http://www.bookwire.com/pw/pw.html

The news magazine of the publishing industry. Publishes a lead feature on mystery publishing trends once or twice a year. In general, a great way to learn what's going on in the publishing industry (forewarned is forearmed). Not cheap — read it in a library or share a subscription with friends.

Quill and Quire
70 The Esplanade
Toronto, ON M5E 1R2
Phone: (416) 360-0044
Fax: (416) 360-8745

The monthly journal of the Canadian book trade.

The Writer
120 Boylston Street
Boston, MA 02116-4615
Phone: (617) 423-3157
Fax: (617) 423-2168
E-mail: writer@user1.channel1.com
Web site: http://www.channel1.com/users/writer/

Articles to help writers improve their craft, along with helpful market information.

Writer's Digest
1507 Dana Avenue
Cincinnati, OH 45207
Phone (subscriptions) (toll free): 1-800-333-0133

How-to articles, practical tips, and market listings for writers whose goal is to get published.

Writers' Journal
PO Box 394
Perham, MN 56573-0394
Phone: (218) 346-7921
Fax: (218) 346-7924
E-mail: writersjournal@wadena.ne
Web site: http://www.sowashco.com/writersjournal/

How-to articles, practical tips, and market listings.

Books

This is a selected reading list. Many helpful books are available on these and related subjects. The ones listed here are a good place to start.

The Mystery Genre

Derie, Kate, ed. *The Deadly Directory.* Berkeley, CA: Deadly Serious Press, annual.

A comprehensive international listing of businesses, publications, and organizations related to mystery, detective, and crime fiction. An excellent resource. Available from:

Deadly Serious Press
868 Arlington Avenue
Berkeley, CA 94707
E-mail: cluelass@cluelass.com
Web site: http://www.deadlyserious.com

Gorman, Ed, et al, eds. *The Fine Art of Murder: The Mystery Reader's Indispensable Companion.* New York: Carroll and Graf Publishers, 1993.

With chapters by many noted authors, this book gives a definitive look at the art, craft, and literary history of the mystery.

Heising, Willetta L. *Detecting Men.* Dearborn, MI: Purple Moon Press, 1998.

Heising, Willetta L. *Detecting Women.* Dearborn, MI: Purple Moon Press, 1994.

Heising, Willetta L. *Detecting Women 2.* Dearborn, MI: Purple Moon Press, 1995.

These books are subtitled "Reader's guide and checklist for mystery series written by men/women."

Swanson, Jean, and Dean James. *Killer Books: A Reader's Guide to Exploring the Popular World of Mystery and Suspense.* New York: Berkley Publishing Group, 1998.

A very readable guide to the contemporary mystery genre.

Wynn, Dylis. *Murderess Ink: The Better Half of the Mystery.* New York: Workman Publishing, 1979.

Wynn, Dylis. *Murder Ink: The Mystery Reader's Companion.* New York: Workman Publishing, 1977.

Delightful compendia of anecdotes, lists, tidbits, and trivia pertaining to mystery literature, writers, and perpetrators of crime.

Writing and Publishing

Appelbaum, Judith. *How to Get Happily Published.* 5th ed. New York: HarperCollins, 1998.

This book has become a classic, showing writers in a clear and encouraging style how the publishing industry operates, what their publishing options are, and how to increase their chances of success.

Bates, Jem. *Canadian Writer's Market.* Toronto: McClelland and Stewart, 1998.

A guidebook to Canadian publishing with market listings to help writers find editors receptive to their work.

Block, Lawrence. *Spider, Spin Me a Web.* New York: William Morrow, 1996.

Block, Lawrence. *Telling Lies for Fun and Profit.* New York: William Morrow, 1994.

These two books are collections of the columns on fiction writing that Block wrote for many years for *Writer's Digest* magazine. A preeminent mystery writer, Block offers advice that is practical, insightful, and fun to read.

Borcherding, David, ed. *Mystery Writer's Sourcebook: Where to Sell Your Manuscripts.* 2nd ed. Cincinnati: Writer's Digest Books, 1995.

A look at the mysterious marketplace, including listings of book and short story publishers, agents, and mystery bookstores.

Cameron, Julia. *The Artist's Way: A Spiritual Path to Higher Creativity.* New York: Jeremy P. Tarcher Books, 1992.

Cameron, Julia. *The Right to Write: An Invitation and Initiation into the Writing Life.* New York: Putnam Publishing Group, 1999.

Two inspirational and encouraging books with practical instruction for discovering and expressing your creativity and keeping the commitment you made to yourself to write.

Conrad, Barnaby. *The Complete Guide to Writing Fiction.* Cincinnati: Writer's Digest Books, 1990.

Drawing on talks and workshops given at the well-known Santa Barbara Writer's Conference over a period of 25 years, this book offers excellent tips and advice from a solid cast of popular authors.

Egri, Lajos. *The Art of Dramatic Writing.* New York: Simon and Schuster, 1977.

A classic on writing technique, as helpful now as when it was published more than 50 years ago. To Egri, dramatic writing means plays, but his advice applies to any writer who wants to tell a compelling tale.

Field, Syd, ed. *Screenplay: The Foundations of Screenwriting.* New York: Dell Publishing, 1979 (expanded edition, 1984).

Aimed at screenwriters, but its information is helpful to novelists too, especially its discussion of plotting and the three-act structure.

Henderson, Bill. *Pushcart's Complete Rotten Review and Rejections.* New York: W.W. Norton and Company, 1998.

An amusing collection of rejection letters and negative reviews received by writers who went on to become (or, in some cases, who already were) well known and highly regarded. A heartening reminder that editors and reviewers are not always wise and that there is life after rejection.

Lamott, Anne. *Bird by Bird: Some Instructions on Writing and Life.* New York: Doubleday, 1995.

Excellent advice and encouragement for writers from an author who is witty, gentle, and wise.

Lucke, Margaret. *Schaum's Quick Guide to Writing Great Short Stories.* New York: McGraw-Hill, 1999.

A concise guide to the essentials of writing captivating, memorable short stories, from finding ideas to developing your narrative voice.

Mettee, Stephen Blake. *The Portable Writer's Conference: Your Guide to Getting and Staying Published.* Fresno, CA: Quill Driver Books, 1997.

A writers' conference between covers, with more than 45 editors, authors, and agents providing insight on the writing craft and the business of getting published.

Tannen, Deborah. *That's Not What I Meant! How Conversational Style Makes or Breaks Your Relations With Others.* New York: Ballantine Books, 1992.

Tannen, Deborah. *You Just Don't Understand: Men and Women in Conversation.* New York: Ballantine Books, 1991.

A noted linguist explores the way in which differences in region, ethnicity, class, culture, and gender affect people's conversational styles, and the misunderstandings that can result. Though not written specifically for writers, these books provide help with dialogue, characterization, and conflict.

Vogler, Christopher. *The Writer's Journey: Mythic Structure for Writers*. 2nd ed. Studio City, CA: Michael Wiese Productions, 1998.

An exploration of what constitutes a story, why stories move us, and how to tell one powerfully. Vogler writes from a screenwriter's perspective but his insights have equal value to writers of short stories and novels.

Writer's Digest Books. *Novel and Short Story Writers Market*. Cincinnati: Writer's Digest Books, annual.

An annually updated guide to fiction markets. Its listings are supplemented with how-to articles and interviews.

Writer's Digest Books. *Writer's Market*. Cincinnati: Writer's Digest Books, annual.

This standard reference volume for writers is a good source of market information. It also can lead you to specialized publications that could be helpful as you do research for your mystery.

You may also want to contact Writer's Digest Books for a catalogue, as it publishes many books on writing and publishing topics, widely available in bookstores:

> Writer's Digest Books
> 1507 Dana Avenue
> Cincinnati, OH 45207

Grammar, Language, and Style

Gordon, Karen Elizabeth. *The Deluxe Transitive Vampire: The Ultimate Handbook of Grammar for the Innocent, the Eager, and the Doomed*. Rev. ed. New York: Pantheon Books, 1993.

Gordon, Karen Elizabeth. *The New Well-Tempered Sentence: A Punctuation Handbook for the Innocent, the Eager, and the Doomed*. Rev. ed. New York: Ticknor and Fields, 1993.

The first book is an excellent — and very entertaining — guide to grammar. Who would have thought that a subject that bored you silly in eighth grade could be this much fun?

The second title is a guide to punctuation, equally as amusing and authoritative as *The Deluxe Transitive Vampire*.

Strunk, William Jr., and E.B. White. *The Elements of Style*. New York: Allyn and Bacon, 1995.

This slender volume, which has become a classic since it was first published in 1957, is a succinct and authoritative guide to presenting ideas with clarity and flair.

Contests

Best First Private Eye Novel Contest
St. Martin's Press/Private Eye Writers of America
175 5th Street
New York, NY 10010
Phone: (212) 674-5151
Fax: (212) 420-9314

This contest, cosponsored by St. Martin's Press and the Private Eye Writers of America, is open to any professional or nonprofessional writer who has never published a private eye novel, by which is meant a "novel in which the main character is an independent investigator who is not a member of any law enforcement or government agency." Contact the publisher for guidelines. The prize is a cash award plus publication by St. Martin's Press.

Best First Traditional Mystery Contest
St. Martin's Press/Malice Domestic
175 5th Street
New York, NY 10010
Phone: (212) 674-5151
Fax: (212) 420-9314

This contest, cosponsored by St. Martin's Press and the Malice Domestic Conference, is open to any professional or nonprofessional writer who has never published a traditional mystery. Contact the publisher for a detailed description and guidelines. Generally, these books feature an amateur detective (or, occasionally, a non-hard-boiled professional) as the protagonist. The prize is a cash award plus publication by St. Martin's Press.

Appendix B
Information and Resources on Researching Crimes and Crime-Solving Techniques

Contact information listed in this appendix is as complete as possible. Some organizations, especially those run by volunteer groups of dedicated mystery writers and fans, may not maintain phone and fax numbers. You can reach these organizations by mail or e-mail or, in some instances, by accessing their Web sites.

Organizations

Mystery Writers of America
17 East 47th Street, 6th Floor
New York, NY 10017
Phone: (212) 888-8171
Fax: (212) 888-8107
Web site: http://www.mysterynet.com/mwa/

Maintains a resource library for members, including a listing, available by mail order, of documents on crime-related topics. See listing in Appendix A.

Web Sites

The Clue Lass Home Page:
A Mystery Lover's Notebook
http://www.cluelass.com

Click the CyberCrime button on this Web site for links to lots of sites dealing with forensics, criminology, police procedure, and related topics.

Cop Net
http://www.copnet.org or http://police.sas.ab.ca

A site with extensive resources for information on law enforcement, including links to the Web sites of law enforcement agencies in the United States, Canada, and elsewhere in the world.

Education in Forensic Science
http://www.forensicdna.com

A site maintained by two top experts in forensic analysis of DNA evidence, whose goal is "to provide both the professional and lay community with education resources in the field of forensic science." Offers information in nontechnical language, links to related sites, and a criminalistics bookstore.

Mysterious Home Page
http://www.webfic.com/mysthome

In addition to links to Web sites on mystery writing and publishing, this site includes many resources on crime and crime-solving.

Mystery Writers of America/NorCal Chapter
http://members.aol.com/mwanorcal/index.html

The site of the Northern California chapter of MWA. A well-organized source of links to connect you to the information you need.

PI Mall
http://www.PIMall.com/pimag/index.html

A promotional page that helps you connect to private investigators and provides a glimpse at their profession.

Zeno's Forensics Page
http://zeno.simplenet.com/forensic.htm

An extensive set of links to informative sites dealing with forensic science, forensic medicine, and forensic psychology.

Government Agency Web Sites

U.S. Department of Justice
http://www.usdoj.gov

U.S. Federal Bureau of Investigation
http://www.fbi.gov

Royal Canadian Mounted Police
http://www.rcmp-grc.gc.ca

Publications

This is a selected reading list. Many helpful books are available on crime, crime-solving, and related topics. The sampling listed here provides a good place to begin.

Brown, Sam, and Gini Graham Scott. *Private Eyes: What Private Investigators Really Do.* New York: Citadel Press/Carol Publishing Group, 1991.
    Written by two PIs, this book looks at the role of the private investigator in American marriage, business, and industry by profiling several colleagues and their modus operandi.

Douglas, John, and Mark Olshaker. *Journey Into Darkness.* New York: Pocket Books, 1997.

Douglas, John, and Mark Olshaker. *Mind Hunter: Inside the FBI's Elite Serial Crime Unit.* New York: Pocket Books, 1996.
    Douglas headed the FBI's Investigative Support Unit and was the model for FBI investigator Jack Crawford in the movie *The Silence of the Lambs.* In these books, Douglas looks back on 25 years of high-profile cases and the development of the art of criminal profiling.

Fallis, Greg, and Ruth Greenburg. *Be Your Own Detective.* New York: M. Evans and Company, 1999.
    An up-to-date guide by a licensed private investigator and a criminal defense lawyer that can help you and your sleuth learn how to conduct a successful investigation.

Gunderson, Ted L., with Roger McGovern. *How to Locate Anyone Anywhere.* 2nd ed. New York: Plume, 1996.
    A step-by-step guide describing how to go about locating missing persons for legal, business, or personal reasons.

Harrison, Wayne. *P.I. School: How to Become a Private Detective.* Boulder, CO: Paladin Press, 1991.
    A slender how-to book full of investigative techniques and tools, from conducting a surveillance to picking locks.

Houde, John. *Crime Lab: A Guide for Nonscientists.* Ventura, CA: Calico Press, 1999.
    An illustrated tour of the crime lab and how it works, following along as evidence from a homicide case is gathered and analyzed.

Jones, Ann. *Women Who Kill.* New York: Holt, Rinehart and Winston, 1980; reprinted by Beacon Press, 1996.
    An investigation of the reasons women resort to murder and the societal conditions that contribute to their crimes and punishment.

Maples, William, and Michael Browning. *Dead Men Do Tell Tales: The Strange and Fascinating Cases of a Forensic Anthropologist.* New York: Doubleday, 1994.
    The subtitle says it all.

McArdle, Phil, and Karen McArdle. *Fatal Fascination: Where Fact Meets Fiction in Police Work.* New York: Houghton Mifflin, 1988.
    A helpful compendium of information about police procedure, anecdotes, recountings of classical cases, and historical tidbits, aimed at helping mystery writers get their facts right.

Norris, Joel. *Serial Killers.* New York: Anchor Books/Doubleday, 1989.
    An intriguing examination of the psychology and sociology of the serial killer and society's response to this phemonenon.

O'Hara, Charles E., and Gregory L. O'Hara. *Fundamentals of Criminal Investigation*. 6th ed. Springfield, IL: Charles E. Thomas Publishing, 1996.

A textbook for professionals that provides detailed information on how the pros investigate various kinds of crimes.

Peat, David. *The Armchair Guide to Murder and Detection*. Ottawa: Deneau Publishers, 1984.

A two-part look at murder. The first half of the book provides a detailed look at how a homicide investigation proceeds, from the scene of the crime to the courtroom. The second offers brief case histories of how some baffling murder cases were solved.

Rachlin, Harvey. *The Making of a Cop*. New York: Pocket Books, 1991.

Rachlin, Harvey. *The Making of a Detective*. New York: Dell, 1996.

For the first book, the author tracked the transformation of four recruits of the New York City police force from civilian to police officer, following them through their training and early days on the job. In the second, the author similarly followed a New York City police officer during his first years as part of the detective bureau.

Simon, David. *Homicide: A Year on the Killing Streets*. New York: Houghton Mifflin, 1991.

From January to December, the author spent a year with the detectives of the Baltimore Police Department. This book inspired the popular TV show *Homicide: Life on the Streets*.

Thompson, Josiah. *Gumshoe: Reflections in a Private Eye*. New York: Fawcett, 1988.

A fascinating look at the world of the private investigator by a man who gave up a career as a philosophy professor at a distinguished university to become one.

Zonderman, Jon. *Beyond the Crime Lab: The New Science of Investigation*. New York: John Wiley, 1998.

A look at the scientific and technical aspects of modern criminal investigation, including areas such as DNA typing, criminal profiling, and computer reconstructions of crimes.

An extensive series aimed at mystery writers is the Howdunit Series, published by Writer's Digest Books. Each volume provides an overview of a topic related to crime or crime-solving. Not comprehensive, but a helpful starting place for your research. Some representative titles:

Bintliff, Russell. *Police Procedural: A Writer's Guide to the Police and How They Work*. Cincinnati: Writer's Digest Books, 1993.

Newton, Michael. *Armed and Dangerous: A Writer's Guide to Weapons*. Cincinnati: Writer's Digest Books, 1990.

Stevens, Sertia Deborah, with Anne Klarner. *Deadly Doses: A Writer's Guide to Poisons*. Cincinnati: Writer's Digest Books, 1990.

Wilson, Keith D. *Cause of Death: A Writer's Guide to Death, Murder and Forensic Medicine*. Cincinnati: Writer's Digest Books, 1992.

Wingate, Anne. *Scene of the Crime: A Writer's Guide to Crime-Scene Investigations*. Cincinnati: Writer's Digest Books, 1992.

You might also want to check out:

PI Magazine
755 Bronx, Toledo, OH 43609
E-mail: pimag1@aol.com.
Web site: http://www.IMall.com

A quarterly trade magazine for private investigators — an insider's look at the people, practices, and issues of the profession.